ANOTHER
WORLD
IS
POSSIBLE

ANOTHER WORLD IS POSSIBLE

**Popular Alternatives to Globalization
at the World Social Forum**

Edited by

WILLIAM F. FISHER
& THOMAS PONNIAH

FERNWOOD PUBLISHING LTD
NOVA SCOTIA

SIRD
SELANGOR

DAVID PHILIP
CAPE TOWN

ZED BOOKS
LONDON & NEW YORK

Another World Is Possible was first published in 2003 by:

in Canada: Fernwood, 8422 St Margaret's Bay Road (Hwy 3),
Site 2A, Box 5, Black Point, Nova Scotia B0J 1B0

in Malaysia: Strategic Information Research Development (SIRD),
No. 11 Lorong 11/4E, Petaling Jaya, 46200 Selangor Darul Ehsan

in South Africa: David Philip Publishers (Pty Ltd),
99 Garfield Road, Claremont 7700

in the rest of the world: Zed Books Ltd., 7 Cynthia Street, London N1 9JF, UK, and
Room 400, 175 Fifth Avenue, New York, NY 10010, USA
www.zedbooks.demon.co.uk

Cover designed by Andrew Corbett
Set in 10/13 pt Monotype Bembo by Long House, Cumbria, UK
Printed and bound in the United Kingdom
by Cox & Wyman, Reading

Distributed in the USA exclusively by Palgrave, a division of St Martin's Press, LLC,
175 Fifth Avenue, New York, NY 10010

A catalogue record for this book is available from the British Library
US CIP data is available from the Library of Congress
Canadian CIP data is available from the National Library of Canada

ISBN 1 84277 328 3 Hb
ISBN 1 84277 329 1 Pb

in Canada
ISBN 1 55266 110 5 Pb

in South Africa
ISBN 0 86486 624 0 Pb

The editors gratefully acknowledge the help and support of the Organizing
Committee of the World Social Forum (WSF) without which the preparation of
this book would not have been possible. Royalties, after the editors'
costs have been recovered, will be donated to the Organizing Committee.

CONTENTS

CONTENTS

Epilogue • SOCIAL MOVEMENTS' MANIFESTO
Resistance to Neoliberalism, War and Militarism; For Peace and Social Justice

PREFACE

This book grew out of our shared interest in and commitment to the approaches of contemporary social movements to alternative visions of globalization. Our plans for the book emerged directly out of discussions around the methodological and theoretical challenges of studying global social movements. We wrestled with the questions of how to discuss, analyse and express the participatory character and multiple voices of large translocal movements, and how to choose case studies appropriate to informing an overall theory of social change in an era of globalization. We considered numerous cases including the Zapatistas, the new innovations in Cuba and the Narmada movement, but we discarded each for one reason or the other.

The impetus to focus on the World Social Forum (WSF) initially arose from discussions Thomas Ponniah had with the great anti-apartheid activist and poet Dennis Brutus who stayed in Worcester in the autumn of 2000 prior to taking up a visiting teaching post at Worcester State University. As we discussed Dennis's ideas and his account of the World Social Forum it became clear to us that the World Social Forum presented a challenging and exciting opportunity for the combination of research and political engagement that we valued.

As described by Dennis, the World Social Forum was an attempt to bring together radicals from all over the world to renew the process of envisioning another world. This process had been interrupted by the opening created for the right wing in the wake of the collapse of Soviet communism. But true to historical form, the imperial system's inherently exploitative nature, the self-destructiveness of the political-

xii   PREFACE

economic elite and the creativity of political activists, had once again established the conditions for a new counter-hegemonic vision to be built. The impossible was suddenly starting to look possible.

Neither of us was able to go to the first Forum but we followed it closely. When it ended we looked forward to the release of a publication from the Forum, outlining what had been proposed, discussed, agreed and critiqued. Unfortunately no English compilation appeared. Later, preparing to go the next WSF to initiate his doctoral research, Thomas proposed that we edit a book of the key documents that would be discussed at the second Forum. We agreed from the start that all the profits from such a book should go towards organizing future Forums.

On 10 January 2001, Thomas arrived in Porto Alegre and worked with the WSF Secretariat for that first month. In late February he officially proposed the book project to the WSF Organizing Committee. The Committee encouraged us to do the book: they promised to provide English translations of all the documents and they assigned two Committee members to provide any help that we needed. They also clarified that we could not speak in the name of the Forum, the Organizing Committee or the International Council. Any analysis of the documents that we wrote would be strictly our responsibility.

Over the months of the internship Thomas had the privilege of listening to and talking with a number of the activists and intellectuals involved in the Organizing Committee and the International Council. He circulated summaries and analyses to them and received many insightful clarifications, comments and critical questions. He also had the opportunity to listen in on many of the debates that took place within the International Council. In solidarity, we dedicate this book to a more just, democratic and sustainable world and to the Organizing Committee, the International Council, and activists like Dennis Brutus, who aspire to it.

William F. Fisher and Thomas Ponniah

ACKNOWLEDGEMENTS

This book would not have been completed without the help of a number of people. First and most importantly we would both like to thank all the writers and movements who have produced the documents in this book. Next we would like to thank Jose Correa Leite of the WSF Organizing Committee for his regular comments, criticism and friendship throughout the vast majority of the writing. Other members of the Organizing Committee who were very helpful were Francisco Whitaker, Sergio Haddad, Maria Luisa Mendonça, Atila Roque, Kjeld Jakobsen, Candido Grzybowsky, Oded Grajew, João Pedro Stedile, Fátima Mello and especially Gustavo Codas. Jai Sen, Meena Menon, Vijay Pratap, Anriette Esterhuyssen and above all François Houtart of the International Council, provided thoughtful comments, discussion and guidance.

We also thank the members of the 2002 and 2003 WSF Executive Secretariat for their support and friendship: Alessandra Ceregatti, Verena Glass, Carol Gil, Carla Lyra, Diego Azzi, Andrea Haddad, Maira Junqueira, Patricia Giuffrida, Mariangela Graciano, Adriana Guimarães and Luana Vilutis. Thanks to the numerous WSF volunteers who translated documents and offered their support. They are central to this book and to the success of the World Social Forum. Special mention goes to the generosity and friendship of Eliane Carmen Lima, Flavia Miranda Falcao, Margarete Noro, Gabriella Noro and Mathieu Glayre. As well, thanks to the volunteer work of Veronique Rioufol, Peter Lenny and the Committee Gaucho in Porto Alegre. Thomas Ponniah extends his gratitude to the Ceregattis (Reiko, Alessandra, Gracia, Amanda, Gustavo, Alexandre, Roseli, Airton, Ônix and Sem-teto) for the home, the warmth and friendship they provided.

Special thanks to the life-saving and extraordinarily reliable editorial assistance of Sonja Pieck and Lisa Meierotto. Thanks as well to Kris Allen for her careful reading of the text. We extend our heartfelt gratitude to Robert Molteno, Managing Editor of Zed Books, for his enthusiastic support for this project.

William Fisher's involvement in this project and his continuing interest in global activism have been sustained and enriched over the years by his intellectual engagement both within and out of the classroom with a large group of exceptional students, especially those who have taken his courses at Harvard and Clark on contemporary social movements and globalization. Many of these students have made a lasting impression through their intellectual insights and political commitment. In addition to Thomas, Sonja and Lisa, these include Pooja Bhatia, Carleton Dalley, Elizabeth Faust, Sameera Fazili, Kendra Fehrer, Matt Feinstein, Steve Fischer, Kathleen Gallagher, Bret Gustafson, Trina Hamilton, Akash Kapur, Mekhala Krishnamurthy, Robyn Long, Susannah McCandless, Menzie McEachern, Navin Narayan, Daniel Niles, Zuzanna Olszewska, Ben Penglasse, Robert Pike, Balakrishnan Rajagopal, Josie Shagwert, Saubhagya Shah, Brian Shillinglaw, Sam Sternin, Rebecca Stich, Sarah 'Raz' Tsien, Kweli Washington, Sarah Wood and Miranda Worthen.

Thomas Ponniah also makes the following acknowledgements. His internship and research would not have been accomplished without the funding of Clark University's Leir Committee on Globalization and the support of his doctoral committee: Professors William Fisher, Susan Hanson, Yuko Aoyama, Robert Ross, and especially his principal advisor, Richard Peet, whose commitment and teaching are fundamental to this book. As well he would like to thank David Angel, the Dean of Graduate Studies, and Professor Ron Eastman for their regular encouragement.

Thomas's work would not have been possible without leave of absence from, and encouragement by, George Brown College of Toronto, Canada. Thanks to: Michael Cooke, Vice-President of Academic Excellence and Innovation, Marjorie McColm, Director of Academic Excellence and Innovation, Georgia Quartaro, Chair of Community Services, and the professors in the Community Worker

Program: Bob Luker, Lynne Brennan, Bill Fallis, Pramila Aggarwal, Robin Buyers and Johanne Clare.

Thanks to the insight of many past and present teachers: Alain Rodrigue, Sr Gloria D'Andrea, Michael Ekins, Peter Henderson, Victor Garaway, John Laffey, Eric Davis, Chengiah Ragaven, Charles Small, Richard Johnson, Anne Gray, Josephine Diamond, Harvey Waterman, Bruce Robbins, Steve Bronner, Bill Turner II, Diane Rocheleau, Arturo Escobar and Judy Rebick.

Thanks to numerous companions and colleagues for their encouragement: first, the Ponniah family (James, Mary, Ann, Ted and Lyn), Jeff and Rachel Huffines, Geoff and Nancy Ewing, Bonnie Fields, Roya Movafegh, Hooshmand Sheshberadaran, Salim Garin, Manoah Garin, Jaharqa Metaxas, Tina Metaxas, Chelsea and James Parker, Jaedon and Robin Browne, Marva Major, Kim Elliott, Kim De Lallo, Michael Osborne, Scott Milne, Saeed Khan, Laila Smith, Tariq and Munira Khan and their children, Sameen and Salman, Beverly, David and Khembi Maynard, Dorothy and Stevan Boatswain, Maxine Howell, Cory Garfinkle, Liliana Tomaszewska, Iain Macdonald, Grant Zubis, Baruch Zohar, Marize Kenny, Ayman Hassan, Eduardo Zeitune, Julia Schluns, Chiyo Kigasawa, Caitie Dwyer-Huppert, Elizabeth Faust, Trina Hamilton, Scott Jiusto, Carolyn Finney, Winifred Curran, Hao Chen, Pablo Pacheco, Jacqueline Vadjunec, Guido Schwarz, Arvind Susarla, Mary Thomas, Daniel Niles, Mazen Labban, and to the professors and other graduate students at Clark University's Department of Geography.

Last of all, Thomas thanks two of his favourite organizations for their inspiration and friendship: the Worcester Global Action Network (especially Kendra Fehrer, Matt Feinstein, Josie Shagwert, Steve Fischer, Menzie McEachern, Alex Pulsipher, Aaron Pollack, Leah Penniman, Jonah Vitale-Wolff, Susannah McCandless and Ethan Mitchell) and the Network Institute for Global Democracy. The members of the latter group who have been especially helpful are Teivo Teivainen (who provided comments on the introduction to this book), Heikki Patomäki, Katarina Sehm Patomäki, Leena Rikkilä, Mika Rönkkö and Laura Nisula.

FOREWORD

MICHAEL HARDT and ANTONIO NEGRI

The World Social Forum at Porto Alegre has already become a myth, one of those positive myths that define our political compass. It is the representation of a new democratic cosmopolitanism, a new anti-capitalist transnationalism, a new intellectual nomadism, a great movement of the multitude. These are the positive elements of myth-making. The Porto Alegre Forum emerged from the beginning as a great network to bring the members of the Brazilian Workers' Party (PT) together with the 'globalization' protest movements, the local administrators experimenting in new forms of participatory democracy together with the utopian schemers of a global democracy. The Forum is thus the place where the so-called anti-globalization movements in their various guises come together and demonstrate how global they really are. They are, in fact, the real protagonists of globalization today, a truly democratic globalization.

Porto Alegre thus stands opposed to Davos. Davos, Switzerland is the place where, for several years, until the protests made it impractical, the financial, industrial, and political oligarchies of the world attended the World Economic Forum each year for a few days in winter to plan the destiny of capitalist globalization. The contrast between the heat of Brazil in January and the snows of Switzerland echoes the opposition between the two political strategies. The two sites stand opposed, but they are not homologous, they are not mirror images of one another. The meetings at Davos were restricted to a small elite and protected by armed guards whereas Porto Alegre is an overflowing event with innumerable participants. Davos was a small hierarchy blocked on a mountaintop and Porto Alegre an unlimited network expanding across the plains.

There are two aspects that are most striking about the movement of movements or the network of networks that come together at Porto Alegre against neoliberal globalization. The first is that Porto Alegre appears as a nomad point or, rather, as a transitive space. Here the Zapatista slogan 'walk forward questioning' has become a way of life. The networks and the connections among the movements form the horizon at Porto Alegre, and thus here is born a new internationalism. It is no use giving it precise political labels, because here democratic cosmopolitanism, proletarian communism, and anarchist internationalism are linked together while the concept of human rights is redefined and extended, opened to new formulations and experiments. The act of linking together, connecting, has become the fundamental mode of the movements because they are struggling against a structure of power that is unified at a global level. That makes it all the more unfortunate that not all the forces in the world that rebel are present at Porto Alegre and specifically that Africa and Asia are represented only partially! This is only a point of passage, however, an empty space that the network will eventually manage to fill.

The second striking aspect is that the network at Porto Alegre takes the form of a common process. The connections are transformed into discussions and the network becomes a list of demands and projects. Recognizing and constructing what we have in common is what unifies the network. It is not really a matter of fixing a point of unity or, worse yet, identity, but simply finding what is common in our differences and expanding that commonality while our differences proliferate. This proliferation of differences went to Porto Alegre to discover it was a common network, and from this new condition it will go back out to establish new differences everywhere. Every difference is an organizational project.

One should thus read the papers and conferences presented at Porto Alegre like the *Cahiers de Doléances* (statements of grievances) presented to the Estates-General in France in 1789. Over 40,000 Cahiers de Doléances were presented with lists of demands, denunciations, requests, and desires that were the basis for constructing the

Third Estate as a revolutionary force. In pre-revolutionary France they perfected an art of demanding. At Porto Alegre too the statements and lists have the same intensity, full of denunciations and utopian desires. They reveal the horrible state of our present form of globalization, the scandal of neoliberal capitalist power, and the misery of the majority of the world's populations. Three clouds in particular hung over the 2002 meeting at Porto Alegre: Argentina, Afghanistan, and Palestine, poignant examples of the ruins and suffering wrought by the dominant world economic and military powers. But every list of grievances also contains utopian demands. They demonstrate a mature and organized desire to go beyond what we have, to construct a new world that is possible.

The most important aspect of Porto Alegre may not be how it balances the neoliberalism of the World Economic Forum with a counter-forum, but rather how it provides an opportunity to reconstitute the Left in each country and internationally. This year at Porto Alegre there were important encounters and exchanges among the globalization movements, the trade unions, and social democratic political forces. As we have already seen in the struggles that developed in the last few years in North America and Europe, from Seattle to Genoa, working together with the trade unions had allowed the globalization movements to expand their bases and to form a broad social network based on common interests. There is a strong pragmatism in the relationship between the movements and the unions and we think when this practical relationship is proposed honestly on both sides and the needs, interests, and projects are put clearly on the table then it is possible to go forward together. Social democratic politicians and organizations also came to the Forum, but linking with them presents many more difficulties. Social democratic forces in the various countries, especially their conservative elements, have voted for the various wars and approved the capitalist processes of the dissolution of welfare structures, accepting the financialization of all aspects of life, giving rise to various forms of social conflict. The conservative social democrats have thus become inescapably identified with the deepest interests of capitalist power, where exploitation and repression constitute the fundamental political line. The movement of movements cannot find a common ground with these social democratic forces and cannot link together with them in a network.

The encounters at Porto Alegre thus clarify this situation. The globalization movements can attempt with labour unions to construct a new front of anti-capitalist struggle on a global scale. Doing this, the movements would fundamentally oppose the social democratic forces. Porto Alegre would be the grave of social democracy or, at least, the end of any possibility of identifying social democracy with the Left. The encounters at Porto Alegre make clear instead the possibility of reconstructing the Left on the basis of the movements, going beyond every alliance with the existing structures of political and economic power. The movement of movements can create a position of hegemony here, even over the unions. The trade union defends partial interests whereas the movement can represent the general interest of all who work; the union interprets the interests of a limited class, whereas the movements can express the action of the entire multitude. Perhaps this is the moment of the end of the historical cycle of social democracy and the beginning of the democracy of the multitude.

Finally, we should add that the struggle against war is a central element of this program. It is perfectly clear to those at Porto Alegre that the neoliberal world order and the interminable state of war go hand in hand, that they support and legitimate each other. There is no just war. Pacifism at Porto Alegre is thus transformed into an active political stance. We must struggle against war at the same time that we struggle against the neoliberal order. Numerous strategies have been invented by the movements for this struggle against war, such as caravans for peace and operations of 'diplomacy from below', that is, intervening actively in conflicts, outside official state channels. Only the movements can destroy the fascisms, fundamentalisms, and imperialisms however and wherever they appear in the world. Porto Alegre is thus the symbol of a new internationalism, which like others is born and reborn against the war. The networks that are based on our differences and our commonalities create an unbreakable relation not only against war and death, but ultimately for a new form of life.

INTRODUCTION

The World Social Forum and the Reinvention of Democracy

THOMAS PONNIAH AND WILLIAM F. FISHER

As the globalization project unfolds, It exposes its bankruptcy at the philosophical, political, ecological and economic levels. The bankruptcy of the dominant world order is leading to social, ecological, political and economic non-sustainability, with societies, ecosystems, and economies disintegrating and breaking down.

The philosophical and ethical bankruptcy of globalization was based on reducing every aspect of our lives to commodities and reducing our identities to merely that of consumers on the global market place. Our capacities as producers, our identity as members of communities, our role as custodians of our natural and cultural heritage were all to disappear or be destroyed. Markets and consumerism expanded. Our capacity to give and share were to shrink. But the human spirit refuses to be subjugated by a world view based on the dispensability of our humanity.

Vandana Shiva

Global Civil Society

The World Social Forum is the most recent, vibrant, and potentially productive articulation of an emergent global civil society. For many activists, the arrival of the Forum makes possible what previously seemed impossible. Through newly exposed cracks in the armour of neoliberal globalization, movements are beginning to assert that another world is possible.

I

In a world of rapid globalization, where large corporations grow more powerful in their pursuit of economic expansion and profits, there are growing networks of concerned activists who are not dazzled by the promised land of globalization. They are alert instead to the dangers globalization presents to justice, cultural autonomy and the environment.[1] These networks find themselves pitted against well-financed and well-staffed institutions, multilateral development banks, governments and transnational corporations. With limited resources but great tenaciousness, they work to make visible the damage and dangers wrought by rampant and unexamined economic expansion. In recent years the most visible manifestation of so-called 'anti-globalization' protests may be the protests against the WTO, or the World Bank, on the streets of Seattle, Washington DC, or Genoa. But a more lasting impact may emerge from the efforts of some focused coalitions seeking to build participatory processes of sustained dialogue across boundaries.

Transnational alliances of social movements are not new. There are, however, two striking characteristics about contemporary transnational efforts: they emerge with increasing speed and with less regard for geographical distance; and they move along networks that are neither fixed nor symmetrical – things do not move in all directions, flows are unequal, and networks are subject to change.

The growing number of alliances among, and expanding influence of, so-called civil society groups in the global arena is noteworthy. These alliances have arisen without any centrally organized institutions. This arena is not free from power struggles, and it is not easy to keep open a space for rational argument and apolitical decision-making. Indeed, it is a hotly contested political space in which power is in flux. This active engagement in global or transnational arenas stems from two contradictory aims: one is the desire of some civil society groups to be part of the global governance process; the other is the determination of many groups to protest and resist. The World Social Forum has made the most significant effort so far to create a political space for the emergence of a global civil society, a space where interactions and common discourse can evolve that are constructed by movements emerging out of different cultures.[2]

It is tempting to see transnational networks as a new kind of imagined or invented community. But to refit the trope of community to span the spatially discontiguous connections and solidarity that characterize transnational activist networks, we need to ask what is entailed in new kinds of imagining, or, specifically, in the imagining of a transnational activist community. Like the national collectivities to which Benedict Anderson applied the term 'imagined communities', these transnational collectivities are distinguished by 'the style in which they are imagined'.[3] While the shifting construction of space and time, which results from endless capitalist adaptation, may create for some individuals severe problems of identity, and weaken allegiances to local communities, cities, regions or nations, it also creates an opportunity for greater identification with transnational issue networks, epistemic communities,[4] or interest groups.

Unbounded and fluid, some of the emerging global networks differ in significant ways from the imagined communities of nationalism: the values, allegiances and global flows among transnational resistance networks crosscut national, regional, and local collectivities.[5] The communities of activists they engender, while spatially diffuse, nevertheless share values and a sense of belonging. Networks like those which gave rise to the World Social Forum, for example, are organized around shared discourses and shared values, or at least the presumption of shared values.[6]

Yet, despite the sense of belonging and shared goals, emerging communities like those participating in the World Social Forum (WSF) are also marked by an element of heterogeneity, fragmentation and transformation. The networks in which the WSF arose are part of an emerging transnational civil society that is 'an arena of struggle, a fragmented and contested area' (Keck and Sikkink 1998: 33–4). Nevertheless, the social practice of transnational advocacy networks creates space within which new forms of community are possible. The pre-eminent example of this is the World Social Forum.

The World Social Forum

The World Social Forum is the most promising attempt to date to provide a space in which global civil-society groups can become better educated about one another, learn more about the processes of neoliberal globalization, plan collective actions, and develop alternatives to the current world order. The Forum first emerged as an alternative to the neoliberal project represented by the World Economic Forum held annually in Davos, Switzerland. The suggestion for a counter-summit to Davos was first formulated during the twentieth anniversary of the Tricontinental Centre in Leuwen, Belgium, in 1996. Some of these groups organized the first anti-Davos event in 1999. A World Social Forum, to be held in Brazil, was first proposed by Oded Grajew, the coordinator of the Brazilian Business Association for Citizenship (CIVES), Francisco Whitaker of the Brazilian Justice and Peace Commission (CBJP) and Bernard Cassen, the director of the Association for the Taxation of Financial Transactions for the Aid of Citizens (ATTAC, France). These individuals articulated three framing concepts for the Forum: first it should be held in the South, preferably in Porto Alegre; second, its name should be the World Social Forum to counterpose it to the World Economic Forum; and, third, it should be held at the same time as the World Economic Forum (Patomäki and Teivainen with Rönkkö 2002: 120).

A number of Brazilian civil-society organizations formed the Organizing Committee for the Forum. They were: the Brazilian Association of Non-Governmental Organizations (ABONG), Association for the Taxation of Financial Transactions for the Aid of Citizens (ATTAC), the Brazilian Justice and Peace Commission (CBJP), the Brazilian Business Association for Citizenship (CIVES), the Brazilian Institute for Social and Economic Studies (IBASE) and the Social Network for Justice and Human Rights. In March 2000 the city of Porto Alegre's assent was secured. The city and its state government of Rio Grande do Sul were under the governance of the Brazilian Workers' Party.

Porto Alegre was seen as an appropriate site for the World Social Forum because the city had been governed by the Workers' Party since 1988 and is celebrated for its innovative participatory budgetary process, grounded in radical reform of the relationship between the public, the government and business. A 'radical reform' prevents corporate domination of the democratic process and gives progressive governments and popular mobilizations leverage against corporate power.

The annual participatory budget process of Porto Alegre is structured by a number of phases. The process begins in March with citizen forums across sixteen geographic and sectoral areas of the city. Forums of five hundred to seven hundred people elect two representatives and two alternates to serve one year on the budget council. In April and May, the forum representatives organize smaller assemblies to propose the budget priorities of the public for the following year. Between May and mid-July, the proposed budget priorities are forwarded to the current municipal council (33 councillors elected by traditional democratic means). Simultaneously, the forum representatives attend training sessions on municipal finance. A draft budget is constructed by the budget council and municipal bureaucrats and is sent to the mayor and the municipal council for consultation. Between October and December, the participatory budget council amends the budget for final approval from the municipal council and for eventual implementation in January. Altogether the four phases aim at maximizing public involvement in setting the city's social and economic development priorities (Rebick 2000: 26–9). The success of this innovative participatory budget process made Porto Alegre the ideal home for a movement searching for alternatives to the neoliberal world order.

The first World Social Forum was held at the end of January in 2001. It attracted more than 10,000 activists, with half coming from around the world. The second Forum, in January 2002, from which this book's documents emerge, brought together more than 55,000 activists. Since January 2002 there have been a series of regional and thematic forums that have enabled more grassroots groups to discuss alternatives. Through the end of 2002, forums have taken place around the world. The Asian Social Forum to be held in Hyderabad, India, at the beginning of 2003, will serve as a prelude to WSF 2004, which may also be held in India.

Many activists talk about the World Social Forum as if it were a new political agent. It is not an agent, but is instead a pedagogical and political space that enables learning, networking and political organizing. The organizers of the World Social Forum have discouraged any interpretation of it as a deliberative body. They have focused instead on the Forum as a pedagogical space for activists to learn what alternatives are being proposed and enacted around the world. Clearly the WSF has also acted as a political space by giving activists an arena in which to network and develop common projects. But the projects that emerge from networking at the WSF are never carried out in the name of the World Social Forum. The WSF has never produced an official final document, nor has it ever assumed to represent the thousands of activists who attend the conference. The only document that represents the World Social Forum's views is its Charter of Principles, which has been included in this book's Appendix.

The World Social Forum Documents

The World Social Forum 2002 conference proposals and syntheses are best understood as the central part of a work in progress. The individual documents are uneven: some are profound, others superficial.[7] Collectively they contribute to the discussion of alternatives to 'neoliberal globalization', or to what many progressives are now referring to as 'the empire'.[8]

The use of the term by social movements portrays 'the empire' as an entity built and maintained by institutions and groups such as the International Monetary Fund (IMF), the World Bank, the World Trade Organization (WTO), corporations, banks, and the Group of Eight (Globalization and Militarism synthesis).[9] This use of 'empire' places special emphasis on the United States as the central determinant of the neoliberal project ('the Washington Consensus'). It sees neoliberal globalization as a process sweeping all actors along with it. Yet it is a process that could not continue without the efforts of agents all over the planet. Nation-states are both instruments and architects of the global capitalist system. This has become more evident in the current shift from a neoliberal project to a neo-imperial one. The conference proposals and syntheses included here articulate both the rebellion against the neoliberal order, and the desire to produce another world, another imagination, another life that is free of empires.[10]

In some ways, the documents in this volume are specific to a particular time and place. The year 2001 was a year like no other. It included the controversy at the Durban World Conference on Racism, the continuing financial crisis in Argentina, the collapse of multi-nationals such as Enron, the intensification of the conflict between Israel and the Palestinians and, above all, the events of 11 September and the subsequent bombing of Afghanistan. To some degree, the documents are reactions to this year of crisis.

Yet at the same time these documents emerge from years of social-movement efforts. Since the first national uprisings, strikes and riots against the policies of the Bretton Woods institutions in the mid-1970s, and in the context of the failure of three leftist projects (the Soviet Union, the welfare state and the Bandung project [Amin 1995: 36]), social movements have been searching for alternatives to neoliberalism. However, the period of this search, from the late 1960s to the late 1980s, is very different from the periods corresponding to the dissolution and final breakdown of the Soviet Union. The strikes, protests and uprisings against the IMF and World Bank in the first period operated within the ideology of socialism and national liberation. These were movements dominated by the universalist dreams of 1917, decolonization and development.

During the past two decades new forms of social movements became prominent in both the Global North and the Global South. In the North, these movements consisted of environmentalists, urban movements, feminism, the lesbian and gay movement and the anti-racist movement. In both the North and the South these new movements were concerned with questions concerning identity, culture and modernity (Escobar 1992: 62–85). Unlike the universalism of the old left, the new movements argued that radicalism consisted of the liberation of difference.

The period beginning after 1999 is a new epoch in which workers' struggles, the 'new social movements', as well as a new group of young militants (anarchists, anti-sweatshop activists, anti-biotechnology, peace and human rights movements) have come together via an interrelated set of recent efforts. The Zapatista uprising in Chiapas in 1994, the protests in Seattle against the WTO in 1999, the subsequent demonstrations against the perceived agents of corporate globalization in Washington, Melbourne, Prague, Gothenburg, Quebec City and Genoa, and the creation of the World Social Forum, all helped coalesce a series of dispersed struggles against neoliberalism. These events have linked the old left, new social movements and the newest wave of radicalism into a planetary network of networks,[11] 'the movement for global justice and solidarity' or, as the mainstream media has inaccurately framed it, the anti-globalization movement.

These documents are public statements by spokespersons and intellectuals involved in various grassroots struggles around the world. These individuals or organizations were asked by the World Social Forum Organizing Committee to present a summary of the key challenges and alternatives that surround specific issues. An analysis of the documents reveals both the differences amongst the various networks within the movement as well as their points of convergence. We draw attention to five significant debates that emerged from the 2002 conference documents of the World Social Forum.

- **Revolution versus Reform?** Some of the differences are ideological and fall within the familiar leftist debate concerning 'revolution versus reform'. The most familiar manifestation of this kind of debate emerges in the call by some movements for the 'decommissioning' of the IMF (Bello), while others argue for the importance of negotiating with the IMF and other international financial institutions (IFIs). The former group believes that the solution is a pluralist form of global governance that requires the delegitimization of the IFIs, while the latter believe that the current global institutions are not inherently flawed and can be improved through the engagement of civil society.

- **Environment versus Economy?** A second area of difference lies between the environmentalists' call for a reduction of growth and consumption, and labour's demand for more growth and the employment it engenders. This debate can be caricatured as 'saving trees versus saving jobs', or framed as living democracy versus anthropocentrism (Shiva).

- **Human Rights or Protectionism?** A third difference exists within the labour movement itself. Northern labour's call for human rights standards to be included within international trade and investment agreements is often interpreted by Southern workers as a disguised form of protectionism. On the other side Northern labour questions the South's commitment to human rights when the latter refuse to support concrete stipulations (Faux).

- **The Universality of Values?** A fourth conflict lies in the debate concerning the relationship between Western values and universal values. Can the two be simply equated? Is the alternative to the universal acceptance of Western values cultural relativism? Or can a new inclusive process be established for the development of global values that promote diversity? How can universal values be constructed that acknowledge the experience of the marginalized? (Löwy and Betto; Amorós)

- **Local, National or Global?** The fifth significant conflict lies between different geographies of political demands: the local, the national and the global. Different ideological positions focus on the primacy of different scales. Some activists argue that the primary agent of progress lies in localization, hence their call for direct democracy, local governance, subsidiarity, economic self-sufficiency, cultural autonomy and food sovereignty (Parameswaran). Others argue for a new form of state that is run by radical, participatory democratic principles that are regulated by criteria established by civil society (Bello). A third position proposes global forms of regulation such as taxes on financial speculation (ATTAC), world parliaments and referenda (International Organizations synthesis).[12] The emphases on different scales, like the debates mentioned earlier, constitute potential fault-lines in the movement for global justice and solidarity. Whether these differences are fundamentally antagonistic or should be read as *contradictions in process* that can be reconciled into a complementary multiplicity, is unclear at this time in history.

Despite the differences, the movements are unified by several areas of agreement. One is the perception of a common adversary. Mentioned in a number of documents are the problems created by the expansion of corporate capitalism ('neoliberal globalization'). The perception is that corporate dominion has been organized across global space by the most powerful Northern states in the world, in collaboration with Southern economic and political elites. Simultaneously, this expansion is occurring in conjunction with the suppression of political, economic, cultural, racial, gendered, sexual, ecological and epistemological differences. Several authors argue that the striking aspect of the current form of globalization is its capacity to reproduce, rearticulate and compound traditionally oppressive social hierarchies. Neoliberal globalization is not simply economic domination of the world but also the imposition of a monolithic thought (*pensamento unico*) that consolidates vertical forms of difference and prohibits the public from imagining diversity in egalitarian, horizontal terms. Capitalism, imperialism, monoculturalism, patriarchy, white supremacism and the domination of biodiversity have coalesced under the current form of globalization and constitute the primary challenge for the movements represented in the WSF 2002 conference documents. The key instruments of contemporary globalization are the free trade agreements and policies propelled by the WTO, the North American Free Trade Agreement (NAFTA) and other regional trade agreements, and the privatization policies of corporations, the G8 countries, the World Bank and the IMF. Time and again they are identified as the key site of strategic opposition by the various networks within the overall movement, precisely because these agreements, policies and processes have eluded democratic accountability.

These WSF documents begin from the recognition that elite institutions have imposed 'globalization from above'. They understand that neoliberal globalization is a process that imposes neoclassical economic policies, consumerist cultural practices and technological risks. Different strands of activist organizations lay emphasis on economic, cultural and/or technological imposition. For example, socialists lay emphasis on the economic, and therefore define neo-liberal globalization as essentially the globalization of capitalism (Globalization and Militarism synthesis). Identity groups (Cultural Diversity) lay emphasis on consumerism, and therefore define globalization as the colonial expansion of American 'McWorld' culture (Barber 1996). Ecologists lay emphasis on the technological, and therefore view globalization as the spread of risk (Beck 2000). These different analyses do not preclude one another. Yet each has a specific diagnosis and solution to the challenges that neoliberal globalization poses. Where all three – socialists, identity groups, and ecologists – are in agreement is the conviction that uniform economic policies, cultural practices and technological risks are being *imposed* across global space. The world's public did not vote for the leadership of the WTO, nor for advertising billboards to dominate visual space, nor for research that produces genetically modified organisms. All of the movements coincide in their desire for a new democratic process, a 'globalization from below' (Brecher *et al*. 2000; Starr 2000: 83–110) that will respond to the needs of the world's people. These needs have been brought into focus precisely because of the anti-democratic nature of the movements' adversary.

As well as clearly identifying its opponent, a movement must also be clear on what it is struggling for – that is, what kind of society it wants to imagine, produce and experience. A central question to consider while reading these documents is: to what extent do they imply a common vision that can thread together the diverse goals of the various movements across the world? Do these documents propose a common outline for a new global left and a new global society? Laclau and Mouffe (2001: vii–xix) argue that a viable alternative to neoliberalism can arise only if the various social movements' alternatives coalesce. In order for coalescence to occur, the different philosophical/political logics of the alternatives (for example, socialism, anarchism, ecologism, feminism, indigeneity and multi-culturalism) have to establish a chain of equivalence. A chain of equivalence is a new perception, a counter-hegemonic discourse that allows the diversity of movements to recognize that their fundamental aims are similar and can be fulfilled via the implementation of an overarching set of principles, policies and procedures. A chain of equivalence arises when one of the various alternatives demonstrates that it has the capacity to solve the challenges that all of the movements face and that it can produce the new society that all movements want. For example, historically, socialism was the common discourse that established a chain of equivalence amongst the diversity of interests on the left. For the past 30 years, neoliberalism has played this unifying role for the political right by bringing together neoclassical economic theory, libertarianism and social conservatism.

A counter-hegemonic discourse must have a common articulating thread that can weave together disparate movements by demonstrating that their particular long-term interests can best be served by pursuing a common project. It cannot accomplish this if it is simply a resistance discourse. A counter-hegemonic discourse encompasses a resistance discourse: it constitutes a new form of radical subjectivity by demonstrating that what was previously construed as a neutral relation of subordination, simply as horizontal difference, is really a hierarchical relation of oppression (Laclau and Mouffe 2001: 152). However, a counter-hegemonic discourse also demonstrates how that hierarchical relationship can be subverted, made horizontal, by pursuing a larger collective project – that is to say, it offers a visionary discourse. It proposes a utopia.

Because of the failures of the Soviet project, and the rise of the politics of difference in alignment with the post-structural critique of metanarratives, progressive movements are wary of any group playing a vanguard role in defining the society that the overall global movement should pursue. Therefore a contemporary counter-hegemony has to embrace a respect for difference without precluding a capacity to articulate a common vision. If the global movements are to prosper, they have to produce a vision that allows them to maintain simultaneously both their convergence and their difference.

The WSF documents offer a rich variety of alternatives. In our reading, the convergence of difference among the anti-corporate globalization movements lies less in a shared vision of an outcome than in a shared commitment to a process.[13] Essentially, the convergence of difference is best reflected in the widely asserted commitment to *the reinvention of democracy*. We define 'the reinvention of democracy' to mean *the reinvention of society such that the mode of economic production, the structures of political governance, the dissemination of scientific innovation, the organization of the media, social relations and the relationships between society and nature, are subjected to a radical, participatory and living democratic process*. The proposals converge when they call for a democratization of the production of wealth and social reproduction, of access to wealth and sustainability, of civil society and the public arena, and of political power.[14] The integration of a participatory democratic process is repeatedly identified in the World Social Forum documents as the essential step for overcoming elite domination, technocracy, classism, racism, sexism and the apathy generated by bureaucratization and current forms of representative democracy. The development of a participatory process, as exists in the participatory budget of Porto Alegre, and the participatory planning of Kerala (Parameswaran), must also simultaneously involve the pursuit of radically new political and economic structures. 'Participatory democracy' refers to the variety of institutions, networks, processes and perceptions that are needed to democratize representative democracy: participatory budgets, referenda, constituent assemblies, the principle of subsidiarity, the belief in pluralism, the desire for diversity and the affirmation of experience, 'the wisdom of everyday life' (Rebick 2000: 231–2).

'Radical democracy' refers to the radical transformation of the existing class, gender and racialized relations of power that prohibit the full functioning of democracy (Laclau and Mouffe 2001: xv; Peet 1999: 206–8). The fundamental starting point of a radical democracy would be the development of post-capitalist democratic modes of production. Whether those modes of production would be socialist economies, solidarity economies, ecological economies or a combination of the three is unclear. What is essential is that whichever modes of production are employed, they operate by means of radically, participatory democratic processes. Similarly, whether the structures of political governance are localist, statist, internationalist or globalist, they too will operate by means of radically democratic participatory processes. Included in the concept of 'the reinvention of democracy' is the notion of a living democracy, an 'Earth Democracy' (Shiva) – that is, one that is conscious of the needs of every species to the resources of the whole planet as well as the needs of future generations.

A radical, participatory, living democracy involves all citizens in the daily reconstruction of society. It is the transformation of a global society in which decisions are predicated on the current relative monopolies over capital, international financial institutions, the media or technology, into one in which decisions, in every sphere, are determined by directly democratic decision-making.

Some examples of the implicit call for a reinvention of democracy, seen in the documents that follow, include demands for democratic public control over external indebtedness, democratic regulation of corporations, the globalization of collective bargaining, decentralized local solidarity economies, a World Water Parliament, local food sovereignty, civil society monitoring of capital and the state, free education for all, enforceable social, economic and cultural rights, and new values for a civilization of solidarity. All of these point to the reinvention of democracy, such that decision-making is not constrained by elite economic, political, racialized and patriarchal interests.

These documents represent the beginning of the process of building a new left and a new global civilization. This new civilization aims further than the socialist or identity discourses of the twentieth century, in that it asks not only for a post-capitalist democratization of production, but also a democratization of ecological, epistemological, gendered, racialized, ethnic, sexual, cultural, social, political, inter-generational and interpersonal relations. Instead of either unions or identity groups being at the core of the radical project, it calls for networks of all progressive forces, a universalism of difference,[15] to converge and build. This is an ambitious goal. It is too early to judge the long-term capacity of the World Social Forum for sustaining progress towards it. But the Forum has enabled remarkable strides in a short period of time. The World Social Forum has proven to be an effective political and pedagogical space within which this work can progress. It has initiated a process of envisioning a new society. The path to that new society is radical, participatory and living democracy.

Notes

1 Globalization is probably the most overused term in the current political and social science lexicons. The contemporary discussion about globalization emphasizes the intensification of interactions in the contemporary world. Robertson uses the term to refer to 'the compression of the world and the intensification of consciousness of the world as a whole' (1992: 8). Hannerz calls it 'a matter of increasing long-distance interconnectedness' (1996: 17). Appadurai notes that it 'entails a radical acceleration of the flows of images, people, money, technologies across the face of the globe' (1990).

Hannerz notes the widespread concern with homogenization:

> To a great many people, the term 'globalization' means above all this: a global homogenization in which particular ideas and practices spread throughout the world, mostly from the centers of the West, pushing other alternatives out of existence. In the eyes of some, this is the triumphant march of modernity. Others lament it as a takeover by giant cultural commodity merchants, who make sure that Coca Cola can be sipped, *Dallas* watched, and Barbie dolls played with everywhere, in the ex-Second World and the Third as well as in the First where they originated. (1996: 24)

For illuminating insights on globalization see, in particular, Hannerz (1996), Appadurai (1990, 1991, 1996) and Breckenridge (1995). We share with Hannerz the conviction that 'contemporary interconnectedness in the world is really too complicated and diverse to be either condemned or applauded as a whole' (1996: 6), and with Appadurai and Breckenridge (1995: 1) the assumption that 'modernity today is a global experience' and that 'this experience is as varied as magic, marriage, or madness, and thus worthy of scholarly attention and, more generally, of comparative study'. By globalization we mean to refer to social, economic, cultural and demographic processes that transcend nations, such that attention limited to local processes, identities and units of analysis yields incomplete understanding of the local. 'Transnationalism' entails a more limited range; whereas global processes are decentred from national territories and take place in a deterritorialized global space, transnational processes are anchored in but transcend one or more states.

2 Global civil society is a concept of more recent and vaguer usage than globalization. It implies a world-wide social interaction analogous to the form and function of civil societies we find grounded within nation-states, yet for some authors it refers to no more than NGOs flocking together at ad hoc conferences like UNCED (the 1992 UN Conference on Environment and Development in Rio). Unfortunately, even civil society is an often essentialized category used in different ways by different theorists. The idea has always been rife with ambiguity and the term is 'as contested as the social and political institutions it purports to describe' – see Hunt (1999: 11) and Hunt and Schechter (1999: 1).

3 Anderson (1991: 6). With respect to imagined global communities, see also the discussion by Lash and Urry (1994: 314–16), who contrast two understandings of the global – one in which the universal triumphs over the particular, and a second, more fragmented model, built around notions like

Heidegger's 'being-in-the-world' or Bourdieu's 'habitus', a model which provides both the political space for new communities and is at the same time 'the world of racism and ethnic hate' (315). Lash and Urry place global communities in between Heidegger's 'being-in-the world' and Anderson's 'quintessentially modern' imagined communities, characterizing them as 'invented communities' – communities into which we are not so much thrown as communities into which we throw ourselves (316). A full response to the discussion by Lash and Urry is not appropriate here, but our discussion of the term 'invented communities' for global networks is meant not to align them with the imagined communities of nationalism but to contrast them with both these and with the 'worlded' rather than global character of many social movements.

4 Haas (1992: 1–36) and Keck and Sikkink (1998: 1, 30) usefully distinguish epistemic communities (based on shared causal ideas and professional ties) from other activist groups. As described by Haas, epistemic communities are transnational networks of experts characterized by a shared command of potentially instrumental technical knowledge, common values, agreed ways of testing truth and a shared understanding of causality. Epistemic communities are generally limited to groups of scientists and exclude activists.

5 Robert Keohane has argued that the growing number of committed individuals who think and act transnationally is the critical component in globalization (1995: 184). Some of these actions are driven by different ideas and motivations – some by shared principled ideas, others by shared causal ideas, and others by shared understandings about the possibilities for action. The alliances involved in the World Social Forum derive primarily from a set of shared principled ideas – ideas that specify criteria for determining whether actions are right or wrong and whether outcomes are just or unjust. To the extent that the actions of these networks challenge sovereignty, they also draw on ideas about the possibilities for action. See also Sikkink (1993).

6 At the same time, values are contested within as well as by means of these networks. Gupta and Ferguson have argued:

> Something like a transnational public sphere has certainly rendered any strictly bounded sense of community or locality obsolete. At the same time it has enabled the creation of forms of solidarity and identity that do not rest on an appropriation of space where contiguity and face-to face contact are paramount. (1997b:37)

7 Due to space restrictions we have unfortunately not been able to include all the conference documents and syntheses. We have chosen the documents

according to two principles. First, we ensured that each topic within each of the broader Themes is represented by at least one conference proposal or synthesis. Second, we chose the documents that we felt best represent the diversity of discussions that went on at the Forum.

8 This term has been popularized by Hardt and Negri's insightful book *Empire* (Hardt and Negri 2000). For Hardt and Negri, 'empire' refers to capitalism as a decentred yet totalizing process. In this conception, 'no nation-state can today form the center of an imperialist project' (xiv).

9 Titles and authors referred to in parentheses without publication dates refer to documents contained in the book.

10 Social movements' struggles are as much struggles over meanings as they are struggles over material resources. The battle over the public imagination and the cultural codes that legitimize or de-legitimize a social formation are central to all efforts at social transformation (Castells 1997).

11 Manuel Castells in *The Power of Identity* (1997) has predicted that successful social movements will be characterized by a network form of organization that reflects and counteracts the network logic of contemporary globalization.

12 Another group, as noted by Hardt (2002), discerns diffuse global networks as the path to liberation versus the more traditional leftist argument that states are the key instrument for advancing progress. 'Parties versus networks' constitutes an important conflict in the movement but is not one that is highlighted by the WSF 2002 conference documents.

13 The phrase 'the convergence of difference' was first suggested to us by Samir Amin and Jose Correa Leite.

14 The editors of 'Cultures of Politics, Politics of Cultures: Re-Visioning Latin American Social Movements' have also argued that democracy is the key issue of contention among Latin American social movements (Alvarez *et al.* 1998: 1).

15 The phrase 'the universalism of difference' was suggested to us by Richard Peet, Professor of Geography at Clark University.

Bibliography

Alvarez, Sonia E., Evelina Dagnino and Arturo Escobar (1998) *Cultures of Politics, Politics of Cultures*. Boulder, Colorado: Westview Press.

Amin, Samir (1995) 'Fifty Years Is Enough!', *Monthly Review*, 46: 8–50.

Anderson, Benedict (1991) *Imagined Communities: Reflections on the Origin and*

Spread of Nationalism. London and New York: Verso.

Appadurai, Arjun (1990) 'Disjuncture and Difference in the Global Cultural Economy', *Public Culture*, 2(2): 1–24.

Appadurai, Arjun (1991) 'Global Ethnoscapes: Notes and Queries for a Transnational Anthropology', in R. Fox (ed.), *Recapturing Anthropology: Working in the Present.* Santa Fe: School of American Research Press: 191–210.

Appadurai, Arjun (1996) *Modernity at Large: Cultural Dimensions of Globalization.* Minneapolis: University of Minnesota Press.

Barber, Benjamin (1996) *Jihad vs McWorld.* New York: Ballantine Books.

Beck, Ulrich (2000) *What is Globalization?* Cambridge, England: Polity Press.

Brecher, Jeremy, Tim Costello and Brendan Smith (2000). *Globalization from Below: The Power of Solidarity.* Cambridge, MA: South End Press.

Breckenridge, Carol A. (ed.) (1995) *Consuming Modernity: Public Culture in a South Asian World.* Minneapolis: University of Minnesota Press.

Castells, Manuel (1997) *The Power of Identity.* Malden, MA: Blackwell Publishers.

Escobar, Arturo (1992) 'Culture, Economics and Politics in Latin American Social Movements Theory and Research', in A. Escobar and S. Alvarez (eds) *The Making of Social Movements in Latin America.* Boulder and Oxford: Westview Press.

Gupta, Akhil and James Ferguson (eds) (1997a) *Anthropological Locations: Boundaries and Grounds of a Field Science.* Berkeley: University of California Press.

Gupta, Akhil and James Ferguson (eds) (1997b) *Culture, Power, Place: Explorations in Critical Anthropology.* Durham, NC: Duke University Press.

Haas, Peter (1992) 'Introduction: Epistemic Communities and International Policy Coordination', *International Organization*, 46 (Winter 92): 1–36.

Hannerz, Ulf (1996) *Transnational Connections: Culture, People, Places.* London and New York: Routledge.

Hardt, Michael (2002) 'Porto Alegre: Today's Bandung', electronically published in 2002 on the World Social Forum website: www.forumsocialmundial.org/br/eng/balanco. Site visited on 22 September 2002.

Hardt, Michael and Antonio Negri (2000) *Empire.* Cambridge, MA: Harvard University Press.

hooks, bell (1984) *Feminist Theory: From Margin to Center.* Boston: South End Press.

Hunt, Louis D (1999) 'Civil Society and the Idea of a Commercial Republic', in M. Schechter (ed.) *The Revival of Civil Society: Global and Comparative Perspectives.* New York: St. Martin's Press.

Hunt, Louis D. and M. Schechter (1999) 'Introduction', in Michael G. Schechter (ed.) *The Revival of Civil Society: Global and Comparative Perspectives*. New York: St. Martin's Press.

Keck, Margaret E. and Kathryn Sikkink (1998) *Activists beyond Borders: Advocacy Networks in International Politics*. Ithaca and London: Cornell University Press.

Keohane, Robert (1995) 'Hobbes's Dilemma and Institutional Change in World Politics: Sovereignty in International Society', in Hans-Henrik Holm and George Sorensen (eds) *Whose World Order? Uneven Globalization and the End of the Cold War*. Boulder: Westview.

Laclau, Ernesto and Chantal Mouffe (2001) *Hegemony and Socialist Strategy: Towards a Radical Democratic Politics* (2nd edn). New York: Verso.

Lash, Scott and John Urry (1994) *Economies of Signs and Space*. London: Sage.

Marchand, M.H., and J.L. Parpart (eds) (1995) *Feminism/Postmodernism/Development*. London: Routledge.

Mohanty, C (1991) 'Cartographies of Struggle: Third World Women and the Politics of Feminism', in C.T. Mohanty, A. Russo, and L.Torres (eds) *Third World Women and the Politics of Feminism*. Bloomington: Indiana University Press: 1–49.

Moraga, C. and G. Anzaldúa (eds) (1981) *This Bridge Called My Back: Writings by Radical Women of Color*. Watertown, MA: Persephone Press.

Patomäki, Heikki and Teivo Teivainen with Mika Rönkkö (2002) *Global Democracy Initiatives: The Art of the Possible*. Helsinki: Network Institute for Global Democratization.

Peet, Richard with Elaine Hartwick (1999) *Theories of Development*. New York: Guilford Press.

Rebick, Judy (2000) *Imagine Democracy*. Toronto: Stoddard Publishing.

Robertson, Roland (1992) *Globalization: Social Theory and Global Culture*. London: Sage.

Sikkink, Kathryn (1993) 'Human Rights, Principled Issue Networks, and Sovereignty in Latin America', *International Organizations,* 47 (3): 411–41.

Starr, Amory (2000) *Naming the Enemy: Anti-corporate Movements Confront Globalization*. London: Zed Books.

PART

I

THE PRODUCTION OF WEALTH
& SOCIAL REPRODUCTION

OVERVIEW

Key Questions, Critical Issues

WILLIAM F. FISHER AND THOMAS PONNIAH

Key Questions

The key questions in Part I concern:

- external debt;
- repercussions of the colonization of Africa/Brazil;
- necessity of controls on financial capital;
- comparative disadvantage of international trade;
- need to limit the mobility of transnational corporations;
- the attack on the labour movement; and
- the relationship between 'the solidarity economy' and neoliberalism.

With respect to the debt, these papers begin by acknowledging that the neoliberal model of development has led to perpetual indebtedness, stolen wealth deposited in Northern banks, and Southern dependency on international financial markets, the International Monetary Fund and the World Bank. They go on to ask: how does one move from an economy of indebtedness towards financing and building a sustainable and socially just development? What are the different sources for funding development? What is a new development strategy? What are the local, regional and global alternatives to privatization, structural adjustment programmes, external markets and free trade (Toussaint and Zacharie)?

What new rules are needed to ensure fair, transparent and equitable global financial practices between creditors and debtors? Who should formulate new rules? If the background to the problem of perpetual indebtedness lies in the history of colonialism, then should the discourse of debt focus on 'forgiveness/cancellation of the debt' or should it aim for reparations for the North's historical social, economic and ecological debt to the South (Africa/Brazil synthesis)?

The papers argue that the repercussions of colonialism are compounded by the current lack of control over the global economy. How can an alternative globalization, premised on sustainable development and an economics that is in the service of humankind, respectful of the environment and the diversity of people, be constructed? How can development be made to sustain the diversity of life, nature and culture? What is the relationship of the state to development and specifically to financial capital? What are the specific strategies to regulate capital (ATTAC, France)? What radical reforms can be applied to international financial institutions (IFIs)?

Related to questions around development and financial capital are the disadvantages of the contemporary form of international trade. These papers see the 'free trade' policies promoted by the World Trade Organization producing a society that is at the service of the economy (International Trade Conference synthesis). How can the economy be redirected into fulfilling the broader society's needs? In order to challenge international trade there needs to be a discussion of how to regulate corporations democratically. The challenge is that corporations currently have the power to unilaterally direct government. As these papers articulate, their presence in political decision-making is so profound that it has become common sense that their strategies of privatization and investment are the best methods for achieving employment and development. The challenge of regulating corporations is compounded by the potentially divisive varieties of resistance: environmentalist, human rights, labour, and advocates of corporate responsibility versus those of corporate accountability. How can these various approaches be brought into a complementary agenda that promotes 'life values' against the 'profit values' that permeate the current context (Karliner and Aparicio)?

Discussions of debt, trade and corporate power inevitably circle around the question of labour. How should labour respond in light of the World Trade Organization (WTO), the International Monetary Fund (IMF) and the World Bank's policies that promote the interests of those 'who invest for a living' versus the interests of those who 'work for a living' (Faux)? In light of the global reach of the investor class, should unions focus on strategies for national sovereignty or should workers transnationalize their resistance and their alternatives? Two significant aspects of this question relate to the place of African trade unions and women in new strategies of labour organizing (COSATU). What principles should African workers adopt and what forms of solidarity can workers around the world propose to African labour? In relation to gender, it is well known that women are often threatened at work, on the street and in the home. In addition, they are a minority in terms of power and decision-making in the union movement. In light of the history of patriarchy and the current neoliberal conjuncture, what needs to be done to ensure equality between the genders?

The last challenge is the question of the solidarity economy. It is a form of economy that is publicly debated in Latin America and parts of Europe. The question asked is, since neither capital, the state bureaucracy, nor representative democracy place the whole human being, in both its masculine and feminine dimensions, at the centre of social and economic development, what new economic processes and institutions need to be invented (Solidarity Economy Conference synthesis)? Further questions are: is the solidarity economy self-sufficient or is it meant to complement other forms of economic activity? Is it meant to attenuate the failures of the neoliberal project or is it meant to be the building-block of the new society?

Critical Issues

In Part I, there are two significant areas of antagonism that could divide and disarticulate the global solidarity movement: the conflict between 'radicals' and 'reformers', and the potential incommensurability between diverse ideological scales of political demands.

The conflict between today's radicals and reformers is most evident in the debate on whether to abolish or reform the WTO, the IMF and the World Bank. On one side are reformers who believe that civil society should dialogue, negotiate and form partnerships with the international financial institutions. Their underlying beliefs are, first, that change can come through reasonable discussion, and, second, that the global economy needs to be centrally coordinated and these institutions can be used for that purpose. On the other side are radicals who believe that the Bretton Woods institutions and the WTO are fundamentally dysfunctional. To enter into dialogue with these institutions is thus seen as not only pointless but also dangerous because social movements' acquiescence to consultation provides much-needed legitimacy to the IMF, World Bank and WTO. These radicals also believe that the world economy would work better for the poor in a fluid system of checks and balances that were not dominated by any particular configuration of global institutions. Many activists look for a compromise by calling for a 'radical reform' of the financial institutions and their insertion within the framework of a reformed UN system. This hope also asks activists to believe in the reform of a system that has historically not provided Southern countries with even their reformist demands, let alone their more progressive ones. The radicalism versus reformism debate, in terms of the WTO, IMF and World Bank, can appear irreconcilable.

The second contradiction involves the ideology of scale. There is a conflict in calls for change at the local, national and global levels. Many argue for local self-sufficiency, others argue that a nation-state's production should be primarily aimed at satisfying its own population's basic needs, and all agree that there should be universally guaranteed rights to food sovereignty, to consumer choice in relation to genetically modified organisms (GMOs) and to access to natural resources. These various demands are contradictory. How can there be local or national autonomy and universally guaranteed rights? Who will enforce these rights? A Universal Right to Food Sovereignty will have to impose itself on many nations and many locales. In the context of a growing recognition of the long-term impacts of colonialism, who will have the legitimacy, let alone the capacity, to intervene in order to guarantee these rights? Next, how can the local and the national both have economic self-sufficiency? State sovereignty has never meant local sovereignty. In some instances it has meant the opposite. Historically, as the state has become more powerful it has centralized power such that the local has become more and more dependent on the national authority. The demand for the strengthening of the state risks replicating the bureaucratization that both the right and the left have criticized in Eastern and Western Europe, North America and Third World nationalist states.

Most 'relocalist' groups and many proponents of the solidarity economy, despite the aspirations of the 'Resist and Build' document, have as much hostility to the state as they do to capital. They believe that the state is organized and directed by the elite in the North and the South. The return of a strong state will not sit well with these organizations. They believe in the principle of subsidiarity: that is to say, if the decision does not have to be decided at a larger scale, then let it be decided at the smallest scale possible. They recognize the importance of local economic self-sufficiency, local governance, local knowledge and relationships with the local ecology. They recognize that larger scales of governance threaten the sustainability and democratic participation of local levels of governance.

The conflict between the different ideologies of scale, like the radicalism versus reformism debate, can appear irreconcilable, but these antagonisms of scale can also be interpreted in a more positive light if we think of them as politically conditioned. If these antagonisms of scale are politically or historically contingent, we can see them as contradictions in process that could be overcome as a movement intensifies, coalesces new social sectors, articulates a more comprehensive vision, and engages with the continually evolving geometry of forces in global society. While these differences of scale are not natural, they may have a weight or historical persistence that makes them recurrent and irresolvable conflicts that will inevitably arise as a movement attempts to expand and deepen. While the current antagonisms are significant, they are overshadowed by the number of commonalities that the global movement shares. Every document agrees that neoliberal globalization, alone or in alliance with patriarchy, is the central adversary that all the movements have to face. By neoliberal globalization we mean the market-organized and imposed expansion of production that emphasizes comparative advantage, free trade, export orientation, the social and spatial division of labour, and the absolute mobility of corporations. These documents portray neoliberalism as pervading all of the different issues they confront.

Following the critique of contemporary globalization is the agreement that the IMF, World Bank and WTO are the tools of the elite: they exist to help capital realize value, not to serve the cause of development, nor to stabilize the global economy. They are incapable of handling economic crises because their policies produce and reproduce instability, as in the obvious case of the East Asian currency crisis. The minimum common demand is that these institutions are radically reformed, that Third World debt is cancelled and that structural adjustment programmes are terminated.

The critique of neoliberalism also involves a common call to regulate capital flows. National and local economic sovereignty should not be destabilized by external market forces. One initial form of throwing 'sand into the wheels' of capital would be via the imposition of a 'Tobin Tax' on all financial transactions. The tax would caution speculators and thus reduce the volatility of capital flows. Funds raised would go towards funding health care and education in poor countries. Underneath all of these issues is the basic desire to re-embed the economy into a broader socio-political framework. The market needs to be regulated and guided by the democratic control of the public.

All of the authors of the documents agree that the hierarchical, market-orientated paradigm should be replaced by an endogenous model of development that sacralizes life, labour, nature and culture. All agree on the need for a system that does not relegate basic services to the fluctuations of the market but brings them under the coordination of the public sector. All policies and practices should be characterized, as in the case of the Porto Alegre budget process, by a radical and participatory democracy that runs through the local but goes even further than the Brazilian experiment, by extending into the national and the global.

The democratization of every scale must also include the globalization of human and labour rights. In terms of the latter there is specific agreement on the transnationalization of collective bargaining rights for workers. With the extension of the latter's rights would also come the expansion of collective bargaining to the informalized and casualized sectors of workers.

Last and most hopefully, all of the documents agree that progress lies in building solidarity and convergence amongst the diversity of movements without denying differences. There is recognition of the different experiences and perspectives of workers and environmentalists, Southern workers and Northern workers, women and men. With that recognition has come an acknowledgement of the importance of developing trust and communication and building solidarity based on past successes such as the 1999 demonstrations in Seattle. Underpinning this last point is the belief that 'what is not won on the streets, will not be won later in the boardroom'. All of the documents agree that direct action must complement all forms of political negotiation.

To summarize, while there are significant conflicts in Part I, there are more areas of solidarity and convergence. The documents coalesce in their conception of their adversary, neoliberal globalization, and to a large extent agree on their principles and their long term goals. The latter are driven by radical, participatory, democratic principles that build across the local, the national and the international.

EXTERNAL DEBT

Abolish the Debt in Order to
Free Development

ERIC TOUSSAINT and
ARNAUD ZACHARIE

The question we try to answer can be summarized as follows: how does one move from an economy of indebtedness towards financing sustainable and socially just development?[1] The United Nations Development Programme (UNDP) and the United Nations Children's Emergency Fund (UNICEF) estimate that 80 billion dollars a year for ten years would be enough to guarantee every human being on this planet access to basic education and health care, adequate food, drinking water and sanitation and, for women, gynaecological and obstetric care.

Eighty billion dollars represents about three times less than the sum of the Third World's already repaid external public debt; it's about a quarter of the US annual defence budget; 9 per cent of annual world military expenditure; 8 per cent of money spent on advertisements and publicity each year; half the total wealth of the four richest people on the planet.

The laws of the market and profit cannot be expected to satisfy essential needs. The 1.3 billion people deprived of clean drinking water do not have enough purchasing power.

Only resolute public policies can guarantee the fulfilment of basic human needs for all. This is why the public authorities must have at their disposal the political and financial means of honouring their obligations towards their citizens.

Citizens must also be able to exercise fully their right to play a central role in the political life of the state. To bring this about, efficient judiciary mechanisms and economic policies must be implemented in a participatory democracy. The example of a participatory budget as practised in Porto Alegre since the early 1990s should be adopted on a worldwide scale and inspire original policies of radical democracy.

The application of the Universal Declaration of Human Rights and the International Convention on Economic, Social and Cultural Rights has to be backed up by a powerful social and citizens' movement.

Firstly, the haemorrhage of wealth represented by debt repayments has to be stemmed. Next, different sources of funding must be found for socially just and ecologically sustainable development. Finally, we must break away from the old logic which leads to the cycle of indebtedness, to embezzlement and large-scale pillage of local wealth, and to dependence on the financial markets and condition-laden loans of the international financial institutions.

Breaking the Infernal Cycle of Debt

The champions of neoliberal globalization tell us that the developing countries (in which they include Eastern Europe) must repay their external debt if they wish to benefit from constant flows of funding.

In fact, ever since the debt crisis in 1982, wealth has flowed from the periphery to the centre, not the other way round, as the leaders of the international financial institutions would have us believe. In order to estimate real flows the following factors have to be taken into account: repayment of the external debt; capital outflow due to residents of peripheral countries; the repatriation of profits by multinational firms (including invisible transfers, especially via such procedures as 'over-' or 'under-' billing on invoices); the acquisition of privatized businesses in the periphery at knock-down prices on the part of capitalists of the highly industrialized countries; the purchase of raw materials produced by the populations of the periphery at low prices (deterioration in the terms of trade); the 'brain drain'; genetic pillage – the 'donors' are not the ones we are led to believe. It is a gross error of language to consider the OECD (Organization for Economic Cooperation and Development) countries, members of the Committee for Development Aid (CDA) and the Bretton Woods institutions as 'donors'.

Since 1982, the populations of the periphery countries have sent their creditors in the North the equivalent of several times the Marshall Plan (with the local capitalist elite skimming off their commission on the way).[2]

It has become urgent to adopt the opposite view from that of official discourse: the Third World's external public debt must be cancelled. Indeed, the repayment of the Third World's external public debt represents, on average, expenditure of about \$200–250 billion a year, about two to three times the amount required to satisfy basic human needs as defined by the United Nations.

Extra Resources to Finance Development

For debt cancellation to serve the purpose of human development, the money previously earmarked for debt repayment needs to be paid into a development fund, under the democratic control of the local population. However, once this first step of debt cancellation has been taken, the present economy based on international indebtedness must be replaced by a model which is both socially just and ecologically sustainable, and independent of the fluctuations of the money markets and of the loan conditions imposed by the World Bank and the IMF. This development fund, already supplied with money saved through debt cancellation, must also be financed by the following measures.

Restitution of stolen property to the citizens of the Third World
The considerable wealth illicitly accumulated by the ruling authorities and local capitalists in developing countries has been securely deposited in the most industrialized countries with the complicity of private financial institutions and the tacit agreement of the Northern governments (the practice continues to this day).

To operate such restitution implies the completion of legal proceedings in Third World countries and the most industrialized countries. Among other things, they would serve to ensure that people guilty of corruption do not get off scot-free. This is the only hope, if one day democracy and transparency are to triumph over corruption.

Further action would be to support the resolutions made at the international meeting held in Dakar in December 2000 (From Resistance to Alternatives) demanding compensation for the pillage which the Third World has been subject to over the last five centuries. This includes the restitution of economic and cultural property stolen from the Asian, African and South American continents.

Tax financial transactions

ATTAC suggests a tax of 0.1 per cent on such cross-border financial transactions bringing in some $100 billion annually, which could be used to combat inequality, and to provide public health and education services, food security and sustainable development.

Raise Official Development Aid (ODA) to at least 0.7 per cent of the GDP

In 1999, ODA represented a mere 0.24 per cent of the Gross Domestic Product of the most industrialized countries, despite their commitment, frequently reiterated within the framework of the UN, to reach the objective of 0.7 per cent. This means ODA must be multiplied threefold to fulfil the commitments made. Considering that ODA represents a little under $50 billion, it should therefore reach $150 billion a year which should be entirely paid out as grants. Finally, rather than speak of aid, henceforth it would be more appropriate to use the term reparations, the idea being to make reparations for all the damage caused by centuries of pillage and unfair trade.

Levy an exceptional tax on the estates of the very wealthy

In its 1995 report, UNCTAD suggests levying a single, exceptional tax on the estates of the very wealthy. Such a tax levied throughout the world would mobilize considerable funds. This exceptional tax (unlike a recurrent tax on property such as exists in many countries round the world) could be levied on a national scale. A one-off solidarity tax of, say, 10 per cent on the property of the richest tenth in each country could generate very considerable internal resources.

A New Development Strategy

Instead of the present development strategy, which consists of the creditors forcing Southern countries to adopt neoliberal adjustment programmes, an endogenous and integrated development strategy should be embraced. The change would be implemented in the following stages.

End Structural Adjustment Programmes

Structural Adjustment Programmes (SAPs) result in the weakening of states by making them more dependent on external fluctuations (world-market movements, speculative attacks, etc.) and by subjecting them to conditions imposed by the IMF/World Bank duo backed up by the governments of the creditor countries grouped within the Club de Paris.

The UN Human Rights Commission has repeatedly adopted resolutions concerning the debt problem and structural adjustment. In a resolution from 1999, the Commission states that 'For the population of an indebted country, the exercise of their basic rights to food, housing, clothing, work, education, medical care and a healthy environment may not be subordinated to the application of Structural Adjustment Programs and economic reforms generated by the debt' (1999: Art. 5).

The human consequences of SAPs are incontestably negative. The latter must therefore be cancelled and replaced with policies aimed at satisfying basic human needs, giving priority to domestic markets, food security and complementary exchanges on a regional or continental basis.

Ensure the return of privatized strategic sectors to the public domain

Water reserves and distribution, electricity production and distribution, telecommunications, postal services, railways, companies which extract and transform raw materials, the credit system and certain education and health sectors have been systematically privatized or are in the process of being privatized. These companies must be returned to the public domain.

Adopt a partly self-based development model

This type of development involves creating politically and economically integrated zones, bringing to bear endogenous development models, strengthening internal markets, creating local savings funds for local financing, developing education and health, setting up progressive taxation and other mechanisms to ensure the redistribution of wealth, diversifying exports, introducing agrarian reform to guarantee universal access to land for small farmers, and urban reform to guarantee universal access to housing.

Today's global architecture, built on a periphery forced to provide raw materials and cheap labour to a centre that has all the technology and capital, must be replaced by regional economic groupings. Only such self-based development would allow South–South relations to emerge, which is the precondition *sine qua non* for the economic development of the Third World (and, by extension, the world).

Alter trade practices

The historical tendency for the terms of trade to deteriorate must be brought to an end. To do this, mechanisms guaranteeing a better price for the basket of products exported on the world market by developing countries must be introduced. As for agriculture, as demanded by Via Campesina, there has to be recognition of each country's or group of countries' right to nutritional sovereignty, and especially to self-sufficiency in staple foodstuffs.

The rules of global trading must be subordinate to strict environmental, social and cultural criteria. Health, education, water and culture can have no place in the field of world commerce. Public services in the general interest are the guarantee of basic rights and must therefore be excluded from the General Agreement on Trade and Services (GATS).

Furthermore, the Trade-Related Intellectual Property Rights (TRIPs) agreement needs to be abolished, aspects of which allow the North to appropriate the rich natural resources of the South and prevent the Southern countries from freely producing goods (such as medicines) to satisfy the needs of their populations.

New Rules of Financial Good Practice

The repeated financial crises of the 1990s proved by their absurdity that there can be no sustainable development without strict controls over the movement of capital and tax evasion. Several strategies are therefore required to subordinate the money markets to the fulfilment of basic human needs:

- Re-regulate the financial markets.

- Control the movement of capital. Eliminate tax havens and remove the bankers' rule of secrecy to combat more efficiently tax evasion, embezzlement of public funds and corruption.

- Adopt rules to ensure the protection of indebted countries External indebtedness may be justified if decided democratically by the countries concerned. However, the use of the borrowed money must be organized according to principles radically different from those that have hitherto prevailed. Two new principles must be adhered to. First, a 'reverse' conditionality: the obligation to repay, and pay interest on, these loans provided at low interest rates and below market conditions will only be valid if the debt is proven to have enabled sufficient creation of wealth in the countries concerned. Second, the lender countries should organize strong and efficient protection for the developing countries on an international scale to enable the latter to defend themselves against all forms of abuse and despoliation by banks, private international investors or the international financial institutions.

- Democratic control of political indebtedness. The decision by a state to contract debts and the terms under which they are taken out must be submitted to popular approval (by debate and vote in Parliament, and citizens' control).

Further Indispensable Measures

Cancelling the external public debts of the periphery, abandoning SAPs and other measures proposed above are necessary conditions, but insufficient as such to guarantee the authentic human development of the peoples of the world. Further measures are indispensable, beginning with equality between women and men and the right to self-determination for indigenous peoples.

Notes

1 Sustainable development is defined as that which 'allows present needs to be met without compromising the capacity of future generations to meet their own needs'.
2 The Marshall Plan (1948–51) was intended to help reconstruct a Europe devastated by the Second World War. Considering that in 2001, 6.28 dollars are the equivalent of one dollar in 1948, the cost of the Marshall Plan (12.5 billion dollars in 1948–51) would represent 78.5 billion dollars in 2001. If we consider that the sum of repayments made by the Third World in 1999 was 300 billion dollars (Source: World Bank, GDF, 2000), it means that in that year those countries sent the equivalent of four Marshall Plans to their creditors in the highly industrialized countries. Similarly, the populations of the Third World have sent the equivalent of 43 Marshall Plans (more than 3,450 billion dollars) to their creditors in the centre since 1980.

2 AFRICA/BRAZIL
Conference Synthesis

JACQUES D'ADEKSY

The Africa/Brazil Conference, which took place on 1 February 2002, had Taoufik Bem Abdallah, Aminata Traore and Benedita da Silva as discussants and Jacques d'Adesky as facilitator. Pauline Muchina could not be present because, according to information obtained by Nilza Iraci, member of the Afro-National Committee and the World Social Forum International Committee, she was refused a visa by the Brazilian authorities.

Medical reasons prevented Senator Abdias Nascimento from being present. However, he sent his greetings and a message in which he made some remarks about the social mobilization of people in Africa and their Afro-Brazilian descendants in their struggle against racism and colonialism. He emphasized the need to establish a strategic alliance between the people of Africa and their descendants in Brazil in order to strengthen the case for reparations.

The discussants agreed with Abdias Nascimento's proposal. In relation to the Africa/Brazil dialogue, they noticed the spectacular increase in African and Afro-Brazilian participation in the Forum this year, as well as the increased opportunity to debate these issues. This growth also highlighted the fact that the World Social Forum 2002 had assumed considerable importance, in the sense that it carried forward its partnership with the African Social Forum (ASF) and the Afro-National Committee, making this alliance more solid and meaningful for the future.

The discussants reminded the audience that the idea of an

Africa/Brazil Conference had first been proposed by the World Social Forum 2001, and had gained momentum during the World Conference against Racism, Xenophobia and Intolerance that took place in Durban, South Africa, later that year.

Starting from a report from the ASF meeting that had taken place in January 2002 in Bamako (Mali) analysing the socio-economic, political and cultural issues that affect both African and Afro-Brazilian people, the discussants pointed out proposals that would make another world possible. The suggestions could be divided into two complementary groups: the utopian and the pragmatic.

The utopians point out the necessity of understanding that society can no longer be founded on profit and competition, but should be based on the values of equality, equity and social justice. The desired globalization is a humane one; profit can no longer be prioritized over human needs.

However, the construction of a new world that integrates these values depends on the collective action of civil society to put pressure particularly on states and international institutions. Only when the importance of these values is understood, will it be possible to implement concrete and differentiated actions in the economic, social and cultural fields.

Concerning concrete actions, the consensus reached is to go beyond the rhetoric of solidarity, which is ever present in diplomatic parlance. Faced with the social and economic inequalities that affect the African people and Brazil's Afro-descendants, it is necessary to deepen the notion of reparations and to extend the scope of affirmative action.

Reparations and affirmative action are based, above all, on understanding the need to compensate people and group members for the material and moral damage caused by colonialism and slavery. In this sense, it reinforces the idea that reparations and affirmative action must be considered as ethical principles and not just a means of financial compensation. It is possible, then, that both will come to be accepted as an economic right of the people of Africa and their Afro-descendants, albeit that the debts created by colonization and slavery cannot be simply reduced to monetary terms.

Other concrete actions to repair the damage of racism, colonialism and racial prejudice, point to the construction of a world without violence in which the culture of peace can flourish. Among the proposals discussed, equal access to high quality education and the guarantee of proper attention being given to African and Afro-descendants' history in educational books caught people's attention, as well as the importance of ensuring a positive image of Africans and Afro-descendants on television and in movies, theatre and commercials. All these actions were considered fundamental for these people to become the true owners of their destiny.

These urgent proposals also aimed to consolidate the alliance between the ASF and the Afro-National Committee in their respective struggles against racism and cultural superiority, which so gravely afflict both the people of Africa and Brazil's Afro-descendants.

Translated by Claudia Boal, revised by Joris Van Mol

FINANCIAL CAPITAL

Controls on Finance Capital

ATTAC, FRANCE

Introduction

Liberal globalization has entailed increased inequality and instability on a world scale. Liberalized finance has been a powerful vehicle of these global disequilibria. The data speak for themselves: 80 per cent of international financial flows are concentrated among approximately twenty countries, which represent only 22 per cent of the world's population. Furthermore, over the past decade, financial crises have accelerated, repeatedly striking the countries of Asia, Latin America, Africa and Eastern Europe.

The international financial institutions (the IMF and the World Bank) have been incapable of regulating these crises. Indeed, their policies have tended only to exacerbate existing inequalities. The reforms proposed by the so-called international financial community are inappropriate because they do not address the fundamental driving forces of liberal globalization and the power of the financial markets.

Therefore, an alternative approach to international finance is necessary. International finance must be founded on a different conception of globalization, one premised on sustainable development, that is, on an economics in the service of humankind, respectful of the environment and the diversity of peoples.

This means, first, returning to nation-states control over their own policies, which in turn implies controls over capital movements. This goal is attainable by establishing policies to control capital flows, by reinforcing regulations on markets and financial actors, and by radically reforming the existing architecture of the international financial institutions.

Restore Controls over Capital Flows to Nation-States

The international mobility of capital hinders the implementation of economic policy in the North as well as in the South: central banks, as well as budget and fiscal authorities, are dominated by the markets, which are always quick to sanction policies they judge to be contrary to their interests.

The dependence of nation-states on the financial markets results directly from the development model imposed by neoliberal policies: instead of concentrating on their internal savings and their markets, nation-states are constrained to orientate their productive and financial activities towards international trade, especially when they are indebted as a result of prior deficits.

In order to regain some room for manoeuvre, countries must be able to protect themselves, a necessity that calls into question the liberal logic attributing primacy to openness to external forces. This is a matter of guaranteeing, at the international level, the right of individual countries to reduce their openness to the outside in order to implement their own policies effectively. It is also desirable that countries coordinate with one another to implement common policies: groups of countries must have the right to define their own set of rules to allow them to protect their internal markets. The experiences of the European Common Market and Mercosur (the Common Market in the Latin American core) are moving, or could move, in this direction.

Liberalization of the capital account (which reflects the balance on capital flows) must be decided by the sovereign nation-states, not imposed by the IMF or the World Bank. This is a political choice, and is not the only possible option. Any liberalization, if adopted, must be subordinated to development goals. It should be considered a final step, one that is reached when countries have developed robust economic and financial structures (this is the notion of sequencing).

Two conditions must be satisfied for the capital account to be freed up: macro-economic stabilization (control of inflation, and healthy public finances); and a local banking sector that is sound and sufficiently robust to confront international competition.

Liberalization of the capital account, when it is possible, must be modulated by types of operation: not all financial operations can be treated in the same manner. Operations that most benefit economic growth must be privileged. This means liberalizing direct investment first.

Promote Control of Capital Flows

Contrary to how neoliberal doctrine would have it, economic analysis and experience demonstrate the soundness of capital control policies at the national and international levels.

Theoretical Foundations

There are at least five reasons justifying the implementation of capital control mechanisms:

1 The process of international financial integration has profoundly changed the behaviour of banks and international investors, giving rise to alternating waves of capital inflows and outflows with devastating results.

2 The framework of liberalized finance has made it more difficult to regulate financial crises. Unlike the debt crisis of the early 1980s, which involved a limited number of sovereign state borrowers, the more recent crises of the 1990s have involved a large number of private actors that are more difficult to regulate.

3 The crises are often produced by external factors: we know that the crises that afflicted the East Asian developing nations in 1997– 98 were attributable in large part to the appreciation of the dollar.

4 A country cannot simultaneously maintain the stability of its own

currency and the autonomy of its economic policy in a context in which capital is completely mobile (Mundell's impossible trilogy). Controlling capital flows is a means of resolving this contradiction.

5 Capital inflows cause major macro-economic imbalances (surges in credit, consumption and non-productive investments), creating inflationary tendencies and giving rise to speculative bubbles. Preventing such imbalances requires controlling capital inflows.

National-Level Policy Measures

During the 1990s, several countries, notably Chile, Colombia and Malaysia, have successfully adopted temporary measures to discourage inflows and outflows of short-term speculative capital. These policies can serve as examples for developing countries. They allow two goals to be attained: the restoration of room for responses to economic policies that are imposed by external forces; and the stabilization of exchange rates and avoidance of an overvalued currency, which causes economic recession.

International Financial Measures

National capital control policies are inadequate in the face of the sheer financial fire-power of international actors. It is therefore necessary to introduce capital control measures on an international scale. Taxation is particularly appropriate for achieving this objective. Here we would mention the idea of the 'three global taxes', the first of which is the Tobin Tax.

A Tax on International Financial Transactions (Tobin-type). The best-known tax is that proposed by James Tobin, which is applied to all transactions on the foreign exchange market. It is inspired by Keynes's proposition of a general tax on all financial transactions intended to reduce speculation. Its average rate would be low and its annual cost inversely proportional to the duration of the transactions, so as to discourage short-term operations, the sole objective of which is to realize speculative gains on foreign exchange markets. This measure is intended to achieve several objectives. First, it would permit us, in Tobin's words, to 'put sand in the two well-oiled gears' of the international financial markets by hindering arbitrage and speculative transactions.

Second, the measure would accord greater authority to national monetary authorities, which could in turn focus their attentions on their domestic economic objectives. Moreover, the Tobin Tax would allow exchange rates to reflect better their values as determined by fundamental long-term factors because the spreads between market rates and the 'fundamentals' – speculative bubbles – would be reduced.

Finally, the revenues generated by the Tobin Tax could finance an international fund established, among other possible purposes, to finance aid to developing countries adversely affected by the dysfunctionalities of the international financial system.

There are no serious obstacles to the implementation of a Tobin-type tax. There are other proposals that would reinforce the effectiveness of this measure, most notably the institution of a two-tier tax (Spahn). As it is difficult to create a global tax outright, it is proposed – and this is the position of Europe's ATTAC – that the Tobin Tax be first implemented at the level of the euro zone or European Union. Given its size, with a population and GDP that approach US levels, the European region offers an excellent point of departure for the application of this taxation.

Two Other Global Taxes on Foreign Direct Investment (FDI) and on the Profits of Multinational Corporations. A variable tax on FDI is justified by two sets of factors: first, it is one portion of the activity of multinational corporations that does not lend itself to the tax evasion entailed by capital mobility. Second, it allows us to combat 'tax-dumping' caused by competition among countries' taxation systems in order to make themselves more attractive to foreign investors, and enables us to oppose the erosion of workers' rights in FDI recipient countries at the same time. In effect, these countries are also those where wages are lowest, labour legislation most lax, and taxation minimal. This tax would be applicable to all direct investments, in rich countries as well as in poor countries. Its rate would vary from 20 per cent to 10 per cent, and would be indexed on the basis of a scale for each category of country (rich and poor) according to the rating a country received from the International Labor Office (ILO) regarding its observation of fundamental labour rights.

Another form of global taxation on capital would seek to avoid transfer-pricing manipulation by multinational corporations by calculating their profits differently and identifying the jurisdictions within which they are taxable. One method inspired by the unitary tax in the United States could be used here. This global tax on profits has the advantage of being simple and easy to calculate and collect. Both the North and the South would be involved in this mechanism.

These three global taxes thus offer a coherent and complementary array of mechanisms that public opinion could press for in seeking an alternative, more balanced and controlled, globalization.

There are other related proposals to be considered. Most significant is the UN Commission for Trade and Development's (UNCTAD) proposal of a world tax on income from capital or on large-scale wealth, which would serve to finance a World Fund for Development.

Reinforce Control of Markets and Financial Actors

If the power of international financial capital is to be reduced, it is essential that financial markets be supervised. It is also necessary to control closely financial actors who comprise the global financial oligarchy, for they have benefited the most from liberal globalization.

Supervision
Public authorities should act in accordance with some basic principles: they ought to reduce the mobility of investments; render all financial transactions transparent; distance themselves progressively from the financial markets by rehabilitating bank credit and targeting produc-

tive uses including job creation and social security; and maintain single price quotations by daily fixing to avoid continuous fluctuations of exchange rates.

Each of the four principal markets should be targeted via specific measures:

- **The stock market:** limitations on non-resident shareholding in corporations, limitations on the dividends paid out by companies, a stock-market tax, etc.

- **The foreign exchange market:** compulsory deposits on foreign exchange transactions; a Tobin-type tax; prohibition of the maintenance of a hedged position (spreads between credits and actual commitments in currencies); control of capital flows, etc.

- **Derivative markets:** increases in the compulsory guarantee deposits in order to limit the leverage effect of funds used in speculation; and control and limitation of off-balance sheet systems where the majority of speculative transactions are recorded.

- **The bond market:** limitations on sales of securities to non-residents.

Elimination of Tax Havens

Two sets of measures are necessary:

- **Lifting of banking confidentiality at the request of the authorities:** this implies regulating those professions that are protected by banking secrecy, implementing sanctions against those financial establishments that refuse to comply, and keeping track of principals and transactions in derivative products. These controls on capital flows can be implemented effectively with the support of clearing institutions and payment systems.

- **The establishment of obligations on the part of states:** to recognize a right to intervene in states that harbour tax evaders; to cooperate with other states judicially and administratively, in order to centralize information on financial crime; to require the publication of data on tax havens; to deny recognition to shadow companies; and to respect anti-money-laundering laws.

Reinforcement of Controls on Banks

Banks, along with sinking funds, are those institutions which hold the primary responsibility for speculative international capital flows. It is the large international banks that execute the bulk of exchange transactions, most of which are speculative.

The supervision to which banks are already subject appears to be inadequate, however. Several measures have been implemented to restore to banks their role in financing enterprises: more effective integration of supervisory institutions; expansion of prohibitions on certain speculative transactions; compulsory reserve deposits; and increasing the numbers of government tax officials already in place in financial institutions.

We must change the liberal philosophy of the Basel Committee on Banking Supervision, the principal international regulatory authority, which is increasingly basing the supervision of banks on the notion of self-control exercised by banks themselves.

Finally, the measures currently imposed by the Basel Committee are inappropriate for banks in developing countries, which lack the human and technical resources to implement them effectively and are thus weakened by the expansion of their international operations.

Prudential Rules for International Investors

A major limitation of current international prudential measures is that they essentially affect banks but do not directly affect other international financial actors. This is the case with hedge funds – the heavily leveraged speculative funds that are not subject to regulation because it is claimed that they do not solicit funds from the public.

This is a major regulatory black hole that must be filled immediately by imposing on all investors precautionary rules that are comparable to those applied to international banks. Another series of measures could include the following: limiting the proportion of investments in developing countries made by foreign investors and requiring that shares be retained for at least a year after their acquisition (a measure proposed by Keynes during the 1930s).

Make Private Actors Responsible for the Crises Pay

To repair the damage caused by international financial crises, the IMF is implementing bail-out programmes. These plans best protect speculators, for they are thus assured of reimbursement for their losses. One radical policy measure for discouraging speculation on the part of international banks and investors is to involve them directly in the financing of the damage that financial crises have caused in the South. This would, among other things, reduce the phenomenon of 'moral hazard' affecting the behaviour of private creditors inasmuch as they would be sanctioned for losses that they inflict on debtor countries.

Reform the International Financial Institutions (IFIs)

The full gamut of international financial controls cannot be implemented without a radical reform of international organizations, particularly of the IFIs – the IMF and the World Bank. These two institutions have departed increasingly from their original mandates, as defined by the Bretton Woods agreements, which were to ensure the stability of the international monetary system and to promote the financing of development.

The reform of the IFIs necessarily requires, then, that their functions be redefined:

1 **To organize the cancellation of the external debt** of the poorest countries on an international scale.

2 **To assure countries of the forms and conditions of financing that permit sustainable development**. This means making rich countries respect their commitments to development aid and implementing mechanisms of low-interest, non-market financing targeted to specific objectives.

3 **To guarantee to developing countries the right to protect themselves against speculative capital flows** and equipping them technically with the means to do so.

4 **To help developing countries build (or rebuild) the institutions** that

permit them to protect their exports from the hazards of instability in the currency and raw materials markets.

To this end, two new institutions must be created:

- **A Currency Exchange and Raw Materials Market Stabilization Fund**;

- **A Global Fund for Development** charged with financing the most urgent projects and effecting the necessary North–South technology transfers, particularly in the fields of health, energy and the environment. These funds would be financed by the global taxes described above.

A thoroughgoing reform of the IFIs along the following lines is necessary if these objectives are to be attained:

- **Democracy and transparency:** participation of the countries of the South in management and real control by local populations and national parliaments over the policies of IFIs in order to guarantee a balance between creditor and debtor countries.

- **Unification of the IFIs with a United Nations that itself has undergone reform:** it is essential that the IFIs, as well as the WTO, be subordinated to the United Nations system. This would subject them to external controls, on the one hand, and, on the other hand, compel them to respect fundamental rights – human rights, civil and political rights, economic, social, cultural and environmental rights. These take priority over financial and commercial interests in the hierarchy of international norms.

In this view, in order to reduce the now excessive power of the IFIs and the WTO, and to restore power to nation-states and their citizens on a global scale, it is necessary to organize possible recourse in international law for both nation-states and individual citizens in the face of violations of fundamental rights.

Translated by volunteer translator Germaine A. Hoston

INTERNATIONAL TRADE
Conference Synthesis

BERNARD CASSEN

Panellists
Martin Khor   THIRD WORLD NETWORK, MALAYSIA
Dot Keet   AFRICA TRADE NETWORK, SOUTH AFRICA
Jean Lapeyre   EUROPEAN TRADE UNION CONFEDERATION
(ETUC), BELGIUM
Paul Nicholson   VIA CAMPESINA, BELGIUM
Hector de la Cueva   ALIANZA SOCIAL CONTINENTAL, MEXICO
Lori Wallach   PUBLIC CITIZEN, USA

Facilitator
Bernard Cassen   ATTAC, FRANCE

Broad Consensus on Free Trade and the WTO

- Free trade does not guarantee wealth and development for nations and people.

- The WTO favours the rich states and is gathering too much authority and power over matters that should not be negotiated within this organization.

Proposals by Dot Keet, Africa Trade Network

- The development of nations should be based on production and not on commerce;

- States should focus on diversification of their economies and avoid a rush towards concentrating on exports;

- The rules that govern the WTO and free trade have to change fundamentally;

- The nature and roles of the WTO should be reformed and be subordinated to the UN.

Proposals on the WTO by Martin Khor, Third World Network

- Delegitimize the WTO and condemn the conduct of the United States and the European Union in the latest WTO meetings in Doha (November 2001);

- Sign the Declaration of the Non-Governmental Organizations (NGOs) that rejects the Doha Declaration;

- Do everything possible not to allow the WTO to open a new round of negotiations to liberalize the agreements on investments and competition, services and public markets;

- The NGOs of the rich countries should force their governments to pull back.

The Objective of these Proposals is Threefold

- To stop the expansion of the WTO's authority;

- To reform the current WTO agreements;

- To prevent negotiations on services from taking place within the framework of the WTO.

Concerning the Countries in the South, Martin Khor proposes:

- Increase tariffs and subsidies so that these countries can develop a manufacturing sector of their own;

- Create a system with fair prices for agricultural products and natural resources, guaranteeing minimum prices.

Proposals by Paul Nicholson, Via Campesina

Create a Universal Right to Food Sovereignty. This would imply:

- The right to develop an agricultural policy in order to be able to feed the population of each country (a policy of food self-sufficiency);

- Develop a policy to protect local markets;

- The right to have access to the key productive resources (water, land and cereals);

- The right of consumers to decide what type of product they want to consume (for example, not to consume GMO foods);

- Remove the agricultural chapter from the authority of the WTO;

- Question the current rules of international trade concerning agriculture and propose a system with regional food prices.

Proposals by Hector de la Cueva, Alianza Social Continental

Here are Alianza's alternatives to neoliberalism in Latin America:

- Reduction or cancellation of the external debt;

- Rejection of structural adjustment programmes;

- Taxation of financial transactions;

- Protection of the environment and agriculture.

The objective of the Alianza: to coordinate a global movement that includes all sectors of Latin American countries in order to propose alternatives to neoliberalism.

Proposal by Lori Wallach, Public Citizen

- Point out the negative effects of the WTO agreements;
- Stop the current round of negotiations of the WTO and NAFTA;
- Mobilize civil society on a national level to encourage their respective governments to change their positions on the WTO.

Final proposals by the panellists

- An economy at the service of the people;
- The need for a global movement that goes beyond individual countries, NGOs, unions, etc. in order to build a different world together.

And specifically:

- Forbid dumping in the agricultural sector;
- Claim food sovereignty as a universal right;
- Obtain rights to have access to the key productive resources (water, land, cereals);
- Analyse and point out the disastrous effects of IMF and World Bank actions and the WTO;
- Help, advise and pressure our governments to change WTO policies;
- Question every new WTO agreement.

Translation by Joris Van Mol

TRANSNATIONAL CORPORATIONS
Issues and Proposals

JOSHUA KARLINER (CORPWATCH) and
KAROLO APARICIO (GLOBAL EXCHANGE)

Summary Proposal

The current corporation-driven globalization paradigm, which prioritizes corporate profit maximization over human rights, labour rights and environmental rights, should be turned on its head to prioritize these universal life values.

Corporations Have Too Much Power

It is well documented, and widely accepted among those attending the World Social Forum, that transnational corporations and big business in general have increased their power greatly in the last decade. To note just a few indicators of this power:

- In terms of sheer scale of economic activity, the giant corporations now rival all but the largest countries. Comparing corporate turnover to national GNP, 51 of the world's top 100 economies are corporations.

- Royal Dutch Shell's revenues are greater than Venezuela's Gross Domestic Product. Using this measurement, WalMart is bigger than Indonesia. General Motors is roughly the same size as Ireland, New Zealand and Hungary combined.

- There are 63,000 transnational corporations worldwide, with 690,000 foreign affiliates. Three-quarters of them are based in

North America, Western Europe and Japan. Ninety-nine of the hundred largest transnational corporations are from the industrialized countries.

- These corporations profit from and perpetuate what is essentially a racist global system that benefits the North, and a small minority in the South, at the expense of the vast majority of people in the South and a growing number of people (often of African, Latin American and Asian descent) in the North.

- WTO rules overwhelmingly favour giant transnationals. In fact, these companies play a central role in shaping the WTO and other trade and investment agreements that allow corporations increasingly to transcend the state.

- Cultural and media companies such as Disney sell their products almost everywhere in the world, and concentration of media ownership in the hands of fewer companies has accelerated recently.

- US and other big business interests have succeeded in watering down and appropriating international environmental agreements.

Governments and Corporations are Intimately Intertwined

Complicating any attempt to confront corporate power is the widespread support for the status quo among governments. There are few governments that deviate from accepting the basic dynamic of competition to attract investment to create jobs and wealth. At the United Nations, big business's claim to represent a part of the solution to environment and development problems is accepted by the Secretary General and most delegations. The trend towards privatization is virtually worldwide. And political influence by corporations over governments is also widely accepted. The forms that this influence takes include legal campaign contributions (e.g. US), direct representation in government (e.g. Italy) and corruption (e.g. Mexico).

We are fighting corporate power to promote another, more democratic, world.

At the same time, the 'Seattle movement', which corresponds significantly to the World Social Forum, has identified corporate-led globalization, and corporate power in general, as one of the main battlegrounds in our struggles.

Therefore, the movement against excessive corporate power is also a movement to expose its corrupting influence on governments and intergovernmental bodies, in other words, a movement to strengthen democracy, locally, nationally and internationally.

Many, if not most, of the groups represented at the World Social Forum would agree on the need to reduce corporate power at local, national and international levels while increasing the power of the majority classes (e.g., workers, family farmers and the small-business sector).

A key strategic goal of our movements should be the separation of corporations and the state. Just as the intertwining of religion and state can lead to a religious fundamentalist state antithetical to democracy, so can the intertwining of corporations and the state lead to a corporate-fundamentalist (or market-fundamentalist) state – also antithetical to democracy. Separation of corporations and the state should also extend beyond the arenas of local and national governance to global-governance institutions such as the WTO, World Bank, IMF, UN, etc.

Nevertheless, there are significant differences in approach between various sectors of our movements. This paper identifies some of those differences and makes proposals to better unify our efforts.

So let's get together.

Sectors, Individual Corporations, Structural Power

A great deal of the anti-corporate movement is made up of campaigns against the reputations and actions of specific corporations, such as

Nike, Shell, etc. Complementary efforts focus on specific sectors, such as the clothing industry, oil, nuclear power, etc. Some of us focus on the structures of corporate power *per se*, regardless of whether the corporations in question are 'good' or 'bad' actors.

Sometimes, the impression given to the press and public is that some corporations are good and some are bad, and it's just a matter of influencing the bad ones towards being better. As soon as the company does 'better', the campaign is called off. It is difficult to convey the more fundamental message that corporations in general are too powerful, or that an entire sector needs reform.

Proposals

- Campaigns against specific corporations and their activities should include, in the analysis, the company's activities in other sectors;

- Campaigns should contain the message that the rules giving corporations so much power must be changed;

- Campaigns should seek to combine efforts of workers, environmental groups and communities negatively affected by corporations (not just in analysis, but also in devising demands and organizing strategies);

- When appropriate, campaigns should seek to ally with alternative, smaller-scale, local, more accountable businesses that are providing similar goods or services.

Dialogue versus Confrontation

Multi-stakeholder dialogues and similar processes are in vogue, as is the concept of satisfying stakeholders in general. Yet many groups at the community level are still engaged in confrontation with and direct action against corporations. In reality, negotiation with adversaries, corporate or governmental, is inevitable. As Martin Luther King Jr wrote in his letter from a Birmingham jail, negotiation is the purpose of direct action, and confrontations aim to create enough power and tension to force the powerful to negotiate.

Proposals
Negotiations with companies should take place when we have enough power to force concessions, rather than before. Negotiations and dialogue must not sell out the communities and workers affected by a company's actions and policies. Direct action must be seen as an important aspect of engagement by the social movements confronting corporations.

Corporate Responsibility versus Corporate Accountability versus Democratic Control over Corporations

In response to the pressure of public campaigns, transnational corporations have developed diverse programmes of 'corporate responsibility', that is, voluntary programmes to improve their images and activities. These same corporations most often oppose measures for corporate accountability, defined here as mechanisms for enforcing actual rules on companies.

Social movements often endorse the promises of corporate responsibility, and the United Nations is also promoting the concept. One popular approach is to encourage corporate responsibility by rewarding it in the marketplace, through shareholders and consumers. Another approach is for corporations to form partnerships with government and NGOs, so as to promote the shared values of these different stakeholders.

However, these approaches are also a source of frustration for some because the very same corporations promoting their corporate responsibility are also actively working to prevent measures to enforce corporate accountability, such as international treaties and conventions, transnational lawsuits, national legislation, personal liability of company officeholders, and so on.

In fact, it is acknowledged by the corporations themselves that promotion of corporate responsibility in the fields of the environment, human rights, poverty alleviation and community service is, in part at least, a tactic aimed at avoiding accountability measures – legislation and regulation of corporate behaviour.

Proposals

- Campaigns for corporate responsibility should include advocacy of corporate accountability measures;

- Corporate pledges of responsibility to communities, governments or the United Nations must be monitored, not taken at face value;

- Indexes for measuring corporate responsibility must include an evaluation of their stand on accountability;

- Companies lobbying against and evading accountability should not be considered 'responsible';

- An important step towards forging corporate accountability is for countries where transnational corporations are based to require transparency through 'right to know' laws that compel companies to disclose publicly important information about the impacts of their global operations;

- Binding rules on transnational corporate behaviour should be established through a Framework Convention on Corporate Accountability;

- Campaigns for responsibility and accountability should be geared to help build a broader movement for greater democratic control over corporations (e.g., profit maximization being subordinated to human, labour and environmental rights; separation of corporations and the state).

Reform versus Banishment

Some anti-corporate campaigners in the US are promoting the idea of 'de-chartering' corporations that are especially bad. (In the US, corporations are chartered by the particular state in which they are headquartered.) For environmental campaigners, for example, there is great appeal in the idea that a company can receive a corporate 'death penalty' as a deterrent to other companies.

But, for workers, that kind of ultimate punishment of a corporation would cause a loss of jobs without hope of a transition (alternative sources of employment and the like).

On the other side of the coin, organized workers seek to engage corporations in a social dialogue to improve corporate commitment to worker rights. The problem for environmental campaigners is that they do not always have the leverage or access to influence corporations in a dialogue setting. The interests of workers and environmental campaigners are therefore not always the same.

Proposals

- Environmental and human rights campaigns that seek to eliminate a corporation or a major corporate activity should include dialogue with labour and provisions for a just transition for workers and communities;

- We should build communication and trust among the trade union movement, progressive NGOs working on human rights and the environment, and community-based initiatives working for social justice, fair trade, renewable energy, organic food, etc;

- Examples of positive collaboration between these sectors – such as in opposing free trade agreements – should be built on and strengthened;

- Collaboration between social movements in the South and the North fighting for corporate accountability and democratic control over corporations should be strengthened.

6
(i)
LABOUR
A Strategic Perspective on the International Trade Union Movement for the Twenty-first Century

CONGRESS OF SOUTH AFRICAN TRADE UNIONS (COSATU)

This paper is an initial setting out of ideas presented for discussion and debate by the Congress of South African Trade Unions (COSATU). It is a contribution to the discussions on labour in the World Social Forum of 2002 and is based on a paper which was circulated to a number of trade unions and which Cosatu prepared to send to ICFTU. Its purpose is to stimulate discussion within WSF in order to break out of the traditional categories and camps that so much of the international debate has fallen into in the past.

Introduction

The trade union movement represents civil society's most formidable force within contemporary global politics and the world political economy. Trade unions counter the powerful bloc of multinational companies, international financial institutions and industrialized countries that seek to consolidate their hegemony over the world political and economic system at the expense of the weak. Because of this potential, unions always elicit attacks and labels from those who fear their power.

A progressive trade union movement plays a larger role than just representing its members on the shop floor. It must have a central role in democratization, both of politics and economic policy. To fulfill these roles, it has to be characterized by greater internal democracy, ensuring worker control of the operations and decisions of the union.

After the fall of the Berlin Wall, the ideological divisions within the trade union movement decreased, and many trade unions saw the need to build a united global trade union movement. This led to the consolidation of the International Confederation of Free Trade Unions (ICFTU) as the most representative voice of organized labour. Today we bring together affiliates from all five continents representing millions of workers.

This growing consolidation of organized labour is an important and positive development. Yet the international labour movement is still battling with its legacy from the Cold War. Too often the international trade union movement relies on boardroom tactics and diplomacy instead of using the power of the working class. It often replaces open and robust debates in structures with deals between a few financially powerful national centres, and the continuation of an inner circle of trade unions able to influence the direction of the entire movement, which can undermine internal democracy. We have seen a preference for 'off-the-record' discussions on important issues, instead of these being discussed within executive structures.

The single greatest challenge to the international trade union movement is to change its nature and character so it becomes a fighting organization capable of leading the working class around a minimum platform of demands that will reverse the marginalization of workers and the poor.

This paper outlines the perspective that the international trade union movement must embrace to meet the challenges of globalization. Above all, it argues that the trade union movement should work for unity, adopt a minimum platform for social justice, and transform itself to play a critical role in the unfolding struggle for social justice.

Perspective on Transformative Unionism – Values, Ethics, Beliefs and Traditions

The trade union movement should combine bread-and-butter struggles with broader social, political and economic campaigns. A working-class movement solely concerned with workplace struggles is bound to lose, since the broader political context is shaped by capital's agenda. Experiences in many parts of the world demonstrate that engagement and struggles on a broad platform have delivered more to the working class than a narrow, parochial approach. On the other hand, a high-flying trade union movement interested in broader political issues only, at the expense of its members' daily concerns, is bound to find itself in the margins of history, the victims, not the shapers of history.

In order to survive, unions must find a balance between their broader socio-political role and the daily needs of their members.

To play its role, the trade union movement should adhere to the principles of organizational independence, democracy, worker control and a transformative political perspective.

- **Free and Independent:** Workers themselves establish unions to defend and advance their interests at the workplace and the broader socio-political level. Because of their power, political forces and capital always seek to influence the unions, co-opting them, neutralizing them, at worst virtually taking them over. Unions can only be free if they are guaranteed no interference from governments, political parties and employers.

  A progressive trade union movement should not only be satisfied with consistent lip-service to its independence. It must jealously guard its autonomy, and be seen by members to be a true representative of their undiluted aspirations.

- **Democracy and Worker Control:** Unions are not established for workers, but are established by workers themselves to defend and advance their rights. A trade union that does not maximize workers' participation is bound to face extinction.

  A serious problem arises if unions purport to represent members on issues while leaving the workers themselves in the dark. This is tantamount to self-mandating, and is undemocratic. Workers must

be able to associate with every activity of the union, and must
have control over whatever is carried through to negotiations.

There is a trend today in some unions for the bureaucracy to
'manage' democracy for workers, on the grounds that this is
'practical' or is 'efficient'. This runs the risk of bureaucratizing the
trade union movement. The principle of worker control has to
become a reality.

- **Freedom and Solidarity:** By nature, a trade union movement should
  be on the side of the weak, marginalized and sidelined, within its
  own country and all over the world.

  Unions are the automatic ally of those who face discrimination
  on the basis of their race, creed, religion and sex, because of the
  continent they come from, or any other reason. Trade unionists
  are inherently internationalists who fight against injustice wherever it exists.

  Solidarity is therefore a guiding principle that can never be
  compromised. Supporting discrimination, or doing nothing about
  oppression and marginalization of any group, disqualifies any trade
  union from the transformative trade unionism referred to in this
  paper.

  But solidarity is not about speeches and resolutions: it is about
  the action we are prepared to take, the resources we commit and
  the sacrifices we make to support working people elsewhere.

- **Retaining the Bias towards the Poor and Working Class in Socio-
  Economic Policy:** Trade unions must always support policies and
  measures that seek to bring the marginalized into the mainstream
  and the weakest into more advantaged positions. In this context,
  unions must advance workers' demands around progressive
  economic strategies that can close the gap between rich and poor,
  set a basic floor of rights for all workers, and ensure gender equity
  and social protection. At the centre should be the need to lift the
  standards of living of the poor and the working class and smash
  inequality within and between nations.

This position pits the union movement against the forces of neoliberalism, which seek to impose stringent adjustment policies for which the workers pay the cost through unemployment, cuts in social protection, and so forth. Unions are by nature against the neoliberal dogma, which represents an attack on gains made by the working-class movement over many decades.

- **Social Justice in the Twenty-first Century:** The international trade union movement must transform itself into a fighting force that is an ally and a real representative of those most marginalized by globalization. This includes international organizations such as ICFTU. By combining lobbying and active campaigns, we must campaign for equity and the elimination of the huge gap in income between countries in the North and South. We must form alliances with progressive governments in the North and South, and campaign for active policies that will bring about equity. But the international organizations, ICFTU included, should recognize that inequalities are not only found between the South and North. Increasingly, the gap in income within developed and, even more, within developing countries, is enormous.

These factors inform our work on an agenda for social justice in the twenty-first century. Linked to this is the need to update our organizational strategy to confront the manoeuvres of multinational companies. At the centre of their strategy is the systematic replacement of formal, secure and well-paying jobs with temporary and insecure work that offers no job security or social protection. On the African continent, this situation is compounded by the fact that informal sector and survivalist activities are often already even bigger than the formal industrial sector. We need to go beyond the protection of our historic gains in order to expand quality employment into new areas.

- **Working in Partnership with Other Progressive Forces:** Unions must acknowledge that, despite their power, they cannot on their own bring about the changes needed to confront the neoliberal agenda imposed by globalization. We need to forge strategic and tactical alliances and partnerships with progressive political parties and NGOs that identify with our vision and minimum platform. Trade unions should avoid retreating into a narrow laager, but instead should challenge for political and social space, should seek out allies and nurture and strengthen them, should lead a progressive alliance of working people.

- **Building the Trade Union Movement:** The working class is faced with a unified force comprising multinational companies, powerful states and international financial institutions. The decades of Cold War left the trade union movement fragmented. Our movement is particularly weak in the African continent and much of the developing countries. Conscious effort is needed to deal with this situation.

- **The Unity of the Trade Union Movement Is Vital:** Nothing is bigger or more important than the unity of workers. It is bigger than the name of our organizations, our logos, bigger than considerations of leadership positions, bigger than our specific history or any other issue.

We must set the goal of consciously working for unity in the international trade union movement and consolidate this march to unity by eliminating divisions at the national and continental level.

The national centres themselves should be pressured to end destructive competition for membership. The proliferation of unions should be eliminated and workers taught that only unity can provide protection against the onslaught of neoliberalism.

The struggle for unity has important organizational implications. The time of general unions that offer workers little prospect of acting in solidarity with one another should belong to the past. Unions should organize broadly along industrial and sectoral lines, with powerful national centres that co-ordinate resources and action on behalf of national unions.

There is another important dimension: unity requires that we strongly pressure countries with more than one national centre affiliated to the ICFTU (the International Confederation of Free Trade Unions) to amalgamate into one centre, within a defined period of time, with tough mechanisms to ensure that this is realized.

- **Promote Participatory Democracy:** It is a difficult challenge to manage a national union movement that prides itself on democratic norms which allow members to dictate their destiny. An even more daunting challenge is to manage an international trade union movement that allows every national centre to feel part of the family and influence the direction of the movement.

We have no choice but to take up this challenge. The trade union movement must operate differently from international institutions of capital – the IMF, for example, or World Bank and WTO. Yet all too often, the culture of managing democracy, lack of democratic debate and fear of different points of view make a mockery of our oft-repeated declaration of being a democratic organization.

Our congresses and other structures must deliberately open space in a structured fashion to allow debates, and our resolutions must reflect the debates within our structures. Congress should not function like the Plenary of the International Labour Conference of the ILO (where we all make speeches for the record), but should be interactive, and should shape policy.

Our Socio-Economic Outlook

In line with the instinct to identify with the marginalized and the weakest, the international trade union movement should develop a comprehensive policy on the great divide between the South and North. Central to such a policy should be the recognition that the system of colonialism combined with the Cold War left most countries in the South devastated, with weak economic and political systems. In these countries, poverty, unemployment, disease, ignorance and general underdevelopment are at their worst. In these countries we can measure in real terms the devastating impact of the 'survival of the fittest' approach to social change.

The trade union movement must develop a comprehensive alternative to globalization, neoliberalism and the structural adjustment programmes of the IMF and World Bank. Our vision should be underpinned by the following:

- International solidarity to address the inequalities between and within countries and regions;

- Within countries, addressing poverty and underdevelopment through comprehensive social protection combined with economic development strategies aimed at creating quality jobs, meeting basic needs for food and housing, and improving workers' access to education and training;

- Globalization of human rights and workers' rights as a cornerstone of development and fair trade;

- Elimination of unfair trade practices and rules, and adoption of deliberate measures to ensure that international trade and investment support equitable development, and that the voices of civil society are actively represented on international institutions that regulate trade;

- An end to the debt burden on the poorest countries;

- Use of social funds and retirement funds to promote investment that combines economic returns with social advances in developing countries;

- Rules on movement of capital that will not only challenge the speculative character of many portfolio flows, but will shift the balance of power that capital has gained through free movement of capital back to democratic institutions.

Once we have developed our minimum platform, we should canvass for its acceptance by the progressive NGOs with which we normally work. Progressive political parties and governments should also be urged to support the framework. The platform should guide our engagement with the IMF, World Bank and other UN institutions. We should have a strategy towards the IMF, World Bank and WTO that combines globally coordinated mass-action campaigns with an engagement strategy.

Organizational Review and Restructuring

In the context of the preceding paragraph, the need for a comprehensive review of structures cannot be overemphasized.

A Platform for Global Organizing

Despite our strength, we must recognize that the trade union movement is unevenly developed between countries. In many parts of the South, unions remain weak and dependent on, and sometimes controlled by, governments. In most industrialized countries, union membership is declining.

There are many reasons for these weaknesses. Some workers take the past victories of the unions for granted. Others find unions unattractive because over the years unions have been bureaucratized and no longer help improve conditions of employment. Unions have generally not modernized their tactics, structures and organizing methods, and as a result are often perceived as irrelevant. In many countries, we have not unionized white collar workers sufficiently. The growth of nonstandard employment, with part-time work, contract work and casual work, has left unions with new organizing challenges. In some countries the industrial base is in decline. The traditional manufacturing sector is shrinking, with growth only in the service or informal sectors, which requires a different organizing strategy.

Our detractors must never be proved right when they accuse us of representing an elite. We must retain the mass character of the unions, not through slogans, but with practical programmes to build the unity and power of workers.

It is critical that a global campaign be launched to recruit more workers into our ranks. The ICFTU should set itself hard targets for the number of unionized members we must achieve, by country and by sector. It must help to set up the structures to achieve this, and reallocate resources to this goal.

The campaigns of national centres should be drawn on as examples from which to learn – both from their strengths and their weaknesses.

One example is the COSATU 'Spring Offensive' which sets aside a month of recruitment and organizing, where shop stewards of affiliated national unions are released from work for between one and four weeks to organize workers at unorganized workplaces in the informal sector and in rural areas, not only in their own sectors but elsewhere too. Over the past three years, this has resulted in 150,000 new members into COSATU.

Another example is the campaign of the AFL-CIO to reverse the decline in membership in the USA, with centrally co-coordinated recruitment campaigns, national company targets, and pooling of resources and organizers.

Such campaigns can draw on other experiences, such as that of the FNV in organizing part-time workers as part of a broader policy of regulating part-time work in the Dutch economy, or the provision of new services by unions in Ghana and South Africa to organize the informal sector.

At a global level, this opens up the opportunity for us to share skilled organizing staff, and target companies globally for unionization. This campaign should be coordinated at sub-regional levels and supervised at regional and international levels.

Campaigns

The international trade union movement must move away from being a lobby group to become an effective organization capable of disciplining capital, governments and other institutions. It must provide and coordinate effective solidarity. It must facilitate a worker-to-worker contact and give workers a sense that they are a single family and do not exist in isolation.

Our experience in South Africa, and indeed the working-class movement's experience globally, shows that what you have not won in the streets, you will not win at the boardroom table. The recent past, highlighted by the mass demonstrations in Seattle in 1999, shows that workers are willing to embark on campaigns to support their demands and pledge solidarity with one another. These experiences prove that the problem is not a lack of capacity. Rather, it is a tradition of relying excessively on lobbying, which developed when the movement was weaker than today.

Our choice of leaders, of tactics, of organizational structures, of resource allocation and of allies, must reflect this strategic shift of engagement from diplomacy to the terrain of global campaigning where our latent strength can be realized. Diplomacy and negotiation must be built on this foundation, and not be a substitute for action and campaigning.

We have experiences of successful international campaigns during the struggle against apartheid. The anti-apartheid movements of Europe and Australia relied, not on sending faxes and emails to the apartheid regime, but on active mass campaigns led by workers who refused to handle goods from South Africa in the docks and inland. This is the kind of campaign we need now against the Burmese, Colombian and Swazi regimes.

Within the ILO itself, we should combine our strategy of negotiation with a global campaign on the actual demands we table in Geneva. A Maternity Convention provides an opportunity for the labour movement to make the gender concerns of working women a key part of the agenda, and to unite the women's movement and the labour movement in a common struggle to advance the rights of women and to promote gender equality.

The international labour movement should also identify a list of companies who are the global sweatshop leaders – companies such as

Nike – and run global campaigns with consumer groups, students and others, and provide a unified basis for struggles in all countries where such goods are sold or made, in order to secure commitments around union rights and an end to exploitative labour.

The international union movement must build its capacity for campaigns and actions. This requires a stronger regional capacity to support global campaigns.

Global Collective Bargaining

Multinational corporations (MNCs) are circling the globe in search of cheap labour and resources. In the past, we relied on bilateral relations to track them down and force them to uphold standards. We have established regional organizations, and increasingly (at least in Africa) there is a realization of the crucial role that sub-regional organizations can play in forcing the multinational corporations to observe fair labour standards, protect the environment and embrace good corporate governance. All these initiatives have played a role in ensuring that global capital does not have a free hand to reverse gains made in the past.

In some sectors, International Trade Secretariats (ITSs) have concluded company-level agreements with certain multinationals. In Europe and Mercosur, there is the beginning of cross-border bargaining in some companies. In the maritime industry, there is a global agreement on certain conditions of employment. All of these are very modest and small, compared to the requirements of the times we live in. We should now embark on a substantial programme of global bargaining, identifying key companies in the sectors where we are strong, and concentrating global campaigns on securing global bargaining.

With this should go the setting-up of more global shop steward councils within multinational corporations and other sectors where these are feasible.

We must seriously explore the possibilities and modalities of global bargaining and of global shop stewards' councils. We can also set clear targets and time-frames to result in a concrete outcome that is of help to workers across the world.

The Informal Sector

The international labour movement must address the growing importance of the informal sector and casual or temporary labour. We have seen the replacement of secure, well-paid jobs with an insecure, casual and temporary army of working poor, with fewer rights and less social security. In some countries, employers now believe that the informalization and casualization of labour is the best way to roll back our gains. At the same time, rising unemployment in developing countries increases the pressure on workers to accept lower standards. Because of the nature of their jobs, many of the affected workers are afraid to join unions and are sceptical of the potential benefits.

We need a workable strategy to organize informal and casual workers. Otherwise, all that we stand for will be eroded while we watch helplessly from the sidelines. Already there are small but effective examples of trade union organization of the informal sector in the Netherlands, South Africa, Ghana and India: we can draw on these and see which elements of their approaches are applicable elsewhere.

Gender

For too long, despite the profusion of slogans professing their commitment to gender equality and the elimination of the oppression of women, the unions have taken few practical steps to eradicate these inequities. Whilst some progress has been registered, the time has come to develop decisive measures to change the situation. We have a responsibility to address gender in the unions, in the workplace and in society. Often gender issues are linked to other developmental issues. Structural adjustment often results in tariff liberalization that puts female workers out of work. The informal sector is in many cases a ghetto where women are condemned to working without fair labour standards or legal protection. Trade unions should lead these struggles.

The Perspective for Africa and the South

The vision outlined in the previous sections has ramifications for the trade union movement of Africa and the South in general. Unions in Africa and most parts of the South require special measures to strengthen their organization.

While it is necessary to continue to consolidate the strengths of the unions in the industrialized countries, it is important to recognize the challenges facing unions in the South. For example, unions from the industrialized countries are looking at how best to strengthen worker-to-worker solidarity through emails, internet and sophisticated telephones. In contrast, unions in the South often do not have basic telephone lines or even electricity in their offices.

Solidarity requires that unions in the North debate too how their societies can help the development of the South. Currently, trade policies, the actions of MNCs, the policies of the IMF and World Bank, foreign direction investment flows and prices paid for Africa's resource wealth all continue to undermine Africa's economic and social development. Hard choices need to be made, and workers in all countries should struggle together, and be prepared to make economic sacrifices, to help develop all countries, so that we have a shared prosperity.

A special challenge is to strengthen Africa's union movement so that, working in partnership with ordinary people and other progressive movements, it can help drive the African renaissance. The continent is still largely underdeveloped, ravaged by years of colonial plunder, mismanagement in the post-colonial era, internecine wars and abject poverty. The African trade union movement is weak and fragmented at national and continental level.

Unity of the African union movement is a precondition for labour to take its place in the affairs of the continent. Such unity should result in a vibrant trade union movement that can ensure that worker concerns are taken into account in developments such as the African Union. To play this role, the African trade union movement should learn to champion its own cause, instead of always relying on others to explain its pain. The dependency syndrome should belong to the past.

The Millennium Review process must strengthen unions throughout the South, including in Africa. As the basis for this work, we need to map out the nature of unions in the South – membership, representation, whether national centres and their unions are genuinely independent, free and democratic, and so on. A deliberate process to unify national centres should be based on the results of the research.

In Africa, the Millennium Review must consider the consolidation of continental organizations. The Organization of African Trade Union Unity (OATUU) was formed by African governments, in accordance with the principle of non-alignment. The ICFTU formed ICFTU-AFRO as its regional structure for Africa. In addition, WCL and WFTU organizations still survive in our continent. The challenge is to ensure that these divisions belong to the past, and that we rapidly and with urgency set up a single continental centre, within a clearly spelled-out time-frame.

The ICFTU-AFRO and OATUU should be called upon to shape a trade union strategy for Africa. As a minimum, this strategy should call for:

- Peace and stability;

- Democracy, including participatory democracy;

- A strong public sector to steer and foster development;

- Agricultural and industrial development to exploit the riches of Africa for the benefit of its people;

- Regional development strategies; workers' rights and the abolition of export-processing zones that bring neither development nor substantial job creation;

- Social protection and the eradication of poverty;

- Lifting of trade barriers against African products by industrialized societies;

- Cancellation of foreign debts; and

- A development plan for the continent, on a scale at least as large as the Marshall Plan introduced in Europe at the end of the Second World War, and financed by the international community.

Achieving these aims requires support from the entire international trade union movement. The pursuit of this minimum African and Southern platform should not be limited to unions from the South and Africa, but become the duty of all trade unionists.

Conclusion

We have here proposed a minimum programme that progressive movements across the globe should follow and pursue. The World Social Forum is a golden opportunity, both historic and well-timed, for a debate on all these matters.

6 LABOUR
(ii) *A Global Strategy for Labour*

JEFF FAUX
(ECONOMIC POLICY INSTITUTE)

The overwhelming majority of people in this world must work in order to live. The definition of labour in the global marketplace includes those who are unionized and those who are not. It includes those who work in cities and those who work on farms. It includes those both in the formal and informal sectors. It includes those who work at home and small-business people who live by exploiting their own labour. It follows that full employment, adequate wages and a healthy environment ought to be the common-sense goals of the global economy.

But the global marketplace, like all markets, is built on a set of rules. Indeed, according to a former director-general of the World Trade Organization (WTO), the rules of the WTO represent the 'constitution' of the new global economy. The current rules of the global market – those of the WTO, the International Monetary Fund (IMF), the World Bank, and other global regulators – were not established to promote the dignity and well-being of labour. They were established to protect the interest of those who invest for a living, at the expense of those who must work.

Investor Protectionism

The investor protectionist policies imposed by those who set the rules for the world's commerce include trade deregulation, privatization, weakening of collective bargaining and financial liberalization. Not surprisingly, they – and therefore their clients in the media and the academic world – also measure the progress of globalization according to the interests of the investor class, such as rising stock markets, increasing volume of trade, lower taxes for the rich, and the elimination of any restrictions on investment. The rationale for such a narrow perspective is that these policies will automatically create faster growth and greater equality and expand democracy.

After more than twenty years of intense investor protectionism policies, these promises remain unfulfilled. Over the past two decades of neoliberalism, global economic growth has actually slowed. Those countries that grew the fastest were the most resistant to the advice of the bankers, the economists, and the consultants who control credit and aid and set the trading rules according to the Washington Consensus.

In the past twenty years, equality has actually got less. As Christian Weller, Robert Scott and Adam Hersh have shown,[1] the median income of the richest ten countries was 77 times those of the poorest ten countries in 1980, and 149 times in 1999. The incomes of the richest 10 per cent of the world's people were 70 times those of the poorest 10 per cent in 1980, and 122 times in 1999. Within nations, inequality also seems to have worsened. Accurate global data are not available, but in the countries where the data are most reliable, the trend is clearly towards more inequality.[2]

Neither has the claim about democracy been fulfilled. As one scholarly article in a neoliberal publication recently reported, the evidence does not support 'a strong and direct connection between globalization and democratization. The evidence is mixed and will continue to be so for some time. For every society in which a "people's power" revolution is helped along by international cheers and the publicity given it by satellite television, another is daily becoming more cosmopolitan while adhering to traditional (and often authoritarian) practices'.[3]

Even World Bank president James Wolfensohn in 1999 was moved to admit, 'At the level of people, the system isn't working'.

By 'people', Wolfensohn meant working people. Clearly the system is working for some people. It is shifting the benefits of new technologies and the efficiencies from the natural expansion of trade and communication to the world's investors and shifting the costs to the world's workers.

No one can deny the existence of a global investor class. Electronic technologies and modern transportation and communications systems allow for extremely effective business and financial networking. Increasingly, multinational businesses are managed by multinational personnel, who have little or no loyalty to the country whose passport they happen to hold.

A global investor class implies a global working class, even though the international organization of workers across borders is far behind that of investors. Therefore we cannot fully judge the impact of globalization without reference to the share of benefits and costs going to capital and labour. The question of who wins and who loses from particular policies – such as the WTO round or the North American Free Trade Agreement (NAFTA) or the proposal (currently under negotiation) for a Free Trade Area of the Americas (FTAA) – cannot be answered on the basis of separate national economies alone because every country has an investor and a working class, i.e., there are rich people in poor countries and poor people in rich countries. In 1996, for example, 22 per cent of the world's billionaires were from the developing nations.

In most cases, international agreements are negotiated by elites that have more in common with each other than with working people in the countries that they represent. As a retired US State Department official put it to me bluntly a few years ago: 'What you don't under-stand', he said, 'is that when we negotiate economic agreements with these poorer countries, we are negotiating with people from the same class. That is, people whose interests are like ours – on the side of capital'.

Thus, the fundamental purpose of neoliberal polices of the past 20 years has been to discipline labour in every country in order to free capital from having to bargain with workers over the gains from rising productivity. Such bargaining is the essence of a democratic market system. Although labour is obviously better served when it is organized into trade unions to bargain with a unified voice, the bargaining between labour and capital goes on even if workers are unorganized.

As in any bargaining, both sides are constantly manoeuvring for advantage. But labour is typically at a disadvantage because it usually bargains under conditions of excess supply of unemployed workers. Moreover, the forced liberalization of finance and trade provides enormous leverage to capital by giving it a threat it can brandish of fleeing the economy altogether – by freeing it from responsibility to the firm, the community or the nation.

Uncontrolled globalization puts governments' domestic policies decisively on the side of capital. In an economy that is growing based on its domestic market, rising wages help everyone because they increase purchasing power and consumer demand – which is the major driver of economic growth in a modern economy. But in an economy whose growth depends on foreign markets, rising domestic wages are a problem, because they make it more difficult to compete internationally.

Capital's Gains

Although one can find a mass of data on the financial interests of the relatively tiny investor class, the mainstream media carry little systematic information on what is happening to the huge class of the world's workers as a whole. But a look at the trends within countries shows a general deterioration of the position of labour relative to capital – in both developing and developed economies.

The Global Policy Network, a new group of non-profit research organizations linked to national trade unions movements, has so far posted reports on labour conditions in 27 countries on its web site (www.gpn.org). The countries examined include some of the poorest (e.g., Lesotho, Zambia), the most rapidly developing (e.g., Korea and Ireland) and the most developed (Canada, United States). The exact manifestation of labour's shrinking share of income differs from country to country but there is a common pattern in the concentration of economic growth in the informal sector – where workers are unorganized, contingent and unprotected. That is, where they have little or no bargaining power with capital.

Argentina is, of course, the latest example of this relentless downward pressure on workers' living standards. No other country has embraced the neoliberal paradigm as much as Argentina. The suicidal tying of the peso to the dollar was for years celebrated as the example of what a developing country had to do in order to gain the confidence of foreign investors. One result has been the nearly doubling of the share of the population in extreme poverty as capital relentlessly squeezed labour's income share. As a report from the Instituto de Estudios y Formación in Buenos Aires shows, labour productivity among Argentina's 500 largest firms – which dominate Argentina's international trade – rose 50 per cent from 1993 to 1998, while real wages rose only 20 per cent. So where did the benefits of increased efficiency go? Within those firms the share of income going to labour dropped from 35 per cent to 28 per cent in five years, while capital's share rose from 65 per cent to 72 per cent.[4] Moreover, much of this capital found its way overseas. Many so-called foreign investors are in fact Argentinians who have been buying high-interest Argentine bonds with accounts in banks in the United States and Europe.

Another vivid example of how neoliberalism negatively affects workers at all levels of development is NAFTA. Like most recent agreements, NAFTA protects investors at the expense of workers and the environment. Seven years after its implementation, the political protectors of capital in all three countries judge NAFTA a great success, and support the efforts to expand it to all of the Western Hemisphere through the Free Trade Agreement of the Americas.

But as a recent collaborative study by economists in Canada, Mexico and the United States shows,[5] from the perspective of the working people in all three countries, NAFTA has been a failure. All three countries saw a decline in real wages, an upward redistribution of income in the direction of more inequality and a dramatic expansion of the informal sector jobs characterized by insecurity, low pay and no bargaining power.

Global Class Politics

All markets require rules and policies. Consequently, they are political institutions. Therefore, just as a global investor class implies a global working class, a global marketplace implies a global politics. Global politics in turn implies global political 'parties', even though they are not formally organized as such.

The meetings in Davos, and now New York (in 2002), of the World Economic Forum are in some ways the convention of the global party of capital. We might call it the Investors' Protection Party. Their convention in New York is paid for by the world's largest multinational corporations and will be dominated by 1,000 corporate executives, along with 250 government officials, including 20 heads of state. They will be accompanied by lawyers, consultants, journalists and academics who will do business with each other at the receptions and dinners and in the corner of hotel lobbies, just as in any political convention.

Similarly, this meeting of the World Social Forum here in Porto Alegre is in many ways a convention of a global political party in opposition, which is now searching for a common programme with which to oppose the investors' agenda. The difference between these two 'parties' is not, as the media would have it, the difference between globalizers and anti-globalizers. Globalization – in the sense of people exchanging goods and ideas with each other – has been going on for several thousand years and will continue. Neither is it a concern with social as opposed to the economic issues. This meeting of the WSF is also about economics – but an economics that serves society, rather than one that is served by society. In that sense, the core point of contention between Davos/New York and Porto Alegre is over the rules of the global marketplace – and who will set them.

Because the Investor Protection Party dominates the global financial institutions, the party in opposition has little real access to forums which might force those institutions seriously to consider alternatives. Demonstrators can temporarily obstruct the workings of the global institutions' managers. But as the WTO showed by moving its last meeting to the remote location of Doha, international agencies have the resources and the will to circumvent street demonstrators.

As a consequence, the leaders of the NGOs, trade union, anti-poverty and religious groups in opposition find themselves drawn into largely fruitless efforts to achieve social justice by lobbying the IMF, the WTO, the World Bank and other financial and development institutions, which have no intention of making significant changes in their programme. NGOs may be put on public advisory committees, but the real work goes on in private where representatives of multi-national businesses negotiate the rules.

The Party of Opposition is thus constantly forced back into a defence of national sovereignty as the only available instrument for achieving social justice. Yet sovereignty is steadily eroding under the relentless pressure of global markets. Moreover, a nationalist politics undercuts the cross-border cooperation needed to balance the cross-border political reach of business and finance. Nationalism perpetuates the myth that national identity is the only factor in determining whether one wins or loses in the global economy. It obscures the common interests of workers in all countries when faced with the alliances of investors in rich and poor nations that now dominate the global marketplace.

Still, human rights and social justice will become part of the 'constitution' of the global marketplace only when enough nation-states demand it. Therefore, if the global opposition is to develop an alliance of its developing and developed country wings, it must pursue a common global programme for working people of all nations that reinforces their national struggles for economic and social equity. Such a programme would support national democratic movements and leaders who understand that national social contracts cannot be maintained in a global market that lacks one of its own, and that a global social contract cannot be established in the absence of effective social democracy at the national level. We cannot demand democracy at the IMF and not within the nations that belong to it.

The strategy for labour must change the framework of current global political debate in which the investor class pursues its interest across borders, while the working class is constricted by those borders. The creation of a true global alternative requires a perspective through which the interests of workers in all countries are linked. In a global marketplace, workers' living standards increasingly rise and fall together. When workers in Brazil win a wage increase, it raises the bargaining power of workers in Germany. When workers in Indonesia improve their working conditions, workers in Nigeria benefit. Likewise, when the social safety net is strengthened in one country it helps those struggling for human economic and social rights in other countries as well.

So long as the struggle is seen as a struggle of nation against nation, the Party of Opposition will never be able to mount a credible alternative to the neoliberal paradigm. Only when workers in all countries see that they ultimately have more in common with workers in other nations than they have with the owners of capital in their own country, will they be able to organize effectively. When investors are faced with similar demands for decent pay, healthy working conditions and human dignity at the workplace everywhere, they will be forced to have a serious debate about the economic future of the planet.

Trade Unions' Role

The definition of the global working class cannot be restricted just to unions. Nonetheless, the free trade union movement – that is, the movement of unions democratically elected by workers and accountable only to their membership – plays a crucial leadership role for the world's workers. Labour unions are critical in part because they have the power to deny capital the human resource that is necessary for the generation of profits. The capacity to strike is the ultimate threat to the investor class.

And just as the Party in Opposition needs the support of organized labour, so labour needs the support of the NGOs and other organizations that rise in opposition to the neoliberal programme.

In recent years, trade unions and other parts of the Party in Opposition have been working closer together. The coalition of workers and environmentalists in Seattle in 1999 symbolized this effort. And local struggles against multinational corporations around issues of privatization, pollution and injustice all over the world reflect similar partnerships. One recent example is the coalition of US and Mexican union activists and university Students against Sweatshops that forced a company producing for Nike to recognize an independent trade union whose leaders had been persecuted for protesting against abominable working conditions.

Through the International Confederation of Free Trade Unions (ICFTU) and its regional networks, unions have stepped up their efforts at global collective bargaining and joint organizing campaigns against multinational employers. The global trade union movement was crucial in the struggle against apartheid in South Africa and dictatorships in Korea and Indonesia. Today, unions all over the world are aiding in the struggle against oppression of workers' voices, from Burma to Colombia to Zimbabwe.

To move forward in partnership with the other parts of the opposition to neoliberalism, we will need to pay attention to areas that have sometimes divided trade unions and their allies. One area is the environment. At times, differences have been interpreted as reflecting philosophies of growth versus no growth in which trade unions are seen as willing to sacrifice the environment in order to save jobs and environmentalists are seen as willing to sacrifice jobs in order to save the environment. This of course allows the investor class to play off one group against the other.

The real question is not growth versus no growth but the creation of a full employment economy that respects and sustains the environment and resource base. By now it is obvious that competitive markets driven by self-interest will maximize the use of resources for immediate consumption. That is what makes them so efficient. Individual firms do not typically accept higher costs in order to preserve the environment, because doing so would put them at a competitive disadvantage. Moreover, there is little incentive for investors who live thousands of miles away from their investment to reduce their profits in order to avoid the environmental costs. Thus, any programme to create a sustainable economics that relies on the voluntary efforts of profit-maximizing firms is doomed to failure.

The solution therefore lies in the democratic regulation of capital and the development of long-term planning – not just land-use or water-resource planning, but one that includes provision for social safety nets and job opportunities as well. At the margins, of course, there will always be some differences between those whose primary concern is worker security and those whose primary concern is the environment. Just as there will be differences within the environmental and labour movements. But the key task in building an alternative vision is to create a democratic forum for negotiation, in which those who will pay the price of failing to protect the environment or providing sufficient employment are the ones making the ultimate decision over the allocation of natural resources.

Another tension that must be resolved involves labour rights and standards in international trade and investment agreements. Although virtually all trade unionists and their allies support such rights and standards, many in the Third World see the effort to enforce them with trade and financial sanctions as a vehicle for First World protectionism.

As one Asian economist observed: 'The US Treasury runs the International Monetary Fund, and for years urged them to make loans to dictators who squandered the proceeds and are now dead, or retired in the South of France. Then the IMF tells us that the only way to pay their debts is to increase exports made with our cheap labour. When we do, US unions complain that we are undercutting labour standards'.

On the other hand, trade unionists from developed countries see their Third World brothers and sisters as being too willing to align themselves with multinational capital in opposing social protections through trade and financial agreements. They are sceptical when those in developing countries who claim to be supportive of human rights resist economic sanctions – which, in practical terms, are the only way to preserve those rights.

One strategy for overcoming this disagreement is to design a 'grand bargain' that gives the working people in both developed and developing countries what they need. The bargain starts with the distinction between rights and standards. Collective bargaining is a right that every worker is entitled to, regardless of how rich or poor his or her society. The wages and benefits that a union settles for, however, will depend on what the particular enterprise can pay. Likewise, all workers should have a right to a minimum wage. But the level of that minimum wage will depend on the economic development level of the country or region.

Once that distinction is understood, it may be possible for labour organizations and their allies in all countries to reach agreements that would provide enforceable labour rights in exchange for guaranteed commitments of long-term development aid and debt relief. Thus, the developed world would get protection for its social standards, and the developing world would receive the flexibility and capital investment it needs for growth. Incidentally, the issue of labour rights and standards is not just an issue for developing countries but developed ones as well.

This 'grand bargain' that links development with broadly increasing living standards would be connected to planning for sustainable development to create the programme elements for a global social contract. Other elements would include:

- **Flexible Development:** The one-size-fits-all policies of the international financial agencies have not only failed to produce faster growth, they have allowed the leaders of recipient countries to escape responsibility for their own policies by blaming all their problems on the IMF or World Bank. Therefore, once human and political rights are ensured, countries should have the flexibility to choose their own development path, for which their leadership should be held accountable – to their citizens.

- **Winners Compensating Losers:** As long as workers who have to bear the costs of open markets expect that they will be abandoned by the society that profits at their expense, they will resist globalization. So countries need social policies that compensate those who must pay for the benefits of economic integration. Such policies would include increased public spending on health care for the uninsured, worker retraining, adequate pensions, and community redevelopment, as well as more generous unemployment compensation and wage insurance to cushion the blow of moving to lower-paying jobs.

- **Regulated Finance:** Volatile financial markets must be tamed. Since no system of global banking regulation is in sight, the simplest solution is the Tobin Tax – a tax on international financial transactions. The proceeds would be used for long-term investments in education and health care in poor countries. Such a tax, which has the virtue of being easily understood and can be administered with minimal bureaucratic discretion, is already supported by many influential people around the world. Several years ago, in fact, the government of Canada proposed a discussion of the Tobin Tax for the agenda of the Group of Seven (the major economic powers) meeting in Halifax, but the US Treasury quickly quashed the idea.

- **Coordinated Economic Policy:** A fully functioning global economy – like a fully functioning national economy – needs central banking and counter-cyclical public budgets in order to maintain overall growth. But there will be neither a global central bank nor a global government budget for a long time, so these functions must be performed by the governments of the three largest economies – the United States, Europe, and Japan – acting together. Having pressured the world into a system of brutal competition, the major powers have an obligation to maintain sufficient global demand with low interest rates and other macro-economic policies. Putting pressure on their governments to act is the special responsibility of worker organizations in those countries.

Conclusion

A major strategic task before us is the strengthening of the alliance of working people – North and South, East and West – through a common programme. This should rest on a 'grand bargain' in which the interests of developing and developed country workers are both served. Such a grand bargain for labour would also help raise consciousness among the majority of the world's citizens of the need for international solidarity with each other.

The task is difficult. But the world's working majority has two great advantages. One is that it is the vast majority – in every country. The second is that the world's workers are indispensable. One can imagine a world without multinational investors. It is impossible to imagine a world without workers.

Thus the world's workers, broadly defined, have the power to change radically the rules of the global economy. To do it, we need a common programme, strong organizations and the realization that – whatever country we live in – we are all in the struggle together.

Notes

1 Christian E. Weller, Robert E. Scott and Adam S. Hersh, *The Unremarkable Record of Liberalized Trade* (Washington, DC, Economic Policy Institute, October 2001).

2 Jeff Faux and Lawrence Mishel, 'Inequality and the Global Economy', in Will Hutton and Anthony Giddens (eds), *On the Edge: Living with Global Capitalism* (London, UK, Jonathan Cape, 2000).

3 Catherine Dalpino, 'Globalization & Democracy', *Brookings Review*, Vol. 19, no. 4 (2001), pp. 45–8.

4 Claudio Lozano and Eduardo Manjovsky, 'Highlights of Labor Market Conditions in Argentina', Global Policy Network, Washington, DC, Economic Policy Institute. Available at http://gpn.org/data/argentina.html.

5 Jeff Faux and Robert Scott (US), Carlos Salas (Mexico) and Bruce Campbell (Canada), *NAFTA at Seven: Its Impact on Workers in all Three Nations* (Washington, DC: Economic Policy Institute, 2001).

7 A SOLIDARITY ECONOMY
(i) *Resist and Build*

ECONOMIC SOLIDARITY GROUP OF QUEBEC

Social, solidarity-based economics, by aiming at reclassifying actual people as the main actors in and beneficiaries of the economy, contributes to a socially just globalization. It is in this sense that we are presenting here the main proposals for this approach derived from the Final Quebec Document (October 2001). This second International Meeting on Solidarity-based Globalization brought together 327 people from 37 countries: 12 in the North and 25 in the South.

Social, Solidarity-based Economics

Social, solidarity-based economics represents a group of economic initiatives with the social goal of helping build a new way of experiencing and considering the economy. It grows out of the practical experience of tens of thousands of projects in countries in both the North and the South. Meetings in Lima (1997) and later in Quebec (2001) agreed on a definition that states that social, solidarity-based economics puts the human being at the centre of social and economic development. Solidarity economics is built on a collective economic, political and social project that brings about a new way of conducting politics and establishing human relationships on the basis of consensus and the activity of citizens (Lima Declaration, 1997).

This definition echoes a highly diversified set of practices. What, however, they have in common is:

- Uniting productive activity and satisfying the needs of populations by responding first to social needs rather than maximizing returns on capital;

- Producing goods and services by actively calling upon populations or sections of these populations within communities and grassroots social networks that are built on and promote the participation of women and men;

- Setting up associational-type (community) networks at the local, regional and national, as well as international, levels, organized on the basis of dialogue and cooperation rather than decision and control;

- Helping to bring out new economic and social rules and institutions that are collective and democratic in their methods of corporate and developmental management.

Social, solidarity-based economics includes all activities that are built on:

- Collective ownership that is indivisible;

- Distribution of wealth as a function of people rather than capital;

- Freedom of membership and democratic management;

- Decision-making and managerial autonomy in relation to the state.

It also consists of micro-business and small business activity that, while private property in their forms of ownership, do involve social relations and reflect aspects of local or regional communities.

No sector is immune from possible social, solidarity-based economic initiatives. They are evolving both in urban centres and rural settings and in very varying forms both in what is called the informal sector as well as the formal sector. Their activities, commercial or non-commercial, may involve the whole of a village or neighbourhood, or only a specific group such as women, young people, merchants, farmers, craftsmen, etc. They may have formal rules as an association or cooperative, but quite often they do not. They are made up of those men and women who contribute their actual labour, rather than just capital, and their investment revolves around the fact of their collective cooperation.

The following examples illustrate what these organizations' initiatives in different sectors of the economy are about:

- The creation or preservation of jobs in production workshops in Latin America, craftsmen's groups of West Africa, and the inclusion companies in Europe and Quebec;

- Agricultural and food production by village groups, producer cooperatives, and agricultural producer unions;

- Marketing agricultural products and inputs by village grain banks and other forms of group self-organization for marketing;

- Cultural activities developed by theatre groups, artistic cooperatives, companies for marketing home-made products, training schools for street art or other forms of artistic production;

- Group marketing of handicrafts by women's associations in India, groups of craftsmen in Andean America, and fair trade organizations between the North and the South;

- Solidarity-based savings and loan institutions in the shanty towns of Africa and Asia; savings and loan cooperatives and village banks in French-speaking Africa; credit unions in English-speaking countries; solidarity-based lending systems like Grameen Bank in Asia, Africa and Latin America; financial cooperatives in European and North American countries;

- Collective health-care services in Africa, and similar institutions in Europe and North America;

- Collective environmental protection undertaken by reforestation associations; resource reutilization, recycling and other social ventures for recapturing and recycling in the North as in the South;

- Community living environments created by self-help construction associations and cooperatives in Latin America and neighbourhood associations in Africa, and housing cooperatives in the countries in the North;

- Food security through shared kitchens and community gardens in Latin America, Quebec and elsewhere;

- Local development associations and organizations in both rural and urban settings.

Thus social, solidarity-based economics operates as part of a pluralist economy and calls into question the traditional way of viewing development as favouring either 'everything being in the private sector' or 'everything in the public sector'. The market and the state are not the only poles governing development. Social, solidarity-based economics adds to both by society itself taking economic action that embodies a prospective group interest. The recognition of society's own contribution to economic and social development makes us aware of the reality of pluralist economics, and more disposed to putting the economy in the service of society by promoting an 'economy with a market' rather than a 'market economy'.

As part of the process of updating and remodelling state intervention, the society is contributing by its action to social, solidarity-based economics. This may even extend to collective ownership of the instruments of development as well as protection of the common good.

Social solidarity-based economics allows for defining and promoting group interests without reducing them simply to being in the public sector. It also constitutes an alternative to private sector business ventures in sectors where the market should not be the determinant of everything and where the state, while assuming its responsibilities to regulate and redistribute, does not intervene directly by providing services. In this area social, solidarity-based economics and the public sector are not in competition. If well-organized, they reinforce each other and act as complements in order to guarantee the public good.

By its commercial activity in other lucrative sectors of the economy, social, solidarity-based economics is increasing its market share. Wherever there is a level playing field between it and globalized market forces, solidarity-based economics can protect our collective ownership of our resources and give us a means of responding to the needs of our communities.

Social, Solidarity-Based Economics and Development of Communities

Social, solidarity-based economic initiatives are a step towards basic economic development by means of which participation in the market can actually foster a better economic and social organization of communities. They encourage setting up new institutions and show the capacity of local initiatives to have an impact on the development process even at the national and international level.

The initial stage is an 'economy of the people' based on local exchange systems in simple urban markets and small handicraft workshops as well as other small production activities. All this forms the indispensable basis without which progress to another level is impossible. Numerous local development and socio-economic initiatives in the South and the North are working on reinforcing this initial development, thus proving that it is possible to start from an existing economy of the people. Since they maintain close links with local communities and the industries in which they are set up, social, solidarity-based economic businesses are often best placed to recognize new needs and to respond to them in a coordinated way. They are the place where true social innovations happen, which are often taken over by the public and private sectors.

Social, solidarity-based economic projects also offer prospects for sustainable development. Responding to the ecological threat that faces our planet, social, solidarity-based economic businesses radically question our production and consumption patterns. Since they do not have to satisfy stockholders greedy for short-term maximum yields, social, solidarity-based economic businesses can more naturally set their development strategies and their daily activities on the path to sustainable development.

The neoliberal organization of markets and development processes of the present are caught up in failures that are opening the door for the contribution of social, solidarity-based economics. The lack of regulation in the world's economy, the massive poverty that brings about the exclusion of a significant part of the population – particularly women and children – and the threats to the ecological balance of the planet constitute the failure of neoliberal and patriarchal economics. Social, solidarity-based economics is in many ways committed implicitly and explicitly to working out responses to the problems brought about by the new dynamics of globalization and is taking part in the construction of a new economic paradigm.

In the same breath it must be recognized that the war on terrorism is creating a market cycle where militarism and national security, with their aim to increase control over society, impede the creation and maintenance of favourable conditions for the activity of networks such as ours.

7 A SOLIDARITY ECONOMY
(ii) *Conference Synthesis*

SANDRA QUINTELA

Panel members
Discussion leader: Sandra Quintela, Brazil INSTITUTE OF
ALTERNATIVE POLICIES FOR THE SOUTHERN CONE (PACS) AND
BRAZILIAN SOLIDARITY SOCIOECONOMY NETWORK (RBSES)

Hostess of Organizing Network Conference
Carola Reintjes NETWORK FOR ALTERNATIVE AND SOLIDARITY
ECONOMY NETWORKS (REAS), SPANISH GOVERNMENT

Discussants
Jean Louis Laville, France CENTRE FOR RESEARCH AND
INFORMATION ON DEMOCRACY AND AUTONOMY (CRIDA) AND IRES
José Luiz Coraggio, Argentina UNIVERSIDAD GENERAL
SARMIENTO
Rosa Guillén, Peru LATIN AMERICAN WOMEN'S NETWORK
FOR ECONOMIC CHANGE

Conference and Seminar Lead Networks
Rural Coalition Mexico and the United States
Latin American Confederation of Workers' Coopera-
tives and Mutual Benefit Societies (COLACOT)
FAMES Senegal
FINANSOL France
Solidarity Economy Group of Quebec (GESQ) Canada
Solidarity Economy Group of Peru (GRESP)
Solidarity Economy Internetworks (IRES) France

MAG2 Finanza, Italy
Solidarity Socioeconomy Group (PSES) Global
Brazilian Solidarity Socioeconomy Network (RBSES),
   Brazil
Network for Alternative and Solidarity Economy
Networks (REAS), Spain
Solidarity Exchange Network, Argentina

Questions

The questions which participants talked about in the ensuing discussion addressed the problem of whether the Solidarity Economy, in its varied forms, is an occasional practice of merely micro-economic impact and significance, or whether it constitutes a development project with the potential to promote individuals and social groups on a much more ambitious scale sustainably to become active subjects as regards the means, resources and tools for producing and distributing wealth, preserving nature and the environment, and ensuring a sufficiency for the needs of all:

1 Is the Solidarity Economy directed merely at alleviating social
   problems generated by neoliberal globalization, or does it have the
   potential to underpin a different humanizing globalization, with a
   pluralistic and sustainable human development that is socially just
   and aimed at meeting needs rationally while unleashing the
   potential of every individual and citizen on Earth to improve the
   quality of their lives and those of generations to come?

2 Are knowledge, human creativity, work and meeting needs
   sustainably the core values of Solidarity Economics? How can the
   oppressive division of labour based on sexual, ethnic, cultural and
   other types of discrimination be overcome, as well as the unjust
   distribution of the means of consumption?

Originating largely among those that states have excluded from material well-being, with no access to goods, markets, technology and credit, the Solidarity Economy is revealing its potential as a paradigm for another globalization, one that shows in practice that another world is possible. In this regard:

1 Is it a proposal for an economy in parallel with other economic systems? Does it merely complement other forms of economy? Or will it expand in conflict with them, coexisting but confronting them in a long process of change, and capable of eventually replacing them? Does it contain its own contradictions and conflicts, or does it claim to be pure solidarity? And if conflicts exist, are they intrinsic to Solidarity Economics? How can it coexist with capitalism, without being integrated or absorbed?

2 How can we deal with solidarity in a society imbued with the consumer values of the market, and how can we disseminate the proposal of living in networks of Solidarity Economy? What are the educational challenges involved in sensitizing people to the culture of solidarity as an indispensable strategy for practising Solidarity Economics?

3 How can we bring together the wealth of insights contained in Social Economics, Solidarity Economics, Popular Solidarity Economy and Solidarity Socio-economics to consolidate this body of theory and practice in an emancipatory direction, while respecting regional and cultural diversities, and the distinguishing characteristics of South and North, East and West?

4 How can we reinforce practices and encourage mutual support among the various initiatives in an orderly fashion, by interlinking sectors and practices? How can we evaluate them, and by what criteria and indicators? How can we convey the wealth of these practices to society as a whole? How can we coordinate and expand the experiences and networks at the local, national, continental and international levels? How can we integrate the local and global scope of solidarity undertakings and networks?

The Social Groups Referred to

The people involved in these networks include (a) those who can no longer live in the dominant system, because they are excluded, threatened, exploited – they include urban and rural workers, the jobless, working women, the landless and the homeless; and (b) those who no longer want to, because they are struggling against every form of exclusion and dehumanization, and in solidarity are becoming part of this project.

Analyses

- The past 30 years have seen the emergence of solidarity economic practices that embody, and innovate creatively on, more than a century of workers' struggles to organize. In order to deal with social problems created by the market, these past and present collective actions have shown that another economic principle can be mobilized to serve society.

- Solidarity is the result of mutual action among free people, and can be an economic principle in opposition to the liberal principle that recognizes only the market and competition.

- Innovations include the insight that Solidarity Economics comprises solutions ranging from the local to the global levels, and including a multiplicity of human dimensions and potential. Intrinsic to economic solidarity is its ability to link the socio-political and economic dimensions constantly, always with a concern for the environment.

- Central to Solidarity Economics is the valuing of human labour, knowledge and creativity, rather than capital. When, however, it empowers workers as the subjects of the means and resources to produce and distribute wealth, it has to deal with objective and subjective risks and obstacles that make this process slow and complex. Patience and perseverance are required of everyone involved in this endeavour, which also entails incorporating new values, attitudes and types of relationships, and thus personal change on a day-to-day basis.

- We shall never progress towards building another economy until we consider gender relations in depth – what they have been and what is still present that we want to change: the sexual division of labour and patriarchal culture.

- Solidarity Economy networks refuse to permit their practices to be defined by the market economy; they refute the myth that all human relations and the economy itself can be reduced to the market. Solidarity Economics does not define itself as anti-market or anti-government, but instead as an endeavour to build new economic practices and power relationships where labour plays the leading role.

- It is an open proposal to be enriched by change in moving towards new realities. It calls for the state to be democratized and placed at the service of society.

- Unless a Solidarity Economy is built, globalization in solidarity will be impossible.

Proposals

Strategic proposals

- Integration, consolidation and interlinking of Solidarity Economy networks at the local, national, continental and intercontinental levels;

- Alliances among organizations and networks in the various segments of the economy;

- The connection between the Solidarity Economy and a new education: learning to learn, learning through experience, changing the study programmes and methods of formal education by introducing cooperative and solidarity-based practices, and so on;

- Dispute the use of funds that organizations make available for solidarity;

- Build awareness of our modes of consumption, and how they connect with production processes, so as to transform them in the light of the ethics of solidarity and sustainability;

- Public policies that foster the empowerment of society and of action for building a Solidarity Economy;

- Bilateral or multilateral agreements with public authorities;

- An ethical World Bank;

- A World *Fair* Trade Organization;

- Solidarity pension plans.

Proposals for integration

- Prepare a history of Solidarity Economy;

- Prepare a Solidarity Economy map and collective database;

- Consolidate successful practices in exchanging solidarity goods and services organized at the international level (portals, marketing);

- Link the different forms and sectors of the Solidarity Economy movement, from the local to the global level, building and reinforcing networks for collaboration in solidarity that facilitate interaction among the various participants and foster the spirit in people that they are the active subjects of this collective construction.

Proposals to facilitate a process of consensus-building on concepts and an ethical framework

Promote international debates on:

- Ethical criteria and distinguishing features of Solidarity Economy;
- Ethical criteria and codes of conduct for business;
- Concepts of employment, labour, value, wealth, scarcity, need, the market, state, democracy, etc.;
- International methodology on innovative evaluation indicators (indicators of wealth, labour, job quality and quantity).

Proposed alliances to help the Solidarity Economy forge linkages, project itself externally and introduce itself into societies and economies as an agent of change

- Compilation and publication of data and studies at two levels – national (networks) or sectoral (solidarity financing, fair trade, local currency, etc.) – regarding data, realities, impact;
- Rethink international cooperation using the paradigm of solidarity South–South, South–North, consumer–producer and worker–entrepreneur, thus replacing the dominant logic of mere financial or technical transfers;
- Strategic alliances with social movements for international cooperation, globalization in solidarity, pressure on holders of power (e.g., tax on financial transactions) and on multilateral institutions (the UN, IMF, World Bank, World Health Organization, International Labor Organization, etc.) so that they integrate into Solidarity Economy as a component indispensable to sustainable, multidimensional social and human development;
- Strategic alliances with academia and other research agencies, to expand research on the topics set out here;

- Joint undertakings with political authorities (e.g., participatory budgets), and bilateral or multilateral agreements with public/political authorities, to foster specific legislation on Solidarity Economy, or occasional collaboration.

Care must be taken in every action and collective construction not to neglect fundamental, crosscutting concerns

- To be patient, to know how to wait: major political, cultural and social projects take a long time, and firm, measured steps;

- Start at the bottom and work up, go from individuals to groups, from local to global levels;

- Establish relationships that are horizontal, transparent and participatory.

Consensus and Differences of Opinion

Points of agreement

- Organize another economy and production structures proactively;

- Meet the challenge of business management and the overall economy;

- Foster an economy that will integrate already existing endeavours;

- Strengthen a shared, synergistic strategy that will nourish the Solidarity Economy as a whole;

- Make it one of the main objectives of the Solidarity Economy to meet everyone's basic material needs, with respect for the environment;

- Foster empowerment of producers and consumers;

- Deconstruct the science of economics;

- Take into consideration the wealth of experience that women have in the everyday practice of solidarity;

- Build economic and educational practices aimed at promoting new – empowered and self-managed – subjects;

- The Solidarity Economy is not just an economic programme but also a social and political one: consequently, it is essential to democratize the state and relationships within civil society as a whole;

- Building globalization focused on human beings and labour is a day-by-day process. It has the potential to integrate all social segments, with a view to decent conditions of life, the fulfilment of all human and social rights, and equity with respect for diversity.

Points of disagreement

- Questions were posed regarding the scope of Solidarity Economy and the danger it runs of being co-opted by the capitalist system.

Lead Participants

Self-managing workers' associations; organic agriculture movements; trade-union and popular movements; pastoral and ecumenical movements; organizations promoting fair trade, ethical and solidarity consumption; trade networks with or without social currencies; ethical banks; people's banks; solidarity micro-credit; solidarity financing networks; solidarity buyers' groups; cooperative and associative movements; community kitchens; community radio stations; freeware manufacturers' organizations; neighbourhood associations; multi-cultural restaurants; collective gardens; artists' spaces; local networks of small and medium-size businesses; community childcare centres; youth and environmental movements; solidarity tourism and others that share in this project.

Translated by volunteer translator Charles Johnson, reviewed by Peter Lenny

PART

II

ACCESS TO WEALTH
& SUSTAINABILITY

OVERVIEW

Key Questions, Critical Issues

WILLIAM F. FISHER AND THOMAS PONNIAH

Key Questions

The key questions in Part II concern:

- Environment and sustainability;

- Access to water;

- Knowledge and intellectual property rights;

- The availability of essential medicine,

- 'Food sovereignty';

- The public's right to benefits associated with cities;

- The sovereignty of indigenous peoples.

With respect to sustainable development, the documents argue that the neoliberal project is inconsistent with nature's renewability. Corporate globalization has led to the enclosure of the ecological commons, the privatization of nature via the WTO's agreements, the dilution of democracy and a culture of violence and death (Shiva). What institutions, principles and processes need to be implemented to create sustainable development? How do we reduce current levels of production and consumption? How do we reimagine the economy? How do we finance sustainability? A specific issue, perhaps the most significant one, in regard to nature–society relations is the fact that over one billion people lack access to clean drinking water. How can universal access be guaranteed ('Water – a Common Good' conference synthesis)? What is the relationship of democracy to universal access? How should we evaluate large dam projects with respect to long-term sustainability?

Related to the question of the environment's renewability is the challenge of the privatization of nature. The documents note that the World Trade Organization's Trade-Related Intellectual Property Rights (TRIPs) Agreement is denying the poor of the Global South access to knowledge goods and innovation in terms of medicine, seeds and educational material, thereby amplifying the technological gap and leaving global research ever more focused on the consumer markets of the affluent, silently appropriating the biological knowledge and traditional wisdom of peasants and indigenous people, and reproducing the North's imperial relation to the South (Knowledge, Copyright and Patents synthesis). What are the alternatives to be fought for within the TRIPs Agreement? Are there possible agreements alternative to TRIPs? How can the mass public and Southern governments be mobilized to support alternatives (Oxfam)?

Related to the unsustainability of neoliberal development, the lack of access to drinking water, seeds and research, is the challenge of hunger and malnutrition. The documents argue that the latter are increasing because of the exploitative economic, agricultural and trade policies imposed by international financial institutions, Northern countries and corporations. What alternatives are needed in order to guarantee people the right to define their own sustainable food production, distribution and consumption policies in order to ensure that the whole population has the right to food, respecting their own cultures and the diversity of traditional and indigenous methods of farming and fishing, of trade and management of rural areas, in which women play a crucial role? How do we approach the crisis that confronts small and indigenous farming, traditional fishing and sustainable food systems (APM World Network)? Due to neoliberal policies and its 'food standards imperialism', export fishing and farming

is subsidized, while small farmers who produce for their own populations are not protected against international competition, thus forcing
them to leave the countryside and abandon traditional modes of self-
sufficiency.

As the documents observe, the impacts of neoliberal policies are
not only on peasants and fishermen and women. The policies have
encouraged the consolidation of agriculture and food industries, thus
homogenizing food and developing increasingly complex food
systems that depend on longer production chains. How do we confront the fact that longer, more interdependent networks transform
local food crises into international problems? How do we tackle the
health risks that are being produced not only by under-consumption
in the South but also by over-consumption in the North? Com-
pounding these dangers to health are the new risks being generated by
genetically modified organisms. What are these risks and what are
their solutions?

The documents in Part II assert that, along with the right to nature,
the right to knowledge and the right to food sovereignty, the public
also deserves the right to the benefits of the city. How has corporate
globalization reshaped the city (Cities, Urban Populations synthesis)?
What are the new responsibilities that the citizen has to bear? In terms
of alternatives, how can a new type of city be built? How can we
construct a city that is in harmony with nature and in continual
dialogue with its citizenry?

The last set of questions concerns the rights of indigenous peoples.
What alternatives need to be built in light of the historical effect on
indigenous sovereignty of colonialism, the proposed Free Trade Area
of the Americas (FTAA) agreement, Plan Colombia, the Andean
Initiative and the 'empire's' attempt to control water? How can the
indigenous be guaranteed recognition and redistribution (Indigenous
Peoples synthesis)? How do we build states that are multinational,
multicultural and multilingual?

Critical Issues

As elsewhere there are many convergences in this section and a few key differences. We will focus first on the dissimilarities and then outline the many agreements. The immediately obvious conflict in Part II, as in Part I, is between radicals and reformers. This antagonism is implicit in the discussion of agrarian reform. There is an acknowledgement that there can be no food sovereignty without a redistribution of land. The question is, as the synthesis states, who will effect the redistribution and how will they do it? During the twentieth century, substantial agrarian reform was implemented only as part of a broader revolution (Russia, China, Cuba) or as a conservative strategy aimed at preventing revolution, as in the case of the US encouraging change in South Korea, Japan and Taiwan. There are no examples of successful reformist land redistribution. The belief in agrarian reform is a convergence in the global justice and solidarity movement, but the different strategies to achieve it may become sources of disagreement in the future.

Another more serious contradiction is one between Parts I and II, that is, the conflict between labour's call for a full-employment economy versus the environmental call for a reduction of growth and consumption. The workers' movement rightly wants everyone to have economic independence whereas the green movement understands that the planet cannot endure the current level of resource appropriation. Faux, in 'A Global Strategy for Labour', points out that the differences between the two strands should not be overemphasized: both would like a full-employment economy built on sustainable growth. This is correct but it does not discuss how the North can achieve sustainability in a culture permeated by consumerism. Workers and others in the North consume more than the planet can sustainably allot to each human being. Therefore the challenge for these movements is to effect a simultaneous transformation of materialist values into ecological values. That change in the politics of consumption is necessary for these two strands of global civil society to become mutually compatible in the long run.

In the short term, the above conflicts are not necessarily divisive. In their document 'Intellectual Property and the Knowledge Gap', Oxfam proposes a strategy to transcend differences between radical goals and current possibilities. The organization focuses on what it calls 'wedge' issues:

A wedge provides a concrete illustration of a problem caused by global policies in a form that can easily be understood by the broader public. The idea is that once people understand the grassroots, human impact of particular policies, they will be encouraged to campaign for broader policy change. So, for example, the problem of patents and access to medicines is a 'wedge' issue for the reform of TRIPs. (Oxfam, UK).

The wedge strategy allows organizations to focus on concrete, available changes in the short term, while building public opinion for fundamental changes over the long term. This tactic, along with other methods mentioned in the documents, may offer paths that reconcile conflicting agendas.

There are many convergences in Part II. The documents agree that as the knowledge of nature increases, the nature of knowledge and the knowledge of nature are transformed: both are patented and become commodities. The rights to the two are transferred from humans, via the World Trade Organization, to corporations. The rights themselves become commodities. Where this is most evident is in the case of the indigenous. Their land, the nature they co-exist with, and their knowledge of their land are taken away, drained of their collective value, and exploited as economic value for the benefit of the multinationals. Against this conception of nature, knowledge and rights as objects of purchase, against the nihilism of neoliberalism, against its 'culture of death', the various documents build a new conception of what constitutes progress, development and solidarity for both the North and the South. It is a collective vision of advance that has faith in the Earth; that desires decommodification; that argues for common goods (genes, seeds, water, as the heritage of all humanity); that argues for people's right and sovereign capacity to feed themselves; that asserts natural rights; that asserts every individual's right to health and essential medicines; that stipulates that the citizen is a bearer of rights and has rights to the benefits of the city, and that citizenship is not simply to bear obligations; that wants to construct a town, a country, a world in harmony with nature; that aspires to the indigenous concept of unity in diversity via the promotion of multinational, multicultural, multilingual states; that creates genuinely accountable institutions, that is, introduces a new form of national and international governance; that wants democratized access to invention, technology, science; that promotes traditional knowledge; that sees identity as interwoven with ecology, and so identifies with the planet; that believes in cultural, environmental and biological diversity; that envisions an alternative form of knowing, doing and being that experiences all of life as sacred; and that nurtures the infinity of relations to create the possibility of the future.

8 ENVIRONMENT AND SUSTAINABILITY

(i) *The Living Democracy Movement: Alternatives to the Bankruptcy of Globalization*

VANDANA SHIVA

Bankruptcy of Globalization

Globalization was projected as the next great leap of human evolution in a linear forward march from tribes to nations to global markets. Our identities and context were to move from the national to the global, just as in the earlier phase of state-driven globalization, it was supposed to have moved from the local to the global.

Deregulated commerce and corporate rule were offered as the alternative to the centralized bureaucratic control under communist regimes and state-dominated economies. Markets were offered as an alternative to states for regulating our lives, not just our economies.

As the globalization project unfolds, it exposes its bankruptcy at the philosophical, political, ecological and economic levels. The bankruptcy of the dominant world order is leading to social, ecological, political and economic non-sustainability, with societies, ecosystems and economies disintegrating and breaking down.

The philosophical and ethical bankruptcy of globalization was based on reducing every aspect of our lives to commodities and reducing our identities to that of mere consumers in the global marketplace. Our capacities as producers, our identity as members of communities, our role as custodians of our natural and cultural heritage were all to disappear or be destroyed. Markets and consumerism expanded. Our capacity to give and share was to shrink. But the human spirit refuses to be subjugated by a world-view based on the dispensability of our humanity.

The dominant political and economic order has a number of features that are new, which increase injustice and non-sustainability on scales and at rates that the earth and human community have not experienced.

● It is based on enclosures of the remaining ecological commons – biodiversity, water and air, and the destruction of local economies on which people's livelihoods and economic security depend.

● The commodification of water and biodiversity is ensured through new property rights built into trade agreements like the WTO, which are transforming people's resources into corporate monopolies, viz. TRIPs and trade in environmental goods and services.

● The transformation of commons into commodities is ensured through shifts in governance, with decisions moving from communities and countries to global institutions, and rights moving from people to corporations through increasingly centralized and unaccountable states acting on the principle of eminent domain – the absolute sovereignty of the ruler.

This in turn is leading to political bankruptcy and anti-democratic formations and constellations. Instead of acting on the public-trust doctrine and principles of democratic accountability and subsidiarity, globalization is leading to governments usurping power from parliaments, regional and local authorities and local communities.

For example, the WTO TRIPs agreement was based on central governments hijacking the rights to biodiversity and knowledge from communities and assigning them as exclusive, monopolistic rights to corporations.

The WTO Agreement on Agriculture was based on taking decisions away from farming communities and regional governments.

The WTO General Agreement on Trade in Services (GATS) takes decisions and ownership over water from the local and public domain to the privatized, global domain.

This undemocratic process of privatization and deregulation has led to increased political bankruptcy and corruption and economic bankruptcy.

A decade of corporate globalization has led to major disillusionment and discontent. Democracy has been eroded, livelihoods have been destroyed. Small farmers and businesses are going bankrupt everywhere. Even the promise of economic growth has not been delivered. In fact, economic slowdown has been the outcome of liberalizing trade. Ironically, some corporations that led the process of trade liberalization and globalization have themselves collapsed.

Enron, which came to India as the flagship project of globalization with the full force of backing – and blackmail – by the US Trade Representative, has gone bankrupt, mired in corruption scandals. Chiquita, which forced the banana wars on Europe through a formal US/Europe–WTO dispute, has also declared bankruptcy.

First South East Asia, now Argentina, have exposed how vulnerable and volatile current economic arrangements are.

The non-sustainability and bankruptcy of the ruling world order are fully evident. The need for alternatives has never been stronger.

Creating Alternatives to Corporate Globalization

During the last decade of the twentieth century, corporate-driven globalization shook up the world and the economic and political structures that we have shaped to govern us.

In December 1999, citizens of the world rebelled against the economic totalitarianism of corporate globalization. Social and economic justice and ecological sustainability became the rallying cy of new movements for citizen freedoms and liberation from corporate control.

The events of September 11, 2001, however, shut down the spaces that people's movements had opened up, though they brought into focus the intimate connection between violence, inequality and non-sustainability, and the indivisibility of peace, justice and sustainability.

Doha was rushed through in the shadow of global militarization in response to the terror attacks.

As we face the double closure of citizen spaces by corporate globalization and militarized police states, by economic fascism aided by political fascism, our challenge is to reclaim our freedoms and the freedoms of our fellow beings. Reclaiming and recreating the indivisible freedom of all species is the aim of the Living Democracy movement. The Living Democracy movement embodies two indivisibilities and continuums. The first is the continuum of freedom for all life on earth, without discrimination on the basis on gender, race, religion, class and species. The second is the continuum between, and indivisibility of, justice, peace and sustainability – without sustainability and a just sharing out of the earth's bounties there is no justice, and without justice there can be no peace.

Corporate globalization ruptures these continuities. It establishes corporate rule through a divide-and-rule policy, and creates competition and conflict between different species and peoples and between different aims. It transforms diversity and multiplicity into oppositional differences both by breeding fundamentalisms through spreading insecurity, and then using these fundamentalisms to shift humanity's focus and preoccupation from sustainability and justice and peace to ethnic and religious conflict and violence.

We need a new paradigm to respond to the fragmentation caused by various forms of fundamentalism. We need a new movement which allows us to move from the dominant and pervasive culture of violence, destruction and death to a culture of non-violence, creative peace and life. That is why in India we have started the Living Democracy Movement.

Creative Resistance

Seattle was a watershed for citizens' movements. People brought the negotiation of a new international trade agreement and the WTO – the institution that enforces it – to a halt by mobilizing globally against corporate globalization. Seattle was the success of a strategy focusing on the global level and on protest. It articulated at the international level what citizens do not want. Corporations and governments responded quickly to Seattle's success. They killed off possibilities of protest by moving to remote venues like Doha where thousands could not gather. And they started to label protest and dissent of any kind as terrorism.

The biotech industry has called on governments to use anti-terror laws against groups like Greenpeace and Friends of the Earth and groups critical of the industry.

Mr Zoellick, the US Trade Representative, has called the anti-globalization movement terrorist.

A different strategy is needed post-September 11 and post-Doha. Massive protests at international meetings can no longer be the focus of citizen mobilization. We need international solidarity and autonomous organizing. Our politics needs to reflect the principle of subsidiarity. Our global presence must not be a shadow of the power of corporations and the Bretton Woods institutions. We need stronger movements at local and national levels, movements that combine resistance and constructive action, protests and building of alternatives, non-cooperation with unjust rule and cooperation within society. The global, for us, must strengthen the local and national, not undermine it. The two tendencies that we demand of the economic system need to be central to people's politics – localization and alternatives. Both are not just economic alternatives, they are democratic alternatives. Without them forces for change cannot be mobilized in the new context.

At the heart of building alternatives and localizing economic and political systems are the recovery of the commons and the reclaiming of community. The Living Democracy Movement is reclaiming people's sovereignty and community rights to natural resources.

Rights to natural resources are natural rights. They are not given by states, nor can they be extinguished by states, the WTO, or by corporations, even though under globalization, attempts are being made to alienate people's rights to vital resources of land, water and biodiversity.

Globalization has relocated sovereignty from people to corporations, through centralizing, militarizing states. Rights of people are being appropriated by states in order to carve out monopoly rights for corporations over our land, our water, our biodiversity, our air. States acting on the principle of eminent domain or the absolute sovereignty of the state are undermining people's sovereign rights and their role as trustees of people's resources on the basis of the public-trust doctrine. State sovereignty, by itself, is therefore not enough to generate countervailing forces and processes to corporate globalization.

The reinvention of sovereignty has to be based on the reinvention of the state so that the state is made accountable to the people. Sovereignty cannot reside only in centralized state structures, nor does it disappear when the protective functions of the state with respect to its people start to wither away. A renewed national sovereignty needs empowered communities which assign functions to the state for their protection – such is the basis of a new partnership between state and community. Communities defending themselves always demand such duties and obligations from state structures. In contrast, transnational corporations (TNCs) and international agencies promote the separation of the community interests from state interests and the fragmentation and divisiveness of communities.

The Living Democracy Movement

We started the Living Democracy Movement to respond to the enclosure of the commons that is at the core of economic globalization. The Living Democracy Movement is simultaneously an ecology movement, an anti-poverty movement, a recovery of the commons movement, a deepening of democracy movement, a peace movement. It builds on decades of movements defending people's rights to resources, movements for local direct democracy, and our freedom movement's gifts of *Swadeshi* (economic sovereignty), *Swaraj* (self-rule) and *Satyagraha* (non-cooperation with unjust rule). It seeks to strengthen rights enshrined in our constitution.

The Living Democracy Movement in India is a movement to rejuvenate resources, reclaim the commons and deepen democracy. It relates to the democracy of life in three dimensions.

Living democracy refers to the democracy of all life, not just human life. It is about earth democracy not just human democracy.

Living democracy is about life, at the vital everyday level, and decisions and freedoms related to everyday living – the food we eat, the clothes we wear, the water we drink. It is not just about elections and casting votes once in three or four or five years. It is a permanently vibrant democracy. It combines economic democracy with political democracy.

Living democracy is not dead, it is alive. Under globalization, democracy – even of the shallow, representative kind – is dying. Governments everywhere are betraying the mandates that brought them to power. They are centralizing authority and power, both by subverting democratic structures of constitutions and by promulgating ordinances that stifle civil liberties. The September 11 tragedy has become a convenient excuse for anti-people legislation worldwide. Politicians everywhere are turning to xenophobic and fundamentalist agendas to get votes in a period when setting economic agendas has been taken away from national governments and assumed by the World Bank, IMF, WTO and global corporations.

The Living Democracy Movement is about living rather than dead democracy. Democracy is dead when governments no longer reflect the will of the people but are reduced to anti-democratic, unaccountable instruments of corporate rule under the constellation of corporate globalization, as the Enron and Chiquita cases make so evident. Corporate globalization is centred on corporate profits. Living democracy is based on maintaining life on earth and freedom for all species and people.

Corporate globalization operates to create rules for the global, national and local markets which privilege global corporations and threaten diverse species, the livelihoods of the poor and small, local producers and businesses. Living democracy operates according to the ecological laws of nature, and limits commercial activity to prevent harm to other species and to people.

Corporate globalization is exercised through centralizing, destructive power. Living democracy is exercised through decentralized power and peaceful coexistence.

Corporate globalization globalizes greed and consumerism. Living democracy globalizes compassion, caring and sharing.

Democracy emptied of economic freedom and ecological freedom becomes a potent breeding-ground for fundamentalism and terrorism.

Over the past two decades, I have witnessed conflicts over development and over natural resources mutate into communal conflicts, culminating in extremism and terrorism. My book, *Violence of the Green Revolution*, was an attempt to understand the ecology of terrorism. The lessons I have drawn from the growing but diverse expressions of fundamentalism and terrorism are the following:

Non-democratic economic systems that centralize control over decision-making and resources and displace people from productive employment and livelihoods create a culture of insecurity. Every policy decision is translated into the politics of 'we' and 'they'. 'We' have been unjustly treated, while 'they' have gained privileges.

Destruction of rights to resources and erosion of democratic control of natural resources, the economy and the means of production undermine cultural identity. With identity no longer coming from the positive experience of being a farmer, a craftsperson, a teacher, or a nurse, culture is reduced to a negative shell where one identity is in competition with the 'other' over scarce resources that define economic and political power.

Centralized economic systems also erode the democratic base of politics. In a democracy, the economic agenda is the political agenda. When the former is hijacked by the World Bank, the IMF, or the WTO, democracy is decimated. The only cards left in the hands of politicians eager to garner votes are those of race, religion, and ethnicity, which subsequently give rise to fundamentalism. And fundamentalism effectively fills the vacuum left by a decaying democracy. Economic globalization is fuelling economic insecurity, eroding cultural identity and diversity, and assaulting the political freedoms of citizens. It is providing fertile ground for the cultivation of fundamentalism and terrorism. Instead of integrating people, corporate globalization is tearing apart communities.

The survival of people and democracy is contingent on an effective response to the double fascism of globalization – the economic fascism that destroys people's rights to resources, and the fundamentalist fascism that feeds on people's displacement, dispossession, economic insecurities and fears. On September 11, 2001, the tragic terrorist attacks on the World Trade Centre and at the Pentagon unleashed a war against terrorism promulgated by the US government under George W. Bush. Despite the rhetoric, this war will not contain terrorism because it fails to address the roots of terrorism – economic insecurity, cultural subordination and ecological dispossession. The new war is in fact creating a chain reaction of violence and spreading the virus of hate. And the magnitude of the damage to the earth caused by smart bombs and carpet bombing remains to be seen.

Living Democracy is true freedom of all life forms to exist on this earth.

Living Democracy is true respect for life, through equitable sharing of the earth's resources among all those who live on the planet.

Living Democracy is the strong and continual articulation of such democratic principles in everyday life.

The constellation of living democracy is people's control over natural resources, a just and sustainable utilization of land, water, biodiversity, and communities having the highest sovereignty and delegating power to the state in its role as trustee. The shift from the principle of eminent domain to the public-trust doctrine for functions of the state is the key to localization, to recovery of the commons and the fight against privatization and corporate takeover of land, water and biodiversity.

This shift is also an ecological imperative. As members of the earth family, *Vasudhaiva Kutumbhakam*, we have a share in the earth's resources. Rights to natural resources in order to meet our basic need for sustenance are natural rights. They are not given or cannot be assigned. They are either recognized or ignored. In contrast to this, the eminent domain principle inevitably leads to the situation of 'all for some' – corporate monopolies over biodiversity through patents, corporate monopolies on water through privatization, and corporate monopolies over food through free trade.

The most basic right we have as a species is survival, the right to life. Survival requires guaranteed access to resources. The commons provide that guarantee; privatization and enclosures destroy it. Localization is necessary for recovery of the commons. And Living Democracy is the movement to relocate the focus of our minds, our production systems and consumption patterns, from the poverty-creating global markets to sustainability and sharing of the earth community. This shift from global markets to earth citizenship is a shift of focus from globalization to localization, a shift of power from corporations to citizens. The Living Democracy Movement is a movement to establish that a better world is not just possible, it is essential.

ENVIRONMENT AND SUSTAINABILITY
(ii) *Conference Synthesis*

SARA LARRAIN

Initiators of the Discussion
Friends of the Earth International RICARDO NAVARRO,
CESTA, EL SALVADOR
Greenpeace International GERD LEIPOLD, DIRECTOR GPI,
AMSTERDAM

Facilitator
Sara Larrain PROGRAMA CONO SUR SUSTENTABLE/
INTERNATIONAL FORUM ON GLOBALIZATION, CHILE

Discussants
Vandana Shiva FOUNDATION FOR SCIENCE, TECHNOLOGY AND
ECOLOGY, INDIA
Robert Bullard CENTRE FOR ENVIRONMENTAL JUSTICE, USA
Wolfgang Sachs WUPPERTAL INSTITUTE, GERMANY
John Cavanagh INTERNATIONAL FORUM ON GLOBALIZATION

Summary Document

The following were the principal themes and the proposals which
achieved the most consensus from the presentations by the committee
and the contributions by attendees of the Conference on the Environment and Sustainability.

**The Marrakesh meeting on global warming destroyed Rio by putting the
environment and economic, social, political and cultural human rights in**

125

the framework of economic competition and in effect providing companies with unconditional access to the resources of the planet.

Socio-environmental problems have continued to worsen in spite of the agreements on sustainable development signed at Rio 1992. This is the consequence of the ever deeper influence of neoliberal economic policies over the international financial and commercial system. The Rio Agreements were the product of twenty years of citizen pressure on governments and we recognize their value as a guide to implementing sustainable development.

The principal obstacle to progress in alleviating poverty and promoting social justice, protecting the environment and strengthening democracy as established in the Agenda for Sustainability at Rio 1992 is the economic and trading system established by the International Monetary Fund (IMF) and the World Trade Organization (WTO). To progress towards sustainable development, it is necessary to change structurally the rules of the World Bank, the IMF and the WTO.

There can be no justice without sustainability. The human species consumes more than the planet can produce. The consumer class in the countries of the North and the South has created a type of consumption that cannot be replicated. Equity worldwide cannot be constructed on the basis of the patterns of production and consumption of the countries of the North. The planet's environmental space on the planet is finite and lifestyles and styles of production and consumption must be redesigned.

More specifically, the North American lifestyle is oligarchic and cannot be spread, since to do that we would need the resources of two more planets. Instead, we need to establish styles of well-being that can be universalized.

We recognize the equal right of all human beings to have access to air, land and water. The redistribution of environmental rights to give practical effect to this requires that the societies of the North and the wealthy of the South lower their levels of production and consumption so that the inhabitants of the South may also achieve well-being and a decent life. To make progress towards equity requires a reduction of consumption, a dematerialization of our concept of what constitutes well-being, and convergence towards equal environmental rights for every human being. Socio-environmental justice and sustainability also require eliminating the external debt.

Democracy is a prerequisite to sustainability. Sustainability requires moving from practising representative democracy to practising living democracy.

- A focus on democracy and environmental justice requires a recognition of the right of all human beings to be actors in defining their own development and realizing a democratic negotiation of what constitutes national and international development.

- Styles of well-being and development that cannot be democratized must not continue to exist, since they destroy the planet on which we all depend for life.

- Sustainability involves a return of power to the citizens, and the regulation of national and international regimes to ensure that they benefit people.

- Sustainability requires consistency between talk and action and between human needs and politics.

Sustainability requires putting the environment and society above the market. To make progress towards sustainable societies requires policies based on the inclusion of all races and cultures, equity and solidarity among societies, and cooperation among governments. The first step in meeting this challenge is repairing the environment and society. This requires:

- Recognizing the ecological debt, eliminating the external debt, and reversing the logic of economic development based on competition, economic growth, and the accumulation of wealth;

- Re-establishing the human, social, labour and environmental rights set out in national constitutions and within the framework of the UN (the FAO, UNICEF, UNESCO, UNEP, OMS, the Rio Summit, the Social Summit, the Beijing Summit, etc.), and not allowing the new economic agreements established by the WTO, NAFTA, and the FTAA to threaten the advancement of these rights.

A convention establishing the international commons and recognizing the right of communities to the common cultural and environmental assets is needed. These resources must not be allowed to be privatized.

We propose a convention, within the framework of the UN, that recognizes and establishes the rights of human communities to land, water, air and natural resources; to produce food; and to reproduce knowledge, the local economy and their cultures generated through the generations. This convention must establish these sovereign rights of the people and mandate governments to protect them. Any appropriation or patenting of life, nature, or the knowledge of the people must be prohibited.

Corporations must recognize these rights and adjust their activities to the requirements of democratic negotiations. (This treaty could be called the Porto Alegre Treaty.)

Pre-eminence of Multilateral Environmental Agreements (MEAs) over the regime of the WTO and the international financial system (World Bank and IMF). The regimes established within the framework of the WTO contradict the various multilateral environmental agreements. Currently, the regulations of the WTO take precedence over MEAs, and the World Bank and International Monetary Fund are not obliged to respect MEAs. Environmental sustainability must, however, be a condition of the economy. There are more than 200 MEAs for the protection of the environment, ecosystems and the biophysical systems that maintain life on the planet: these agreements must regulate trade and the international financial system, not the other way round.

Implementing sustainability requires radical changes in the political and regulatory structures of the WTO, World Bank, and IMF.

Implementation of the Precautionary Principle. The Precautionary Principle must be a pre-condition for any economic activity. Corporations, and not communities, must provide evidence, before beginning their activities, that they will not pollute or cause damage; it must be possible to verify this evidence legally.

Individuals, communities and the environment must be protected. The planet's environmental space is not just for the human species based on equal rights for every person; it is also for the subsistence of other living organisms. Environmental sustainability and the rights of individuals come before the right of corporations to do business.

A new financial system to finance sustainability. The resources and technology necessary to make progress towards sustainability currently exist, but there is a lack of political will on the part of governments, especially those of the North, to commit to them. At the next meeting on Financing for Development, to be held in Monterrey in March 2002, the necessary resources and financial cooperation must be committed to solve the problem of poverty, change the world's energy system, develop ecological agriculture and decentralize and clean up human settlements. In addition, it is necessary to establish new economic instruments needed to internalize social and environmental costs, such as the Tobin Tax on financial transactions and eco-taxes on fossil fuels and chemicalized agriculture. New agencies are needed – and must be funded – like an Agency for Renewable Energy, an Agency for Ecological Agriculture, and an Agency for Local Economies.

Translated by volunteer translator Jeanne S. Zang

WATER –
A COMMON GOOD
Conference Synthesis

GLENN SWITKES and
ELIAS DÍAZ PEÑA

Facilitators

Glenn Switkes   RÍOS VIVOS/INTERNATIONAL RIVERS NETWORK, USA

Elias Díaz Peña   RIOS VIVOS/AMIGOS DE LA TIERRA, PARAGUAY

Co-Coordinators

Ricardo Petrella   INTERNATIONAL COMMITTEE FOR THE GLOBAL WATER CONTRACT, ITALY

Medha Patkar   NARMADA BACHAO ANDOLAN, INDIA

Discussants

Pablo Solon   FUNDACIÓN SOLON, BOLIVIA

Luis Gonzaga Tenorio   FEDERAÇÃO NACIONAL DOS URBANITARIOS, BRAZIL

Maude Barlow   COUNCIL OF CANADIANS

Gabriel Herbas   COORDINADORA DEL AGUA DE COCHABAMBA, BOLIVIA

Marco Antonio Trierveiler   MOVIMENTO DOS ATINGIDOS POR BARRAGENS, BRAZIL

Wenonah Hauter   PUBLIC CITIZEN, US GLOBAL WATER CONTRACT, USA

Mark Ritchie   INSTITUTE FOR AGRICULTURE AND TRADE POLICY, USA

Serge Roy   ASSOCIATION QUÉBECOISE POUR LE CONTRAT MONDIAL DE L'EAU, CANADA

Key Themes

- Water as a common good;

- Water as a social, economic, and human right;

- Water shortage as a consequence of the degradation and destruction of water sources;

- Social and environmental impacts of large dams;

- Privatization and commodification of water;

- Export of water;

- National and international conflicts over water;

- International organizations comprising corporations, governments and international financial institutions to promote the commodification and unsustainable use of water;

- Coalitions, a popular parliament, a new world agreement and specific treaties as ways of bringing together civil society at the international level in defence of water;

- Social control, particularly by local communities, as a way of achieving sustainable management of water sources and supplies;

- Criticism of the French model of water management which is being implemented in various countries.

Social Groups Involved

The groups involved represented local communities, farmers and *campesinos*, indigenous peoples, populations affected by the construction of dams, social and environmental organizations, consumer groups and labour unions

Analysis

Water is a fundamental resource for life, and is thus the common heritage of all. Therefore it cannot be privatized or converted into a tradeable commodity. The right to water is an inalienable social, economic and human right.

The existing economic system has caused the degradation and destruction of water sources, inequality in access to water, and its growing scarcity, particularly for the poorest sectors of the population, as a result of destructive development projects which have had big impacts on local populations and the environment. These projects include large dams, polluting industries, large-scale agriculture, industrial waterways and mining.

The international financial institutions and the WTO are the financial engines behind this process, which has resulted in the destruction of water courses, the privatization and commodification of water resources, and their transfer into the hands of transnational corporations.

Sustainable water resources management, including its distribution and use, is vital to people's survival.

In order to achieve sustainable water management, the current economic system will have to change. This sustainable management will also require the effective participation of local communities in decision-making processes.

Civil society organizations should join at local, national, regional and international levels to promote changes in the economic system and establish sustainable alternatives.

The victories in local struggles, like that of the Coordinadora del Agua de Cochabamba in resisting water privatization and re-establishing sustainable community-based water management systems, demonstrates the importance of organizing and forming alliances at the level of local communities.

The fight against dams is an important part of the struggle by local communities and civil society for the control of water resources and the right to water, and against the current economic model.

In order to achieve change at the global level, local voices must be heard at that level, and local struggles taken to the global level.

Proposals

The Fight against the Commodification and Privatization of Water and for the Right to Water requires that we:

- Globalize the struggle against the economic system which is promoting the destruction of water supplies, degradation of water quality, and inequality in its distribution. This requires forming a broad civil society coalition including local communities, indigenous people, and national and international organizations in the fight for water, in order to:
  - oppose the neoliberal policies of the international financial institutions, the WTO, and new regional free trade agreements such as the FTAA, and the commodification and privatization of water;
  - oppose unsustainable development projects, such as large dams, industrial waterways, large-scale mining, large-scale agribusiness and other projects which destroy and degrade water sources;
  - propose and promote sustainable water management alternatives.

- Establish a World Water Parliament (representing various sectors, popular, and under grassroots control) which would implement a global water contract;

- Establish an international convention at the United Nations on water as a fundamental human right;

- Organize protests throughout the world during the week 14 March (International Day of Struggle versus Dams) to 22 March (World Water Day), promoting the fight for water, in opposition to the privatization of water, and for the universal right to water, with the slogan 'Water for Life, Not for Death';

- Establish an international treaty between nation states and indigenous peoples on water as a common good;

- Form an alliance of social movements on water which would submit to the Sustainable Development Summit in Johannesburg (scheduled for August 2002) a proposal for a global water agreement;

- Ensure adequate supplies of clean water for all individual, community and national water needs (domestic, food production, energy, recreation and for maintaining environmental quality);

- Support and promote global solidarity with those peoples who suffer the consequences of desertification and drought;

- Support the struggle of local communities and national movements, like the Coordinadora del Agua de Cochabamba, for control of their water sources and distribution systems, in resistance to the privatization process and for the re-establishment of sustainable community-run water management systems;

- Denounce the Bolivian government's systematic persecution of leaders of the Coordinadora del Agua de Cochabamba, including Oscar Olivera.

Sustainable Water Management

This requires the following steps:

- Manage water all the way from its source through the territories through which it flows by means of the effective participation of civil society, in particular indigenous communities, in decision-making processes;

- Require companies that destroy water sources – including those responsible for unsustainable land use, mining, and production of toxic industrial, mining, and agricultural waste, to repair the social and environmental damages they have caused and to restore the quality of these water sources;

- Prohibit the use of chemical products that destroy water quality;

- Promote campaigns against the conversion of rivers into industrial waterways;

- Use experiences gained during climatic disasters, such as El Niño, to promote campaigns for sustainable water management and also campaigns of resistance to the present economic system;

- Implement alternative biological systems for sewage management;

- Promote rainwater harvesting methods for domestic and agricultural use.

The Fight against Dams

Here we call for the following steps:

- Establish a moratorium on new dams until all the economic, social, cultural and environmental impacts they have caused are resolved;

- Pressure national governments, export credit agencies and international financial institutions to adopt the recommendations of the World Commission on Dams;

- Promote a new energy model, based on efficiency, conservation and the use of alternative energy sources such as wind, solar power and biomass;

- Support and express solidarity with the people fighting the Sardar Sarovar dam on the Narmada River in India.

10 KNOWLEDGE, COPYRIGHT AND PATENTS

(i) Intellectual Property and the Knowledge Gap

OXFAM, UK

This paper discusses the impact of intellectual property rules in the developing world, and possible campaign strategies to change them. These rules matter because they affect people's access to medicines, seeds and educational materials, and the ability of poor countries to develop and participate effectively in global markets. Oxfam hopes that the paper will be a useful contribution to others working on the issue, and will prompt feedback for its own work on WTO patent rules.

The First Problem – The Rules

One of the most intense struggles in the campaign to reform globalization concerns the control of knowledge. Will knowledge be monopolized by corporate interests for private profit, and shaped by the markets of rich consumers, or will it be kept within the public domain, and used to help end poverty, hunger and disease? At a time when millions of people are deprived of basic rights to health, food and education, and inequality is growing, this question could not be more critical.

The World Trade Organization's TRIPs Agreement, introduced in 1995 after intense corporate lobbying, is at the centre of this controversy. It is the main international treaty determining rights over intellectual property (IP), which includes patents, copyright and trademarks.

TRIPs obliges all WTO members to grant patent holders – which are mainly large Northern-based corporations – temporary monopolies for their 'inventions'. This system is supposed to stimulate innovation, as it allows patent holders to prevent competition, raise prices and thereby recoup the costs of their investment.

Bilateral trade agreements such as the (proposed) Free Trade Area of the Americas (FTAA) are also being used to ratchet up national IP standards to even higher levels than those required by TRIPs.

All these rules will affect the lives of billions of people, yet until recently they have been introduced with minimal public debate.

The Second Problem – Their Impact

IP protection can be one useful incentive, alongside others, to stimulate investment and innovation. Unfortunately, TRIPs and other trade agreements require all countries to implement very high minimum standards of protection, irrespective of their level of development, or of a sector's potential contribution to the realization of human rights. This one-size-fits-all approach is damaging to both welfare and innovation. It has shifted the balance too far towards the private interests of corporate IP holders, and away from the users of knowledge.

Many of the damaging effects of international IP rules will be most acutely felt in poor countries. Oxfam fears the new regime will:

- **Exclude poor people from access to vital 'knowledge goods'** such as medicines, seeds and educational materials. TRIPs will result in higher prices for knowledge-rich goods, further excluding poor people from access to medicines, seeds, computer software and educational materials. The high price of HIV/AIDS medicines graphically illustrates the iniquitous effect that patents can have. Higher prices also limit the ability of developing-country governments to meet basic human rights to food, health and development.

- **Exacerbate the technological divide.** There is already a wide technological gap between rich and poor countries. Although developing countries are rich in informal knowledge, they are net importers of the kinds of high-tech goods and know-how protected by TRIPs. Industrialized countries, on the other hand, account for 90 per cent of global research and development (R&D) spending, an even higher share of patents, and are the main exporters of IP.

- **TRIPs will exacerbate this divide by increasing the cost of knowledge-rich goods imported by developing countries.** Royalties and licence fees paid by developing countries to patent holders in the industrialized world have been climbing rapidly since the mid-1980s. In 1998, the US received a net surplus of more than $23 billion from its IP exports.

- **TRIPs will further skew R&D towards rich-consumer markets rather than the basic needs of the poor.** There is a massive 'market failure' in R&D into medicines and agriculture. Most global R&D is targeted at the markets of rich consumers rather than at the basic needs of the poor. Less than 10 per cent of global spending on health research addresses 90 per cent of the global disease burden. Similarly, much agricultural research aims to improve the appearance and taste of produce for consumers in rich markets, rather than to support the sustainable farming of staple foods such as sorghum and cassava, on which many poor farmers depend.

- **Global IP rules will worsen this problem by further concentrating R&D into profitable areas such as cures for obesity or impotence.** Even with stronger IP protection in place, women and men living in poverty in developing countries simply do not have sufficient purchasing power significantly to influence the direction of R&D. Only large-scale public funding, and public/private partnerships, will ensure that R&D is directed to meeting their basic needs.

- **Restrict the ability of poor countries to innovate and participate effectively in global markets.** Supporters of TRIPs say that short-term welfare losses caused by higher prices will be offset by longer-term benefits through increased innovation and technology transfer for poor countries. But the lack of technological capacity means that foreign companies will capture most of the benefits of stronger IP protection. Moreover, by restricting the scope for developing countries to imitate and adapt new technologies, TRIPs will inhibit future innovation, development, and the ability of countries to compete effectively in global markets. There is little evidence to suggest that higher levels of IP protection in developing countries will prompt greater foreign direct investment or licensing by TNCs, even in pharmaceuticals and chemicals.

- **Encourage piracy of biological resources and traditional knowledge of farmers and indigenous people in the developing world.** TRIPs were designed to prevent so-called piracy by developing countries of the inventions and products of rich countries. But it is silent about the systematic appropriation of biological knowledge and informal forms of traditional knowledge from developing countries by large Northern companies.

Campaign Strategies

This section draws on Oxfam's recent experience of campaigning on the issue of patents and access to medicines (the Cut the Cost campaign) and raises some questions about the future focus of civil society campaign strategies.

What Should be the Focus for Campaigning on TRIPs?
A key question is whether it is more effective to campaign for broad reform/abolition of TRIPs, or to focus on achieving change in specific areas, such as patenting of medicines, patenting of plant genetic resources, or patenting of life forms.

Oxfam tends to focus its popular campaigning on what it calls 'wedge' issues. A wedge provides a concrete illustration of a problem caused by global policies in a form that can be easily understood by the broader public. The idea is that once people understand the grassroots, human impact of particular policies, they will be encouraged to campaign for broader policy change. So, for example, the problem of patents and access to medicines is a 'wedge' issue for the reform of TRIPs. The fact that no poor country could afford expensive, patented HIV/AIDS medicines provided a particularly dramatic illustration of the problem.

Prior to the launch of Cut the Cost, Oxfam's research showed that few people knew what a patent was, and that if they did know, they were more likely to think that it was a good thing than a bad thing. Even fewer people knew what the WTO or TRIPs were. On the other hand, many more people were concerned about health in poor countries.

Focusing popular campaigning on wedge issues does not stop Oxfam from raising broader concerns in its publications and lobbying. It also believes it is important to form cross-sectoral alliances with different groups campaigning on TRIPs – whether on seeds, medicines, genes, or software. This allows groups to coordinate campaigning but without losing the specificity of each campaign. The TRIPs Action Network (TAN) formed last year is a good example of this approach. It has coordinated days of actions on TRIPs and developed an NGO statement calling for wide reform of TRIPs.

Incremental or Fundamental Change?

Various strategies for campaigning on IP rules are possible, and can be complementary. In the case of TRIPs, the demands range from outright abolition of the agreement, through to re-interpretation (as in the Doha Declaration on TRIPs and public health). Oxfam pursues a twin-track strategy, focusing on concrete changes that are achievable in the short term, while also pressing for more fundamental change in the long term. Our experience is that small gains can

strengthen rather than undermine the momentum for more fundamental change.

In the case of the Cut the Cost campaign, the policy aim is to
reform the TRIPs agreement in favour of public health. The short-
term goal is to strengthen the existing public-health safeguards in
TRIPs, and to stop rich countries and TNCs bullying poor countries
over their patent laws. The longer-term goal is a substantive review of
TRIPs with a view to introducing longer transition periods for
developing countries to comply with TRIPs, and allowing developing
countries much greater flexibility in determining the length and scope
of pharmaceutical patenting, including the option to exempt
medicines altogether. While some groups and governments fear that
reopening TRIPs may result in something worse, Oxfam believes that
growing public pressure will prevent this from happening.

Some groups have expressed concern that the Doha Declaration on
TRIPs and public health could undermine the case for more radical
reform by legitimizing the TRIPs Agreement. However, Oxfam
believes that the declaration, though limited, will result in some
concrete health gains, set a precedent to reinterpret TRIPs in favour
of other fundamental rights, and build momentum among the public
and developing countries at the WTO for further reforms to TRIPs in
the future.

TRIPs out of the WTO?

Oxfam has not so far made the removal of TRIPs from the WTO a
focal point of its popular campaigning, for three reasons. First, although
there is a strong rationale for such a proposal, not least because TRIPs
is inherently protectionist, the arguments seem unlikely to mobilize
public opinion. Second, the idea is unlikely to win concrete backing
from developing-country members of the WTO. Finally, a public
campaign on such a position would also require that a coherent
alternative to TRIPs be put forward. Giving control of all IP treaties
to the World Intellectual Property Organization (WIPO), for example,
would not necessarily be desirable, given its narrow pro-IP stance.

However, Oxfam will argue in its lobbying that the future review of TRIPs should look seriously at this issue, and welcomes other groups campaigning on it, because this provides a strong indication of NGO concern and adds to the pressure for change.

Global, Regional or National Campaigns?

Campaigns should not stop or start with TRIPs. Strong campaigns about national and regional-level IP rules are also vital. Many developing countries have been or will be pressured to introduce national laws that grant levels of IP protection that go beyond TRIPs. Increasingly, countries are also signing up to bilateral or regional economic agreements that mandate levels of IP protection that are at least comparable to TRIPs, and are often even higher. This means that even if TRIPs were reformed in the future, countries would still be locked into anti-developmental IP rules. National-level campaigning can be based on a broad social base, including small and medium enterprises that are prejudiced by the high cost of technology.

The United States has been particularly aggressive in pursuit of 'TRIPs-plus' rules, employing direct political and economic pressure, and formal trade treaties such as the US–Jordan agreement and the FTAA. If developing countries win further concessions on TRIPs, one can envisage converting the WTO TRIPs Council into a body whose purpose is to police a ceiling for IP standards, rather than a minimum – a role entirely consistent with the pro-competition philosophy of the organization.

In the case of medicines, now that greater clarity has been won on the issue of what TRIPs does and does not allow, it is important that governments use the flexibility within TRIPs to implement national legislation in support of access to medicines. Strong national campaigns in South Africa, Brazil, and Thailand have shown what is possible at this level.

Other Action

If TRIPs reforms are to translate into real gains for poor people, campaigners will also need to press for increased debt relief and international aid, and for governments to finance R&D in health and agriculture which seeks to work with people living in poverty to address their needs. More funds are also urgently needed to help finance the purchase of medicines in least-developed countries. Groups could also campaign for a technology transfer fund financed by a small tax on patents to help the poorest nations.

Conclusion

Worldwide concern about the effects of patents on the price of life-saving drugs has led to victories in the South African court case, in the US–Brazil WTO dispute and at Doha. This has created a political climate in which it is much harder for rich countries to intimidate the developing world over patents, though we still have the task of reforming the rules.

The tide is turning in the patenting debate. There are now greater opportunities to increase ordinary people's understanding of the other ways in which current IP rules contribute to poverty and under-development, and to increase political pressure for reform. This will be a significant step towards a world where knowledge and innovation are social assets that serve people, above all those in need, rather than corporate assets that serve shareholders.

10 KNOWLEDGE, COPYRIGHT AND PATENTS

(ii) *Conference Synthesis*

FRANÇOIS HOUTART

The conference brought together the following contributors:

Michael Bailey OXFAM INTERNATIONAL, UK

Jean-Pierre Berlan NATIONAL INSTITUTE OF AGRONOMIC RESEARCH, FRANCE

Wilson Campos VIA CAMPESINA, COSTA RICA

Richard Stallman FREE SOFTWARE FOUNDATION, USA

Alexander Buzgalin UNIVERSITY OF MOSCOW, RUSSIA

Facilitator

François Houtart TRICONTINENTAL CENTRE, LEUWEN, BELGIUM

Context

This conference followed the one on global trade, held the day before, where Martin Khor made reference to intellectual property (a concept called into question by some members of the panel), recalling that in the framework of the WTO there have been three principal areas: the agreements on investment, on trade and on intellectual property. According to him, it is particularly necessary to separate out this latter aspect of the WTO, not only because the principle is inadmissible, but also, ironically, because it goes completely against the logic of free trade.

The first thing to note is that the privatization of knowledge serves to confuse the process of development: Thai peasants believe they should hide the seeds that they use; Egyptian students are unable to pay for their course books; the Peruvian businessman cannot acquire the software necessary for his work; the Kenyan woman has no access to the medication which will save her child. All this because property rights are claimed and monopolized by multinational businesses.

The holding of patent rights is a relatively recent development. In the nineteenth century, the United States took over British technology without any problem and without paying for it; in the twentieth century, Japan copied Western technologies. But in the twenty-first century, we hold back developing countries from doing the same thing. The WTO agreements provide a collection of rules which have to be adopted as a whole. In fact, however, the most powerful nations introduce protection indirectly, while huge pressure is brought to bear, especially by the main multinational companies, on developing countries to 'free up' their economies.

The Problem

The problem of TRIPs is framed mainly by North–South relations. In practice, the rules on intellectual property will set up transfers of resources from the South to the North. TRIPs formed part of the Uruguay Round negotiations, and for twenty years, poor countries have been subjected to periodic economic downturns caused by Northern countries, especially the United States, in order to ensure that they will adopt laws protecting intellectual property. Efforts to achieve sustained industrial development of Southern countries have been counter-productive.

One of the arguments for protecting intellectual property through patents is the need to reward innovation – assuming that is something to be encouraged. What results, however, is the opposite. In the nineteenth century, patents aimed to stimulate competition, as well as to systematize knowledge and make it public. Today, they reinforce monopolies and paralyse scientific research. Progress in the pharmaceutical field occurs three or four times more quickly in a socialist country like Cuba, because discoveries are immediately shared and become common property, whereas in the world of market capitalism they are just as immediately made private property.

Indeed, the result is more withholding of knowledge, more creation of monopolies and less competition. This contradicts the very principles which neoliberalism upholds.

In the pharmaceutical field, the imposition of this right to intellectual property leads to appalling situations, for very little of the industry's profit goes into research, but rather serves to reward shareholders or increase market share at the expense of rivals, with the result that the needs of hundreds of millions of human beings go unmet. The partial victory secured in South Africa when the multinationals eventually withdrew their proceedings against the government is an illustration of this situation.

In agriculture, the introduction of sterile seeds by corporate seed manufacturers, combined with the prohibition on peasants reusing their own seeds, introduces an economic relationship which gives transnational corporations a monopoly over the reproduction of agricultural products. Happily, public opinion has reacted adversely to the introduction of this *Terminator* seed promoted by the multinational Monsanto. The European directive on the subject, however, is not acceptable because it amounts to separating production (farmers) from reproduction (the cartel of multinational firms). While it is dangerous to encourage a transgenic agriculture which monopolizes research outcomes, it is desirable to promote such research in the field of conventional agriculture, which runs counter to the cartel's interests.

On the other hand, respect for biodiversity is essential, and covers not only living animals and vegetation, but also cultures, production systems, ways of life and social relations. This is a fundamental right of people.

As for the monopoly over computer software, it is also unacceptable: knowledge must be able to be shared. Copyright laws prevent people from exchanging computer programmes, which is an obstacle to progress and innovation. The same principle ought to be adopted in education – for textbooks, manuals, dictionaries, encyclopedias, etc.

To conclude, it is important to delegalize the issue of patents, by putting it in context. Public opinion understands a patent in the abstract. As in the case of Third World debt, to understand fully what is at stake, these questions must be seen in the context of unequal relationships, both within nations and between them.

The Alternatives: Three Levels

The Utopian Level: what kind of society do we want?

- To call into question the basic premise that protecting innovation encourages innovation. Innovation grows when systematized and made public, thereby fostering competition and new technical innovation;

- To reaffirm that living organisms are a public and inalienable asset;

- To recognize biodiversity as a fundamental right of peoples;

- To ensure recognition for the rights of farmers and rural communities to ownership, use and improvement of natural resources, including all techniques and knowledge developed in relation to those resources;

- To have it recognized that genetic resources are a patrimony of humankind and a responsibility of all members of society; and

- To reject all monopolistic appropriation of knowledge and natural products.

Medium-term Aims

- To reform the TRIPs Agreement radically so that every country can establish and adapt patenting and marketing laws for specific products according to their level of development;

- To influence the behaviour of transnational corporations through pressure from consumers, producers and public opinion in relation to their intellectual property policies;

- To reaffirm and protect the link between the production and reproduction of living organisms in agricultural activities: harvested seeds should be reusable;

- To prohibit monopolies and fight cartelization in scientific and technical innovation;

- In the debate on the patenting and privatization of living things, to recognize the United States' and Europe's genetic debt to the Third World;

- To allow free access to software so as to ensure it is shared and improved (bypassing/disregarding copyrights);

- To extend the fight for free access to knowledge into areas other than software: dictionaries, encyclopedias, textbooks etc.

- Increased public funding for research and innovation for social and economic development.

Short-term Aims

- To prevent the United States and the European Union from imposing intellectual property regulations in bilateral or regional 'free trade' agreements;

- To ensure that national and regional intellectual property legislation does not enact the provisions of the TRIPs Agreement ahead of time, particularly in relation to the 49 least developed countries that are exempt from them at least until 2006;

- To run short-term campaigns to educate and mobilize civil society on this issue. To seek to construct alliances across sectors, combining action by rural workers, consumers, the academic world, the medical profession, small entrepreneurs, etc. To reinforce North-South alliances in the same regard;

- Particularly in relation to farming, to redirect research priorities towards improving conventional agriculture rather than systematically encouraging research into genetic engineering solutions;

- To adopt a moratorium on research, production, marketing and the transport of genetic products until tests show that they are not a hazard;

- To ensure recognition of farmers' and rural communities' rights to own, use and improve natural resources, including all techniques and knowledge developed in relation to these resources;

- As regards software, to promote the use of a non-monopolistic operating system like GNU + Linux and freeware;

- To oppose the patenting of software and recognize that this is now an obstacle to progress and innovation; in particular, to fight against the Digital Millennium Copyright Act and its extension to other countries outside the United States;

- To organize a session of the permanent people's tribunal on pharmaceutical industry practices.

Translated by volunteer translators Margaret Eaton and Samantha Tasker, reviewed by Peter Lenny and Owen Beith

MEDICINE, HEALTH, AIDS
11

Conference Synthesis

SONIA CORRÊA

Organizing Network
Doctors without Borders MSF – MÉDECINS SANS
FRONTIÈRES
Michel Lotrowska REPRESENTATIVE OF MSF IN BRAZIL AND
COORDINATOR OF THE CAMPAIGN FOR ACCESS TO ESSENTIAL
MEDICINES

Discussants
Mário Sheffer PELA VIDDA GROUP, REPRESENTING THE
BRAZILIAN ANTI-AIDS MOVEMENT
Mustafa Barghouti PRESIDENT OF THE UNION OF
PALESTINIAN MEDICAL RELIEF COMMITTEES, PALESTINE
Adrian Lovett OXFAM, COORDINATION OF GLOBAL
CAMPAIGNS, UK[1]

Presenter
Sonia Corrêa IBASE and DAWN NETWORK

Originally intended to examine the implications of the recent
global struggles for access to essential medicines, especially
medicines for HIV/AIDS treatment, the conference, in fact, dealt
with issues related to access to health and essential medicines in
general. A wide range of obstacles to the right to health was also
considered. This opening up of the initial theme was due, on the one
hand, to the composition of the organizing group, and, on the other,

to the expectations of the participants. This suggests that the World Social Forum should in future include in its agenda a larger number of big events dealing specifically with health issues in the globalization context – as indeed was demanded by the audience present.[2]

One conclusion from the debates is the recognition that access to medicines and medical services does not imply access to health. Health issues should be seen and thought about in the light of the global political economy. They necessarily imply relations of power: between North and South; between international actors like transnational corporations and national states; between different levels of management of health systems; and, above all, between people, or users of health systems and medicines, and governments and global institutions. Therefore, the issue of access to medicines and health services must be considered in its huge complexity. We can see limits generated by the new global rules related to patents (the WTO's TRIPs Agreement) and to the constraints imposed on individuals and social groups, including the right to free movement so as to have access to a health service. The situation experienced by Palestinians in the Occupied Territories at the hands of the Israeli army is an acute example of these constraints. In the light of this understanding, it is fundamental that all policies and recommendations related to health (in the broad sense) – whether at a global level or at national and local levels – must be guided by the entitlement of people as subjects with rights and as active bearers of proposals for changes in health systems.

Access to Essential Medicines

Despite the breadth of the debate, the main focus of the discussions was still the campaigns around access to essential medicines – especially drugs used for HIV/AIDS treatment – which in recent years have made it possible to overcome some important obstacles, both in the national context and on the global level. The significance of these social mobilizations, though only partially successful, must not be minimized. There are lessons to be learned from the strategies and priorities put forward by civil society in recent years.

Some facts presented by Michel Lotrowska of MSF highlight the potential importance of these recent political achievements:

- Seventy-two per cent of the world's population lives in developing countries;

- These populations represent only 7 per cent of the sales of pharmaceutical products worldwide;

- One-third of the world's population does not have access even to essential medicines, and in the poorest regions of Africa and Asia this percentage rises to 50 per cent.

Table 1 below about the investments made by the major pharmaceutical corporations also tells us that there is a lack of investment in research and development (R&D) of medicines to treat so-called neglected diseases, which are mainly diseases of developing countries.

Table I Company Expenditure on R&D in 2000 (Billions of US$)

Pfizer	4.44
GlaxoSmithKline	3.82
Johnson&Johnson	2.93
AstraZeneca	2.89
Pharmacia	2.75
Research on Tropical Diseases	0.01

(Source: Pharmaceutical Executive April 2001)

Another crucial aspect to be considered is that the difficulties of access to essential drugs were investigated in depth only after the adoption of the TRIPs Agreement by the countries that are members of the WTO. The Agreement:

- Increases patent protection and favours monopolies, which raise the prices of medicines;

- Restrains competition;

- Has serious effects on a country's capacity for local manufacturing of pharmaceutical products;

- Prevents so-called reverse engineering;

- Discourages R&D for neglected diseases suffered by the poor.

In the same historical context in which the TRIPs agreement was adopted at the WTO, the issue of drugs for treating HIV/AIDS gained huge relevance. This was a result both of the global and 'democratic' character of the epidemic – AIDS affects rich and poor, black and white, men and women, homosexuals and heterosexuals – and of the systematic campaigning by global networks and community responses to the epidemic. Yet it is important to remember that, in addition to HIV/AIDS, developing countries are still characterized by near epidemic proportions of other diseases like malaria and tuberculosis, while also experiencing high rates of major health threats like cancer, hypertension and diabetes. In all these cases, access to essential medicines is crucial. For precisely this reason, the networks of people involved in the struggle for access to anti-retrovirals have established solidarity links with groups and organizations fighting for wider access to essential medicines generally. The successes obtained in recent years, especially in the WTO context, must be understood in the light of this popular capacity for coordination and mobilization.

A Brief Note on the Brazilian Experience

With this wider context in mind, the Brazilian experience is relevant in many ways. Although it would not be possible to describe in detail the complexity of a journey of almost twenty years, it is interesting to point out some of its most relevant elements. First, it is important to remember that the struggle for an effective policy response to HIV/AIDS happened, from the 1980s, in a way that was coordinated with the fight for a really free and universal public health system – that is, for health as a human right. These were the conditions that led to the adoption of legislation that guaranteed the free availability of medicines. Second, Brazil has manufactured some of these drugs for HIV treatment since the early 1990s, because they had been the subject of reverse engineering before the national patents law (which is consistent with TRIPs) was approved. In addition, the Brazilian patents law (though compliant with TRIPs in other respects) includes, similarly to North American legislation, a clause that authorizes compulsory licensing in the event of a threat to public health.[3]

Above all, it is important to stress that the course of Brazilian AIDS policy is a consequence of a long process of clashes (and also of cooperation) between civil society and the state. The Brazilian experience is an example of public policy that came from the periphery of society to the centre. At the roots of the fight for public access to medicines in Brazil lie the mobilization and solidarity networks of marginalized and discriminated groups such as gays, transvestites, prostitutes and drug users. In other words, the debate about access to medicines in Brazil was built on the premise of health as a right and respect for human rights generally. This long journey is what supported the daring decision of the Brazilian government to threaten the pharmaceutical industry to break patents in 2000–2001 in order to reduce the costs of anti-retrovirals. Although the Brazilian response to HIV/AIDS still has its limits, and access to prevention and treatment is not always ensured – especially in the case of the poorest groups – the country's experience has clearly converged with and stimulated the global debate about access to essential medicines.

The Global Campaigns and their Results

During the late 1990s, global campaigns for access to medicines had some very important results, namely:[4]

- Recognition of HIV/AIDS as a human rights issue and a humanitarian crisis (the UN's Commission on Human Rights, 2001);

- Creation of the Global Fund for HIV, Malaria and Tuberculosis (Extraordinary Session of the UN General Assembly on HIV/AIDS, June 2001);

- Adoption in Doha, at the most recent round of WTO negotiations (November 2001), of a text about rights to intellectual property and public health that can be used to justify widening public access to medicines in the coming years.

Although these achievements are neither complete nor definitive, it is important to examine the lessons we have learned. One is to recognize that it is vital for actions and campaigns to be organized in a partnership between North and South countries, ensuring, however, the primacy of the South's agenda and priorities. Another fundamental aspect is that the message of campaigns should be clear and their political and institutional targets well defined, at every step.

Arguments Used by Global Campaigns

- Medicines are not CD-ROMs, Barbie dolls, or computer games: they are a matter of life or death for millions of people;

- There is a huge imbalance between the sanctity of patents and people's health;

- Access to essential medicines should not be a luxury reserved for the rich, but should be enforced as a critical component of *the human right to health*;

- According to Grö Brundtland, Director General of the WHO, the fact that essential drugs exist while millions of people die for lack of them, implies a political problem, a moral problem, and a problem that challenges the credibility of the global market system;

- The primacy of the right to intellectual property is in contradiction with the right to life as set out in the Universal Declaration of Human Rights.

Challenges and Priorities

From the conference discussions a list of challenges and tasks for the future has emerged. Some are general. Others refer more directly to the potential implications of the Doha ministerial meeting.

General Tasks

- It is vital to coordinate every campaign for access to essential medicines with campaigns of public education about the significance of public health policies.

- In the specific case of HIV/AIDS the mobilizations around access to treatment and medicines should be linked to prevention initiatives.

- To demand from governments rigorous quality control of medicines, whether they are trademark drugs or generic copies, and whether distributed through public sector provision or privately, and whether produced locally or imported. There must be agencies to ensure quality control.

- To demand that international organizations (the UN, WTO, Pan-American Health Organization, UNAIDS) and governments of developed countries commit themselves to rules on patents and intellectual property being subordinate to the right to health and life, and not allow commercial interests to be the prime consideration.

- To promote debates, declarations and public action aiming to widen everyone's consciousness about the importance of breaking patents and revising rules on intellectual property in order to guarantee access to medicines, diagnostic examinations of patents and other health issues.

- To define medicines that are essential to the preservation of life as public property worldwide, and thus as non-patentable.

- To link the struggle for access to health and essential medicines to the struggles to cancel the debt; to radically reform multilateral financial institutions, especially those like the World Bank whose directives have harmful impacts on health policies adopted by national governments; to achieve the goal of 0.7 per cent of industrialized countries' GDP being devoted to programmes to help development; and to fair trade.

- Ensuring that the resources of the Global Fund to Combat AIDS, Malaria and Tuberculosis, created in 2001, will not just be spent on prevention, but on widening access to treatment by means of the acquisition of medicines (mainly for the African continent) and investment in production facilities for generic medicines in developing countries. The Fund should be controlled jointly by the rich donor countries, poor countries and NGOs.

Tasks Related to the Implications of Doha

The Doha Declaration of November 2001 opens up the prospect of real flexibility in the TRIPs Agreement. That means that it allows compulsory licensing for any reason and not only in emergency cases. Countries are now potentially free to determine what is a national emergency or an overwhelming priority, which, in turn, allows a simple and quick procedure for compulsory licensing. The promotion of access to medicines for all is clearly recognized as the right of every member country in the WTO to protect its own public health. In the name of access to medicines for all, developing countries and less developed countries will be able without fear of retaliation to use their right to compulsory licensing. The Doha Declaration allows parallel imports and the least developed countries now have until 2016 (not 2006) to implement the terms of the TRIPs Agreement.

Therefore, it is crucial in the following years:

- To establish a dialogue and cooperation with other networks active around the WTO issue. This is necessary because there are controversies concerning the outcome of the Doha meeting and

big questions relating to other definitions that resulted from the
negotiations. While the result offers opportunities in the field of
access to essential medicines and public health, in other fields the
potential new WTO agreements are clearly harmful.

- To enforce the WTO Doha Declaration that asserts that 'the
  TRIPs Agreement must not prevent their members from
  adopting measures to protect the public health and, particularly,
  from promoting the access to medicines for all'.

- To ensure the rights of developing countries not only to obtain
  compulsory licences, but also to produce, import, export and
  transfer technologies related to generic medicines, without any
  obstruction from countries that host the companies which own
  patents. To find a solution for smaller countries without the
  capacity for local pharmaceutical production, mainly in Africa and
  Latin America.

- To encourage developing countries to exercise their sovereignty
  to exclude, by means of national legislation, medicines from the
  patent system, on the grounds of public health.

- To step up the campaign to oppose the proposed Free Trade of
  the Americas Agreement (FTAA), which envisages making the
  standards of protection for patents even more rigid than TRIPs.
  Equally, to condemn any other kind of bilateral or regional
  pressure – as is the case with the Bangui Agreement (in Africa) –
  that prevents developing countries from producing, importing or
  exporting generic medicines.

- To demand a drastic and immediate reduction in the price of
  medicines for poor countries, starting with an end to monopoly,
  and ensuring competition of generic products and transparency of
  information. And to demand that the WHO honour its commitment to the creation and maintenance of a publicly available
  database of comparative prices of medicines in each country.

- To effect compulsory licensing when there is no capacity for national production in a country and to coordinate developing countries in their efforts to complement one another and attain such capacity.

- In the specific case of Brazil it is important to pressure the government to express its solidarity with other countries, especially Latin American and African ones, by exporting medicines already available in the country at reduced cost.

Doha: Challenges that Persist

There are, however, some aspects of the Doha Declaration that are badly defined and need to be explained and debated. For example, there is an acknowledged problem when country A wants to institute a compulsory licence but does not itself have the capacity to produce the medicine concerned. The question is: could another country, B, produce it and export to country A?

In addition, it is recognized that if the TRIPs Agreement for medicines is maintained as it is, there will be hardly any new treatments for neglected diseases developed by the pharmaceutical corporations. This implies two alternatives. The first would be to exclude essential medicines from the TRIPs Agreement. The second, which in the medium term would be better, is to look for alternative ways to fund research on neglected diseases – with public sector participation and the participation of those developing countries which have an R&D capacity.

Palestine: A Motion of Protest

Besides extensively discussing intellectual property and access to essential medicines, the meeting also proposed that the World Social Forum condemn Israel's military occupation of Palestinian territory since it directly infringes the human right to health of the Palestinian population.

Notes

1 Two other specialists unfortunately were not able to make it to Porto Alegre. Dr Zafrullah Chowdhury, from the People's Health Assembly of Bangladesh, one of the organizations that would have helped to introduce the conference, didn't receive his ticket on time, and Dr Mark Heywood, from TAC (South Africa), had some personal problems that prevented him from coming. Therefore we thank Oxfam for having accepted a last-minute invitation to join the staff.

2 The themes debated at the conference suggest a potential agenda for the next forums: Multilateral Financial Institutions and the Reform of Health Systems; Global Inequalities in Terms of Expenses, Investment and Access; Access to Health in Armed Conflicts; Training of Health Professionals and Development of Health Technology; Vulnerable Groups; Globalization and Access to Health.

3 Moreover, this clause supported the breach of the CIPRO patent authorized by the American government during the Anthrax threat in October 2001.

4 It is worth noting that often these initiatives had the support of the governments of developing countries (for example Brazil), and of companies like CIPLA, which produces generics in India (and has not signed the TRIPs Agreement).

Translated by Mariana de Lima Medeiros, revised by Joris Van Mol

FOOD

People's Right to Produce,
Feed Themselves and
Exercise their Food Sovereignty

APM WORLD NETWORK

From 3 to 7 September 2001, some 400 delegates, from peasant and indigenous organizations, fishing associations, non-governmental organizations, social agencies, academics and researchers from 60 countries around the world met in Havana, Cuba, at the World Forum on Food Sovereignty.

This Forum was convened in Cuba by the Cuban National Association of Small Farmers and a group of international movements, networks, organizations and people committed to peasant and indigenous agriculture, artisanal fisheries, sustainable food systems and the people's right to feed themselves. It also served to acknowledge the efforts of a Third World country which, despite suffering for over four decades from the illegal and inhumane blockade imposed by the United States, and the use of food as a weapon of economic and political pressure, has managed to guarantee the human right to food for all of its population by way of a coherent, active, participatory and long-term state policy based on profound agrarian reform, appreciation and support for small- and medium-sized producers, and the participation and mobilization of the entire society.

We gathered to analyse the reasons why hunger and malnutrition grow every day throughout the world, why the crisis in peasant and indigenous agriculture, artisanal fisheries and sustainable food systems has worsened, and why the people are losing sovereignty over their resources. Likewise, we gathered to develop collectively, from the perspective of the people and not the transnational food corporations, viable proposals, alternatives and strategies for action on a local, national and global scale, aimed at reversing current trends and promoting new focuses, policies and initiatives that can guarantee a dignified and hunger-free present and future for all the men and women of the world.

Five years after the World Food Summit, seven years after the agricultural agreements of the General Agreement on Tariffs and Trade (GATT, now WTO) Uruguay Round, and following two decades of neoliberal policies imposed by a large number of governments, the promises and commitments made to satisfy the food and nutritional needs of all are far from being fulfilled. On the contrary, the reality is that the economic, agricultural, fishing and trade policies imposed by the World Bank, IMF and WTO, and promoted by the transnational corporations, have widened the gap between wealthy and poor countries and accentuated the unequal distribution of earnings within countries. They have worsened the conditions of food production and access to healthy and sufficient nutrition for the majority of the world's peoples, even in the so-called developed countries. As a consequence, the most basic human right of all, the right to food and nutritional well-being enshrined in the Universal Declaration of Human Rights, is not guaranteed to the majority of the world's people.

The sustainability of food systems is not merely a technical matter. It constitutes a challenge demanding the highest political will of states. The profit motive leads to the unsustainability of food systems by surpassing the limits on production allowed by nature. The sustainability of food systems is not viable within the current trade system and the context of liberalization promoted by the WTO and international financial organizations.

The hope for a new millennium free of hunger has been frustrated, to the shame of all humanity.

The Real Causes of Hunger and Malnutrition

Hunger, malnutrition and the exclusion of millions of people from access to productive goods and resources, such as land, the forests, the seas, water, seeds, technology and know-how, are not a result of fate, of happenstance, of geographical location or climatic phenomena. Above all, they are a consequence of specific economic, agricultural and trade policies on a global, regional and national scale that have been imposed by the powers of the developed countries and their corporations for the purpose of maintaining and increasing their political, economic, cultural and military hegemony within the current process of global economic restructuring.

In the face of the neoliberal ideological theories behind these policies:

- We affirm that food is not just another market good and that the food system cannot be viewed solely according to market logic.

- We consider as fallacious the argument that the liberalization of international agricultural and fishing trade guarantees the people's right to food.

- Trade liberalization does not necessarily facilitate the economic growth and well-being of the population.

- The underdeveloped countries are capable of producing their own food and could be capable of doing so in the future.

- The neoliberal concept of comparative advantage severely affects food systems. In keeping with this concept, the importing of basic food commodities leads to the dismantling of domestic production, given the possibility of buying them 'cheaper' from the wealthy countries. This in turn leads to the reorientation of their productive resources towards export crops that are 'more competitive and have greater value added' for the First World markets. It is a lie that countries should not be concerned with establishing and implementing state policies to guarantee food security for their citizens. Neoliberal theorists argue that the global supermarket of exporter countries can satisfy any demands with no problems whatsoever.

- They try to deceive the population when they claim that peasant and indigenous farmers and artisanal fisheries are inefficient and unable to meet the growing needs for food production. They use this claim in the attempt to impose wide-scale, intensive industrial agriculture and fishing.

- We denounce as false the argument that the rural population is overly large in comparison with its contribution to the gross domestic product. In reality, this reflects an attempt to brutally expel the rural population from its lands and fishing communities, from the coasts and seas, privatizing natural resources.

- We reject the use of wide-scale, intensive industrial agriculture and fishing as the means to confront the world's growing food needs.

- Supporters of neoliberalism attempt to convince us that the only alternative for peasants, fishers and indigenous peoples is to give way to the privatization of their lands and natural resources. This leads, among other effects, to massive migration to the cities and abroad in order to expand the supply of cheap labour needed to increase the 'competitiveness' of the dynamic sectors of national economies linked to exports and transnational corporations. At the same time, unemployment and the loss of jobs are on the rise in the developed countries.

- There is an attempt to impose the food model of the transnational corporations as the only viable, appropriate and correct model in a global world. This is veritable food imperialism, which threatens the diversity of people's food cultures and their national, cultural and ethnic identities.

- In this context, the hegemonic powers use food as a weapon of political and economic pressure against sovereign countries and popular resistance movements.

- All of the above is taking place within the framework of the systematic weakening of states and the promotion of false democracies that systematically disregard the public interest and real participation of society in general, and the rural population in particular, in the discussion, design, adoption, implementation and control of public policies.

The Consequences of Neoliberal Policies

The consequences of these false and erroneous policies are visible: they have increased the sales and profits of the large corporations of the developed countries, while the people of the Third World have seen the growth of their external debt and heightened levels of poverty, extreme poverty and social exclusion. The concentration of the international agricultural market in the hands of a small number of transnational corporations has accelerated, while the dependence and food insecurity of the majority of people have increased.

There continue to be heavy subsidies for export agriculture and fishing, at the same time that many governments provide absolutely no protection for small- and medium-sized producers who produce mainly for the domestic market.

Policies of production and export subsidies in the developed countries allow the transnationals to acquire products at very low prices and sell them at much higher prices to consumers in both the South and the North.

Neoliberal policies towards the countryside have in fact promoted a process of forced de-ruralization of vast proportions and dramatic consequences, a genuine war against peasant and indigenous agriculture, which in some cases has come to constitute veritable genocide and ethnocide.

Artisanal fishing communities have been increasingly losing access to their own resources.

As a result of neoliberal policies, hunger and malnutrition are growing, not because of an absence of food, but rather because of an absence of rights.

We are witnesses of examples that allow us to assert that the eradication of hunger and malnutrition and the exercise of lasting and sustainable food sovereignty are possible. Likewise, we have seen in practically every country countless examples of sustainable and organic food production in peasant and indigenous communities and sustainable and diversified management of rural areas.

In view of the foregoing, the participants in the World Forum on Food Sovereignty declare:

- **Food sovereignty is the means to eradicate hunger and malnutrition** and to guarantee lasting and sustainable food security for all of the peoples. We define food sovereignty as the people's right to define their own policies and strategies for the sustainable production, distribution and consumption of food that guarantees the right to food for the entire population, on the basis of small- and medium-sized production, respecting their own cultures and the diversity of peasant, fishing and indigenous forms of agricultural production, marketing and management of rural areas, in which women play a fundamental role.

- **Food sovereignty fosters the economic, political and cultural sovereignty of the people.**

- **Food sovereignty recognizes agriculture involving peasants, indigenous peoples and fishing communities** with links to their own territory; primarily oriented towards the satisfaction of the needs of the local and national markets; agriculture whose central concern is human beings; agriculture which preserves, values and fosters the multifunctionality of peasant and indigenous forms of

production and management of rural areas. Likewise, food
sovereignty entails the recognition and appreciation of the
economic, social, environmental and cultural advantages of small-
scale, family-based, peasant and indigenous agriculture.

● We consider the recognition of **the rights, autonomy and culture of
indigenous peoples in all countries as an imperative requisite for
combating hunger and malnutrition** and guaranteeing the right to
food for the population. Food sovereignty implies the recognition
of the multi-ethnicity of nations and the recognition and
appreciation of the identities of aboriginal peoples. This implies, as
well, the recognition of autonomous control of their territories,
natural resources, systems of production and management of rural
areas, seeds, knowledge and organizational forms. In this sense, we
support the struggles of all of the indigenous peoples and peoples
of African descent in the world, and demand full respect for their
rights.

● Food sovereignty further implies **the guarantee of access to healthy
and sufficient food for all individuals, particularly for the most
vulnerable sectors, as an imperative obligation for national
governments** and the full exercise of civil rights. Access to food
should not be viewed as a form of assistance from governments or
of charity from national or international public or private entities.

● **Food sovereignty implies the implementation of radical processes of
comprehensive agrarian reform** adapted to the conditions of each
country and region, which will provide peasant and indigenous
farmers – with equal opportunities for women – with equitable
access to productive resources, primarily land, water and forests, as
well as the means of production, financing, training and capacity
building for management and interlocution. Agrarian reform,
above all, should be recognized as an obligation of national
governments where this process is necessary within the
framework of human rights and as an efficient public policy to

combat poverty. These agrarian reform processes must be controlled by peasant organizations – including the land rents market – and guarantee both individual and collective rights of producers over shared lands, as articulated in coherent agricultural and trade policies. We oppose the policies and programmes for the commercialization of land promoted by the World Bank instead of true agrarian reforms accepted by governments.

- We support the proposal put forward by civil society organizations in 1996, calling for **states to draw up a code of conduct on the human right to adequate food,** to serve effectively as an instrument for the implementation and promotion of this right. The people's right to food is included in the Universal Declaration of Human Rights and was ratified at the World Food Summit in Rome in 1996 by the member states of the United Nations Food and Agriculture Organization (FAO).

- We propose **the most rapid ratification possible, and application** by a larger number of countries, **of the International Covenant on Economic, Social and Cultural Rights**, adopted by the United Nations General Assembly in 1966.

- In defence of the principle of the people's inalienable right to food, we propose the adoption by the United Nations of an **International Convention on Food Sovereignty and Nutritional Well-Being,** which should take precedence over decisions adopted in the fields of international trade and other domains.

- **International trade in food should be subordinated to the supreme purpose of serving human beings.** Food sovereignty does not mean autarchy, full self-sufficiency or the disappearance of international agricultural and fishing trade.

- **We oppose any interference by the WTO in food, agriculture and fishing** and its attempt to determine national food policies. We categorically oppose its agreements on intellectual property rights over plants and other living organisms, as well as its intention to carry out a new round of negotiations (the so-called Millennium Round) including new themes for negotiation. Keep the WTO out of food.

- **We propose the creation of a new democratic and transparent order for the regulation of international trade**, including the creation of an international appeals court independent of the WTO and the strengthening of UNCTAD as a forum for multilateral negotiations on fair food trade. At the same time, we propose the promotion of regional integration schemes among producers' organizations, unrelated to neoliberal goals and parameters.

- **We demand an immediate end to dishonest practices that establish market prices below production costs** and provide subsidies for production and exports.

- **We oppose the FTAA,** which is nothing more than a hegemonic strategic plan developed by the United States to consolidate its control over Latin America and the Caribbean, expand its economic borders, and guarantee itself a large captive market.

- We support the demands made by peasant and social organizations in Mexico for **the suspension of NAFTA concerning agriculture**.

- Genetic resources are the result of millennia of evolution and belong to all of humanity. Therefore, there should be a **prohibition on biopiracy and patents on living organisms,** including the development of sterile varieties through genetic engineering processes. Seeds are the patrimony of all of humanity. The monopolization by a number of transnational corporations of the technologies to create GMOs represents a grave threat to the people's food sovereignty. At the same time, in light of the fact that the effects of GMOs on health and the environment are unknown, we demand a ban on open experimentation, production and marketing until there is conclusive knowledge of their nature and impact, strictly applying the precautionary principle.

- It is necessary **to promote widespread dissemination and appreciation of the agricultural history and food culture of every country,** while denouncing the imposition of food models alien to the food cultures of the people.

- We express our determination **to integrate the goals of nutritional well-being into national food policies** and programmes, including local productive systems, promoting their diversification towards foods rich in micronutrients; to defend the quality and safety of foods consumed by populations; and to fight for the right of all individuals to information on the foods they consume, by stepping up regulations on food labels and the content of food-related advertising, exercising the precautionary principle.

- Food sovereignty should be founded on **diversified systems of production, based on ecologically sustainable technologies**. It is essential to develop initiatives for sustainable food production and consumption generated at the local level by small producers, with the establishment of public policies that contribute to building sustainable food systems around the world.

- We demand **the justly deserved appreciation of peasant, indigenous and fishing communities** for their sustainable and diversified management of rural areas, through appropriate prices and incentive programmes.

- When addressing the problem of food on a worldwide scale, we must **take into account the cultural diversity** that leads to different local and regional contexts, because the protection of the environment and biodiversity are closely related to the recognition of cultural diversity.

- The **development of sustainable food systems must include nutritional considerations**, such as the regulation of the handling of agrotoxins.

- We recognize and appreciate **the fundamental role played by women** in the production, harvesting, marketing and preparation of the products of agriculture and fishing and in passing on the food cultures of the peoples. We support the struggles waged by women for access to productive resources, and for their right to produce and consume local products.

- Artisanal fishers and their organizations will not relinquish their rights to free access to fishing resources and the establishment and protection of reserve areas for the exclusive use of artisanal fishing methods. Likewise, we demand **recognition of ancestral and historic rights over the coasts and inland waters**.

- **Food-aid policies and programmes must be reviewed.** They should not be an obstacle to the development of local and national food-production capacities, nor should they foster dependence, the distortion of local and national markets, corruption, or the dumping of foods that are harmful to health, particularly with regard to GMOs.

- **Food sovereignty can only be achieved, defended and exercised through the democratic strengthening of states** and the self-organization, initiative and mobilization of all of society. It requires long-term state policies, an effective democratization of public policies, and the development of a solidarity-based social setting.

- **We condemn the US policy of blockading Cuba and other peoples**, and the use of food as a weapon of economic and political pressure against countries and popular movements. This unilateral policy must end immediately.

- Food sovereignty is a civil concept that concerns society as a whole. For this reason, **social dialogue should be open to all the social sectors involved.**

- **Achieving food sovereignty and eradicating hunger and malnutrition are possible** in all countries and for all peoples. We express our determination to continue struggling against neoliberal globalization, maintaining and increasing active social mobilization, building strategic alliances and adopting firm political decisions.

- We agree to launch **a call for intensive activity and widespread mobilization** around the following focuses of struggle:

  - Declaring 16 October as World Food Sovereignty Day, known until now as World Food Day;

  - Demanding that the World Food Summit go ahead as planned from 5 to 10 November 2001, and that the FAO fully assume its mandate and responsibility. Social organizations should organize events at the national and continental level to promote their proposals and pressure official delegations;

  - Demanding that the Italian government fully respect the freedom to demonstrate and refrain from repressing social movements opposed to neoliberal globalization;

  - Participating in and mobilizing around the WTO Ministerial Meeting, to be held in Qatar from 9 to 13 November 2001; the Hemispheric Conference against the FTAA, to be held in Havana from 13 to 16 November 2001; and the second World Social Forum, to be held in Porto Alegre from 31 January to 6 February 2002.

Keep the WTO Out of Food. Another World Is Possible.

13

CITIES, URBAN POPULATION
Conference Synthesis

ERMÍNIA MARICATO

Facilitator
Ermínia Maricato

Speakers and Discussants
Guillermo Rodriguez   FCOC, MEXICO
Sudha Sundararaman   AIDWA, INDIA
Cesare Ottolini   HIC, ITALY
Gustave Massiah   ATTAC, FRANCE
Peter Marcuse   PLANNERS NETWORK, USA

Opening Speaker
Ermínia Maricato

Cities are profoundly affected by globalization. This implies:

- Dismantling of the welfare state with the loss of the social, economic and political rights won as a result of a long history of campaigns;

- Privatization of public services, strengthening the dictatorship of the market;

- Weakening of public urban management with the expansion of illegal activities and environmental destruction arising from social exclusion.

The dissemination of international models of town planning rides roughshod over the specific environmental and cultural conditions of each society, especially in peripheral countries, establishing the 'showbiz city', and imposing social relations based on passive individual enjoyment and the interests of real-estate capital.

In peripheral and semi-peripheral countries, the impact of globalization has been particularly dramatic: the process of urbanization is accelerating and elementary rights to housing, sanitation and urban mobility are not guaranteed. Their cities consist of islands imitating the First World, where high- and medium-income households live surrounded by 'shadow cities' ignored by the state and by the social progress of the modern age. The violence and organized crime that grow at a frightening rate in these cities are a direct response to the dismantling and weakening of the public sphere.

The second World Social Forum conference – Cities, Urban Populations – is intended to deconstruct the ideology of the 'single-minded city', and it also seeks to show that another form of city is possible: more supportive, more democratic, more sustainable, and even more efficient in its response to social demands.

Thousands of NGOs, associations and entities of all kinds are building a new militancy, after the era marked by the dominance of large parties and trade unions. The issues of racism, gender and the environment are present on the agenda of the left, as well as the urban issue itself, which has been so frequently forgotten in the past.

The conference presented the analyses, proposals and campaign strategies of some of the largest networks of social movements fighting to democratize power and for the right to the city.

This conference sought to answer the following questions: who are these new fellow activists? How are they organized? What are they fighting for? What difficulties have they confronted? What have they achieved?

Guillermo Rodriguez, from Mexico, who is a member of the Continental Federation of Community Organizations (Federación Continental de Organizaciones Comunitarias, FCOC), an organization founded in Nicaragua to campaign for popular and productive settlements in harmony with nature, emphasized three historical misconceptions: equality before God, law and the market.

For Rodriguez, it is time to reassess these precepts and reconstruct the social fabric of peripheral countries, even questioning the notion of civil society as if it had not been evolved in response to market requirements. While the concept of citizenship is debated to exhaustion, citizens are being deprived of their rights. These postmodern citizens characteristically lack access to health, education, sanitation etc., since these are no longer considered to be the role of the state. Citizenship is no longer based on rights, but on the individual solution of problems. The result is a precarious way of life for most of the urban population – without basic services, without employment, and without infrastructure. For Rodriguez, the campaign by popular movements in various Latin American countries is fundamental to reversing the privatization of water resources, guaranteeing that land tenure is regularized, blocking evictions and ensuring improvements to habitat, all of which are fundamental requirements for building sustainable, just societies. These efforts would also increase the likelihood of electing popular, democratic governments and efforts in sustainable, solidarity production which, on a larger scale, could bring a new type of city into existence.

Sudha Sundararaman then spoke. She represents an Indian women's organization (AIDWA) with 5.9 million members. Unlike Brazil, 60 per cent of India's population still works in agriculture. Even so, 140 million poor people live in cities, of which 100 million live in shanty towns. Despite the astonishing scale of poverty, the reality confronted by most of the population is ignored, or made 'invisible'. Showing evidence of the global character of urban poverty, this Indian activist emphasized similar points to those presented by Rodriguez: the urban population is denied the right to housing, essential services, employment in reasonable conditions, democratic rights and a voice in decision-making. Violence, crime, sexual abuse, drugs and trafficking in women prevail. Tenants are exploited as a result of the dismal quality of housing, high rents and lack of protection from eviction. In shanty towns, no options are considered by the authorities other than the violent removal of the poor for the purpose of 'city-scaping'.

People live in a situation of precarious deprivation, on a knife-edge, and prey to police aggression. Their illegal situation reinforces exclusion and further hinders their access to social security and services through the state or through the market.

Sudha visualizes with clarity the perverse impact of globalization on this urban matrix of poverty: increasing inequality, the feminization of poverty, the shrinking role of the state and social security, the loss of a sense of collectivity, the strengthening of consumer culture, the market society as a positive value, and the idea that there are no alternatives. For AIDWA, resistance should be constructed by means of complementary action at the ideological level – identifying the myths of globalization and combating them one by one; in the political arena – combining local campaigns around specific demands and government policies, and global anti-hegemonic campaigns; and in the cultural field – with interventions in daily life aiming to transform social awareness. Sudha drew attention to the activities of AIDWA in major literacy campaigns, in the campaign to change the model of micro-credit (the creation of production networks), in protests against the privatization of essential services, and in the construction of alternatives to government programmes. As a result of these campaigns, new leaderships have been constituted, several later elected to local and state councils. During some of these activities, which run counter to the dominant interests of global capitalism, leaders have been assassinated and demonstrators injured.

Cesare Ottolini from Italy then asked the plenary session for ideas and proposals for an international movement in solidarity for 'the right to the city'. In the view of this political scientist, who is one of the founders of the European Charter for rights to housing and for the campaign against exclusion, and international coordinator of the International Habitat Coalition (IHC), we must have a right to organize openly, to build the future of our cities. In his speech, Ottolini advised social movements to maintain their independence, recalling that Italy's neighbourhood councils created in the 1970s became bureaucratized, and even left-wing governments asked social movements to exercise constraint in order to avoid reactions from the right. For Ottolini, the movements should be cautious in their relations with governments and international organizations, despite the presence of professionals who are sympathetic to their causes. Like the other discussants, Ottolini stressed the importance of micro-credit, since it demonstrates the capacity of the population to manage resources, but recalled its limits. He alluded to the Tobin Tax and pension funds as sources of financial resources more commensurate with the scale of urban problems. But alliances will be necessary for us to have sufficient strength to approach sources of finance forcefully and claim part of these resources. Another source would be the cancelling of debts, provided that part of these resources was applied to public social policies.

Gustave Massiah (France) stated that the reality of social movements should be the guiding thread in the construction of a new world. Massiah, a professor at the Architectural School of Paris (La Villette) and a member of the Scientific Council of ATTAC, noted that the growing awareness today of what is unacceptable is already a great step forward. At the same time, social movements have moved beyond resistance to positive proposals, and there is now a need for a project that provides an alternative to the neoliberal doctrine. According to him, data from the UN indicate that while the world has become richer in recent years, poverty has not been reduced, but has in fact increased. Contrary to the liberal discourse, according to which the situation would improve, what has occurred in practice is an even faster growth in levels of global poverty. In Eastern Europe, after the return of capitalism, the population classified as poor grew from 4 per cent to 32 per cent of the total. For Massiah, it is essential to have income redistribution, taxation of large fortunes, and global monitoring of financial transactions.

However, Massiah, like all the other presenters, went beyond recognizing the spread of absolute poverty, to emphasize that significant opportunities for change are presenting themselves. For him, public opinion has been coming to its senses since 1995, and today there is a better understanding of social movements. The putting down of the most recent demonstrations failed in its attempt to criminalize their participants, and the idea that another world is possible has made considerable advances. This has allowed an escape from the fatalism of the neoliberal consensus. This growing awareness, a result of the work of urban social movements, has laid bare the causes of poverty and inequality. Urban violence is no accident, but a consequence of the system. Neoliberal leaders have lost their legitimacy. For Massiah, the convergence of urban and rural social movements, which follow parallel paths, creates the foundations for the construction of a new world.

Closing the debate, Peter Marcuse, Professor of Urban Planning at Columbia University in New York, who had just arrived from a student meeting in New York against the Davos Forum, observed that Bush's war on terrorism is being used to reduce resistance to neoliberalism. Marcuse, an activist on several political and social fronts and founding member of the Planning Network, an organization of progressive planners in the United States, emphasized three fundamental issues for the World Social Forum. First, what is wrong with globalization and the system must be exposed – e.g. exploitation, domination and injustice in the economic and political spheres. Then, fundamental issues must be clarified so that urban problems can be correctly understood: issues relating to land ownership and property rights, the role of international institutions, the relation between the state and civil society, the role of the market, the relation between municipal, state, national and international activities; and financing and the organization of the kind of city we want. Third, we must organize ourselves on these issues, and establish links among the various social movements. The World Social Forum is proving an excellent framework for this purpose.

The speakers' presentations were followed by an intense debate, stimulated by countless questions from the plenary participants. Many of them revealed an interest in learning more about the range of experiences in the struggles of the organizations represented here. In conclusion, Ermínia Maricato stressed the importance of identifying the points of commonality between the various presentations, around which the efforts of articulation and struggle should be concentrated:

- Radical redistribution of wealth and access to resources from pension funds and taxation of finance capital as a source of funds to address urban problems;

- Articulation of the day-to-day and localized struggles with those confronting the current global economic system, without which it will be impossible to democratize the world and overcome social injustice;

- The importance of popular, autonomous and independent movements as the guiding thread in the transformation of society;

- Resistance to globalization, through complementary actions in the ideological, political and cultural arenas.

14 INDIGENOUS PEOPLES

(i) *Indigenous Commission Statement*

DIONITO MAKUXI, PINÁ TEMBÉ,
SIMIÃO WAPIXANA, JOEL PATAXÓ,
LURDES TAPAJÓS and
LUIZ TITIÁ PATAXÓ HÃ-HÃ-HÃE

It is with great joy and hope that we, indigenous people from Brazil, are taking part in this World Social Forum. Indigenous peoples from several regions of the planet are here today to join all those individuals who do not want to go on living in a world marked by domination, social exclusion, intolerance, wars, destruction of nature, violence and the threat of extinction of hundreds of indigenous peoples.

Despite having been submitted to a continuous process of violence and extermination, we are alive and are looking forward to contributing to the construction of a new Brazil and a new world, with peace, equality and justice. From an original population of six million 500 years ago, we have been reduced to approximately 550,000 individuals, belonging to 235 different peoples who speak 180 different languages. We occupy 741 pieces of land, most of them still occupied by non-indigenous people or non-demarcated. Unfortunately, the Brazilian government recognizes scarcely a hundred pieces of this land and does almost nothing to help us live in peace, with dignity and autonomy in our territories. Instead of recognizing our traditional territories, as established by the Brazilian Constitution, they are buying small pieces of land for our people. We consider this a trap, a disrespect of our rights.

We keep on suffering at the hands of invaders who take away our riches, abuse our women, despise our cultures and destroy nature. We are not treated with respect in our rights and decisions over our own lands. The government persists in acting as if we were incapable, as if we required tutelage. They impose projects on us, introduce construction sites, make decisions without talking to us and without respecting our will, our culture, our wisdom. We are struggling to change this, and need the help of peoples of good will from all over the world. We are taking back the lands from where we once were expelled, thus reconstructing our lives and identity as people.

Even though we have been victims of all this violence and exclusion at the hands of the government, our population has been growing; as survivors of the past 500 years we believe that we shall win and build a brighter future for our peoples over the next 500 years. In order to be better able to decide about our future paths, we are going to hold a census in order to know how many we are today and how our lands and living conditions stand. The census will be coordinated by the indigenous movement.

We hope that during the World Social Forum 2002 we shall be able to strengthen our friendship and union with other indigenous peoples from all over the world and with other people and organizations that will be here in Brazil to discuss and propose ways in which to fight for a new possible world. We shall leave encouraged and more determined to guarantee our rights, especially regarding our land and the riches present in it, our cultures, our wisdom and our ways of organization and living.

Translated by Margarete M.C. Noro

14 INDIGENOUS PEOPLES
(ii) *Conference Synthesis*

PAULO MALDOS

Facilitator
Paulo Maldos CENTRE FOR POPULAR EDUCATION (CEPIS),
SEDES SAPIENTIAE INSTITUTE, BRAZIL

Support
Yvone Duarte

Debate leaders
Blanca Chancosa CONFEDERATION OF INDIGENOUS
NATIONALITIES OF ECUADOR (CONAIE)
Aurivan dos Santos Barros Truká CONVERGENT
MOBILIZATION OF INDIGENOUS PEOPLES AND ORGANIZATIONS
OF THE NORTH-EAST, MINAS GERAIS AND ESPÍRITO SANTO
(APOINME), BRAZIL

Discussants
Aldo Gonzáles-Unosjo NATIONAL INDIGENOUS CONGRESS
(CNI), MEXICO
Dionito de Souza Macuxi RORAIMA INDIGENOUS COUNCIL
(CIR), BRAZIL

Background

Little by little, the indigenous peoples of the world have undertaken a process of resistance in various forms according to their respective realities. These indigenous struggles have thrown up heroes on every continent, even if they are not recognized by official histories.

Indigenous nations and peoples have been subjected to colonialism right down to the present day. It is not possible to speak about indigenous peoples or nations in the twenty-first century without taking into account the historical development of this massacred, pillaged America from the Conquest to our own times. It is not possible to speak of indigenous peoples or nations in the twenty-first century without remembering the slave role imposed on them in the headlong advance of poverty on our continent.

This situation is now aggravated by the implementation not only of neoliberal programmes and so-called globalization but also of FTAA, Plan Colombia and the Andean Initiative. These all form part of a single strategy in which the sovereignty and self-determination of the region's countries have become negotiable, regardless of the lives and dreams of their millions of inhabitants.

The United States, with its policy of war and military build-up, is attempting to revitalize its own economy at the cost of human life and the appropriation of territories traditionally occupied by indigenous peoples. The latter constitute a daily hindrance to the appropriation process and, in the view of both old and new colonizers, must be eliminated.

This is not just rhetoric, empty words; it is shown by the facts. There is no lack of examples of whole peoples being exterminated in the Amazon, in several countries. Water, the most essential vital resource, has now become a strategic objective for the dominators: in the next 25 years, possessing and controlling it will be the key to ensuring the survival of the 'empire'.

Nowadays, at the local level, indigenous peoples are even more impoverished, with high levels of migration to cities or even moving away from their home countries altogether. In many cases, this has led to the disintegration of the community and, therefore, of the family.

Working from a range of local, regional and national platforms, indigenous peoples' constant struggle for the right to a decent life has given them greater visibility in recent years. The voice of the world's various indigenous peoples and nations has made itself heard and present at the discussion table with the governments of different countries and with international organizations.

Policies towards indigenous peoples devoid of respect and the genocidal policies of governments have pushed the world's indigenous nations and peoples into embarking on a process of organization and, in this way, they have developed alternative policy proposals based on the concept 'Unity in Diversity'.

At the close of the twentieth century, indigenous people presented proposals to governments and international organizations with a view to gaining recognition as nations and peoples, their rights to their land, a healthy environment, self-determination and self-management, and a state that is overtly multinational, multicultural and multilingual.

Together with the above, a new concept of territory has been developed to replace the narrow idea of indigenous lands tied to economic or productive occupation. The sense of identifying with a specific territory is rooted in indigenous peoples' knowledge, cultural heritage and social and religious relationships. Indigenous peoples speak about territorial property rights on the basis not of written laws and rules but as a form of collective identity which envelops the people and their territory, the Mother Earth. An indigenous territory can be inherited, but never sold or mortgaged.

Indigenous peoples are defending their rights not as individuals but as collectivities. Their claim to recognition as indigenous peoples and nations is seen as a threat to the integrity of the nation, the nation-state. But it is the US, free trade and the mighty transnational corporations that are destroying nation-states; it is they who proceed from an integrationist perspective and continue their endeavour to build new bases from which to plunder natural resources, including now the patenting of traditional knowledge.

Neoliberalism, which seeks to integrate indigenous peoples for purposes of economic exploitation, is causing genocide and ethno-cide.

Proposals

Indigenous nations and peoples propose:

- The construction of a new form of relationship with states and their governments in order to establish forms of coexistence based on respect for self-determination; social, cultural, spiritual and linguistic diversity; and legal, territorial and organizational arrangements between indigenous nations and peoples, and between these and states.

- Recognition of collective rights, including territory, autonomy, self-determination, and the fundamental human rights such as education, health and community infrastructure.

- The political and administrative restructuring of the nation-state on a decentralized, culturally heterogeneous and open basis so as to permit participatory representation, by their own representatives, for all indigenous peoples and nations, all social sectors, all those who have been marginalized or excluded.

- Government policies should respect indigenous peoples' autonomy within their traditional territories and recognize their cultures, beliefs, customs and traditions.

- Governments should fulfil their responsibilities, ensuring differentiated social policies, with ample participation by indigenous peoples at all stages of discussion and implementation. Government budgets must guarantee the necessary funds.

- All governments should ratify the International Labour Organization Convention no. 169, which sets standards for relationships between nation-states and indigenous peoples.

- All governments should recognize re-emergent indigenous peoples and demarcate their traditional territories.

- Each government should carry out a census of indigenous populations, to be monitored by indigenous peoples and their organizations, so that the world knows how many peoples exist, their ethnic and cultural diversity, and their respective numbers.

- Crimes against the leaders and other members of indigenous communities and peoples should be investigated and the culprits punished. Mechanisms to combat violence and criminal actions going unpunished should also be established.

- Governments should be accountable for genocide and ethnocide against indigenous peoples.

- The construction of waterways, railways, hydroelectric facilities, highways, military bases and tourist ventures which affect indigenous territories or populations, directly or indirectly, and which cause socio-environmental damage, should be prohibited.

- Governments should immediately remove trespassers from all indigenous territories.

- Governments should create mechanisms to protect and oversee natural resources, conserve ecosystems and biodiversity and prevent the exploitation of our traditional knowledge, water, wood, animals and minerals.

Indigenous nations and peoples reaffirm their willingness and commitment to work together with other peoples and sectors affected by the same realities, aware that only through interlinking and making alliances amongst interested parties can they contribute towards building an international community free from racism, discrimination, oppression and injustice.

Indigenous nations and peoples have marched together, made significant conquests, and made clear their presence and their voice. They are confident that a new world is possible on the principle of unity in diversity, a world that recognizes both the right to be different and the right to be equal.

With these proposals presented to the Second World Social Forum, indigenous nations and peoples intend to contribute towards building a world of justice, peace and equality. The rallying cries of today's indigenous struggles now include the phrase: 'Never again a world without us, the indigenous'.

PART III

THE AFFIRMATION OF CIVIL SOCIETY & PUBLIC SPACE

OVERVIEW

Key Questions, Critical Issues

WILLIAM F. FISHER AND THOMAS PONNIAH

Key Questions

The key questions in Part III concern:

- Democratizing communications and the media;

- Commodification of education;

- Production of cultural homogeneity versus cultural difference;

- The culture of violence, domestic violence;

- Combating discrimination and intolerance;

- Perspectives on the global civil society movement.

These papers ask: how do we ensure the right to information in light of the fact that, despite the profusion of news sources, there is a relative monopoly over the media by a few, mainly US corporations (for example, AOL Time Warner, Disney and General Electric)? The papers react to the fact that the disproportionately large control by corporations over information means that news is vertically conveyed and disseminated in a commodified form. Linked to this challenge is the present attempt to deregulate the information sector and the World Trade Organization and International Monetary Fund's goals of establishing regulation concerning intellectual property that will facilitate the monopolization of the communications media. An earlier progressive alternative to media concentration was the Bandung project of a New International Order on Information which aimed at creating a plurality of news sources. What would a contemporary alternative look like? How can movements construct a 'Social Agenda in Communications and Media' (León)?

Related to the limited range of content in the mass media is the homogenization of education and culture. In light of the progressive belief that knowledge of science, technology and the humanities should be a right for all human beings, how can education be decommodified (Education synthesis)? In light of the global imposition of the Western social, economic, cultural and epistemological model of organizing society, how can monoculturalism be resisted and a pluralist 'world that contains many worlds' be constructed? How can the spread of American consumerist culture be opposed?

The papers identify the most blatant day-to-day expression of the culture of violence as gender violence. Sexism occurs in the home, the neighbourhood, the workplace, the academy and in the proliferation of the global sex trade (World March of Women). A fundamental component of patriarchy (and white supremacism) lies in a hatred of difference which believes that hierarchy is a legitimate form of social reproduction. Can there be a conception of economic production that does not permit social hierarchies, such as sexism or racism, to be perceived as necessary for economic development? How do we create a world where social production is legitimate if it is a product of primarily horizontal, democratic processes that promote the embrace of difference? Two of the prominent agents of patriarchy are the market fundamentalism of neoliberalism and the religious fundamentalism of many groups. Both are underpinned by a belief in universalism. How can the movement for global justice and solidarity develop a global body of human rights law that respects differences without falling into the traps of neoliberal or religious universalism? Can there be a new notion of governance that embraces diversity (Alloo *et al.*)?

On a global scale one of the most insidious expressions of discrimination, insidious precisely because it is not publicized, is the caste oppression of Dalits in South Asia (National Campaign on Dalit

Human Rights). Hundreds of millions of people are subject to caste-based discrimination but it rarely gets much publicity in other parts of the world. What policies need to be applied within South Asia to combat this situation? What strategies should activists in other countries adopt to show solidarity with the plight of the Dalits?

Another form of discrimination is that faced by migrants. Globalization of wealth has led to a globalization of poverty that has afflicted vast numbers of people in the rich countries, most notably persons of foreign origin. These survivors of neoliberal globalization constitute a reservoir of cheap labour. Migration flows are a structural result of the need for cheap workers in the informal economy (Prencipe). Therefore policing and repression will not control illegal migration.

Simultaneously, the criminalization of migration has often meant that poor migrants' entry into wealthy countries becomes dependent on organized criminal networks. These networks employ physical and sexual exploitation (cheap labour and prostitution) of migrants. How can the situation of immigrants be improved? How can the public be educated about the migrant's role in the circuits of capital? How can the racism against them be ended and how can the immigrant be included as a citizen with the same rights as all other members of society?

Related to the discrimination against immigrants is the 'War on Terror'. The newest challenge facing global civil society is the targeting of civilians as well as of progressive activists fighting corporate globalization (Discussion Document on Global Civil Society). How can this be resisted? As well, how can a culture of peace be built in light of the use of militarism as an instrument of economic growth?

Lastly, how can the movement for global justice and solidarity stay unified in the context of the different sectors, scales and visions of struggle involved in the movement? Should the movement negotiate with the international financial institutions? Should it refuse to participate in discussions with them?

Critical Issues

As in Parts I and II, there are many more examples of solidarity than there are of antagonism. The various documents consider the challenge of moving a global movement forward in such a way that it can encompass and respect the different agendas of its diverse constituents. Can the process involve the participation of the traditionally under-represented? Can the movement equitably involve women, people of colour, lesbians/gays/bisexuals, youth, as well as white heterosexual males? As the papers recognize, no other struggle ever has. Perhaps the commitment to diversity will find its greatest challenge precisely in the democracy of its process.

Discourses about civil society tend to position it as the third player, next to business and government, in the dialogue concerning the future. But, as the papers reveal, many social movements do not believe that the governmental and business sectors will ever negotiate in good faith. This tension echoes the reform-versus-radicalism debate mentioned in Parts I and II.

There are many convergences in these papers. The most obvious concern culture, hierarchy, epistemology and the global movement. There is a common conception in the texts that culture, like nature and knowledge, is part of the human heritage that should not be commodified or homogenized. There is agreement that the central world cultural conflict is that between westernization and cultural heterogeneity. There is widespread agreement that the driving component of the Western-style globalization is its commodification of information, education, culture and the consumer. Also widely recognized is the simultaneous spread and, at times, imposition of its political, social, legal and epistemological norms against the rest of the world. Against this 'recolonization' and the abstract universalism that it carries, the documents collectively propose a counter-hegemonic process of building concrete collective values based on a pluralist dialogue that begins at the local level. The essence of a new set of common values would be diversity and peace, hence the goal would be to construct a solidarity, and an always evolving convergence of difference. Such a solidarity would rest on the agreement that convergence does not denote dilution.

Perhaps the most consistent theme in the World Social Forum documents is the argument that social hierarchies such as gender, race, class, culture and political power are not a legitimate form of organizing social and economic production and reproduction. The idea that one person or group possesses the truth is anathema to the overall movement's goals. The texts are against the monolithic thought inherent in all fundamentalisms: religious, market, cultural and political. This does not necessarily imply that the movements are against political or philosophical hierarchies. The texts generally recognize that the public can legitimately vote for political parties that are hierarchically organized. They also acknowledge that some forms of knowledge may have more validity than others. As the texts make clear, the movements are clearly opposed to social hierarchies while they have mixed opinions concerning other forms of vertical organization such as the state.

There is recognition that contemporary capitalism uses the cultural and systemic power of patriarchy, white supremacism and caste to construct a hierarchical and fundamentalist system of profit accumulation that consolidates the distribution of power, money and poverty along colour, ethnic and gender lines. Against this, the proposals argue that neoliberalism's coupling of power and difference must be broken and transformed into a plural, horizontal, culturally democratic system that is always being reconstructed.

The arguments for fundamentalism and hierarchy usually hinge on certain anthropological assumptions. Conservatives frequently argue from the standpoint of genetics or 'cultural essence'. The Part III documents emphasize instead the socially constructed character of oppression and violence. These papers argue that reality is, for the most part, socially and politically constructed and can be deconstructed and reconstructed depending on a movement's organization and vision. Therefore the documents of Part III assert a belief in a political epistemology: our knowledge of the world is profoundly shaped by the interests of the economic, political, media and cultural elite.

The last significant convergence to note is the belief that 'global civil society' comprises a 'movement of movements'. As members of global civil society, they are not opposed to greater planetary interconnectedness but they are against the specific form of inter-connectedness represented by neoliberal globalization. The diversity of the global movement represented by these papers is both a negative response to neoliberal globalization and a visionary, creative process of building new paradigms of utopia. The diversity of the global movement reflects both the differentiating character of capitalism that produces new sites of oppression, as well as the last 30 years of feminist organizing, lesbian/gay activism, anti-racist movements, anarchism and postmodern theorizing that has called for the celebration of difference. These new social movements and their theorists have put immense pressure on trade unions and socialists to transform their processes and their policies. The embrace of diversity alongside the belief in a cultural counter-hegemony, the critique of fundamentalism and hierarchy, and the faith in the power of social change add up to a call not only for redistribution, but also for recognition, that is to say, for the liberation of difference.

THE MEDIA
Democratization of Communications and the Media

OSVALDO LEON

The new spiral of violence and lies that abruptly burst upon the world following the September 11 attacks on the US has created a more difficult environment for democratic struggle. This setback obliges such struggles to step up their efforts, not only for peace and justice, but also for truth. This means challenging 'excesses' in the manipulation and distortion of information, as well as the conditions that allow this to happen.

The World Social Forum, as a networked social process, appears as ideal and legitimate space to catalyse energy and foster the emergence of a social movement under the banner of democratization of communications. With this in mind, we propose that this conference focus its attention on outlining a Social Agenda in Communication. Being a cross-cutting theme that concerns all human relations, the important thing is to situate the central points for definition of strategies and aims, in order to build and give impetus to this social movement.

The Issues

The democratization of communications is above all a question of citizenship and social justice. It is framed by the human right to information and communication. In other words, it is inherent to the democratic life of society itself, whose vitality depends on having a duly informed and deliberative citizenry, able to participate and assume co-responsibility in decision-making on public issues.

In recent times, however, this democratic aspiration has been seriously constrained by neoliberal hegemony, which has put the market at the centre of social organization, thus attempting to emasculate democracies and annulling the meaning of citizenship itself. Moreover, communication has become a key element in this dynamic; so much so that, with the accelerated development of technologies and techniques, the powers that be aim to transform it into a paradigm of the future under the formula of the 'information society'.

In practice, communications have not just undergone substantial internal changes (subordination of the word to the image, live transmissions, multimedia, etc.), but they have also become one of the most dynamic sectors in the economy and society with deep repercussions in all realms of social life.

Communications appear today as one of the cutting-edge sectors of the economy, both because of their profitability and because they appear to hold the key to the so-called new economy. Therefore, in the heat of economic globalization, it is the sector that has proved the most aggressive in expanding business concentration and trans-nationalization, a fact that has resulted in the emergence of veritable media moguls whose reach now extends to all corners of the globe.

These mega-corporations have been formed through the fusion of print media, television chains, cable television, film, software, telecommunications, entertainment, tourism and other activities, such that the products and services of their different branches are able to mutually publicize one another in the quest to broaden their market reach. Today, just seven corporations dominate the world communications market. If checks on this oligopolistic logic are not established, tomorrow there may be even fewer.

Since it is a global project, this process has been accompanied by the imposition, on the one hand, of policies of liberalization and deregulation, especially in the area of telecommunications, designed to eliminate any state regulation or activity that might interfere with transnational corporate expansion, and, on the other hand, of norms – such as the novel interpretation of intellectual property rights –

oriented to safeguarding their interests and to ensuring definitively that information and cultural production are treated as simple commodities.

Under the cover of neoliberal dogma, a highly concentrated media and cultural industry has taken shape, governed by exclusively commercial criteria, where what counts is profitability over and above the public interest, and the consumer paradigm over that which sees people as citizens. It is therefore not surprising that the outlook for the future is one of abundant information that will be free, but banal, degraded and turned into a media spectacle, while quality information will only be accessible to those who are in a position to pay.

This tendency is now so forceful that it has practically swept away media of a public character, privatizing most and forcing the rest to become commercialized, thus eroding their role as spaces to feed into a broad and pluralistic debate open to the variety of perspectives, ideas and cultural expressions present in society.

In the midst of these developments, the media have also become a crucial arena for shaping the public space and the citizenry itself – crucial, in the sense that, although it is not a new phenomenon, it is an intense and influential one due both to the weight they bring to bear on the definition of public agendas and their capacity to establish the legitimacy of certain debates. The predominance of the media is such, with respect to other venues of social mediation (parties, unions, churches, educational establishments, etc.), that the latter can only be heard or seen by continually conforming to the requirements of the media.

In this context, there is a real danger of the dictatorship of the market becoming consolidated through the enormous power it has concentrated in the realm of communications, to win people's 'minds and hearts'.

This trend can only be restrained and modified through forceful, sustained and proactive citizen action. The possibilities of this have been opened by a multiplicity of initiatives on different levels: groups endeavouring to guarantee universal access to and effective appropriation of new information and communications technologies; exchange networks that develop open source software; advocacy organizations seeking to lobby in defence of information and communication rights; monitoring groups acting as watchdogs over sexist, racist or exclusionary media content; education programmes designed to develop a critical reading of the media (what is called media literacy); user associations that seek to influence media content and programming; independent, alternative, community and other media that are committed to democratizing communications; community and information exchange networks linked through the internet; researchers who contribute by understanding how the present system operates and who point out possible alternatives; people's organizations joining in the struggle around communication issues; journalists' associations that raise the banner of ethics and independence in the media; women's collectives that advance a gender perspective in communication; cultural movements that refuse to be relegated to oblivion; popular education networks; human rights organizations in favour of freedom of information; those opposed to monopolies; movements in defence of public sector broadcasting; and many, many others.

All these are the scattered seeds of citizen resistance that need to multiply and grow together into a broad coalition of social movements united by the struggle for the democratization of communication, like soldiers in the trenches where the fight for the future of democracy itself is being fought out. It is not, therefore, an issue that only concerns those who are directly or indirectly linked to the communications industry; it challenges all social actors. And the World Social Forum can become a necessary and urgently needed meeting space.

Proposals for Alternative Approaches

From the experience of the diversity of actions around the issue of the democratization of communications and the media, we have gathered the following points as basic input for advancing towards the formulation of a common agenda:

- The Right to Communicate is now an aspiration representing the next historical step in a process that began with the recognition of the rights of media owners, later extended to those who work as employees in the media, and finally to all persons, who, as set out in Article 19 of the Universal Declaration of Human Rights, have the right to information and to freedom of expression and opinion. The right to communicate starts from a more encompassing conception of all the rights recognized and claimed in the realm of communication, incorporating in particular new rights related to the changing communications scene and a more interactive approach to communication, in which social actors are also information producers and not merely passive receivers of information. Similarly, it assumes that the recognition of this right is necessary to the exercise of all other human rights and an element fundamental to the existence of democracy. The incorporation of this right into the agendas of social movements and the development of strategies to bring it into being is a key challenge in the construction of alternatives more generally.

- Better public policy is a priority: policy that is sustained as a result of democratic control and limits the power of commercial interests imprisoned by the logic of the market place, and also sets out rules for the regulation of the media, establishment of standards and supervision (but not including more questionable dispositions such as censorship). Public policy covers a broad range of issues. These include, on the one hand, the present attempts to deregulate the communications sector and to impose legislation concerning intellectual property, promoted by the WTO, IMF and others, which would result in facilitating the transnationalization and monopolization of communications; and, on the other hand, the need to guarantee the diversity and independence of sources, cultural sovereignty and diversity, democratic access to technology, etc. In this respect, ongoing struggles include those to democratize the airwaves in the face of attempts to privatize them; the defence of internet users' rights with respect to electronic snooping, censorship, etc.; and the setting up of independent regulatory bodies through which citizens can participate in the definition of policy.

- Then there is the important proposal to preserve and promote the creation of public/citizen media. This is media in the public sphere (not necessarily state media), which are under control of civil society and funded according to the principle of economic solidarity (i.e. with public and/or private funds).

- Similarly, actions in the national and international context to restrain the process of monopolization of communications systems and media, and the commodification of information.

- A further priority is the development of diverse, plural sources of information informed by a gender perspective. Actions range from criticism of and pressure on the mass media, to support for alternative and independent media that adopt such criteria as basic principles.

- A priority sector to involve in this movement are journalists, particularly through their associations. Not only are their professional interests threatened by the commodification of information, but it is also crucial to build alliances with this sector around the public service character of communications.

- Another sector with which it is important to develop alliances are consumer movements. Consumers are treated on an individual, isolated basis, depriving them of any other power than that of buying or not buying, switching on or off. Their power could be much greater if it were exercised collectively.

- To develop an informed citizenry requires a capacity for critical appraisal of the media, which is the purpose of media literacy programmes, so that people can have a better understanding of the socially constructed nature of the media.

- A fundamental aspect to accompany this process is research, which makes it possible to focus on new issues and forms of action. A closer link between movements for democratizing of communication and research is needed, as well as the dissemination of research findings in simplified form and exchanges between theory and practice.

- One of the central proposals on communication put forward at the first World Social Forum was the urgent need to open a broad public debate on the impact and consequences of monopolistic concentration in the communications sector, and priorities in the development of new information and communication technologies. Such a debate would make it possible to open public discussion that is essential, but always postponed, concerning the relationship between the media and democracy, the social function of the media, and the consequences of imposing a model based on strictly commercial considerations.

EDUCATION
Conference Synthesis

BERNARD CHARLOT and
PAUL BÉLANGER

Facilitators

Bernard Charlot WORLD FORUM ON EDUCATION
Paul Bélanger INTERNATIONAL COUNCIL ON ADULT
EDUCATION

Discussants

Marta Maffei EDUCATION INTERNATIONAL/ LATIN AMERICA,
ARGENTINA
Jocelyn Berthelot CONTINENTAL FORUM ON EDUCATION,
CANADA
Paula Menezes EDUARDO MONDLANE UNIVERSITY,
MOZAMBIQUE
Sérgio Haddad ABONG AND EDUCATIONAL ACTION (AÇÃO
EDUCATIVA), BRAZIL
Leslie Toledo WORLD EDUCATION FORUM (FÓRUM MUNDIAL
DE EDUCAÇÃO)

Support

José Luiz Ribeiro WORLD EDUCATION FORUM (FÓRUM
MUNDIAL DE EDUCAÇÃO)
Maria Clara di Piero EDUCATIONAL ACTION (AÇÃO
EDUCATIVA), BRAZIL
Salete Valessan Camba PAULO FREIRE INSTITUTE
(INSTITUTO PAULO FREIRE), BRAZIL

The session was opened by Bernard Charlot, who introduced the analysis, conclusions and main purposes of the World Education Forum (WEF) which had taken place in Porto Alegre from 24 to 27 October 2001, with about 15,000 people (education workers, researchers, students, social movement representatives) from 60 countries and representing over 900 organizations. They built a meeting marked by the diversity of its representatives as well as its themes and, at the same time, by the convergence of hopes and the fight for a society and a world where there is more justice, more democracy, more solidarity.

Charlot presented an analysis of the educational situation today, in a world that is a victim of neoliberal globalization. He also introduced the fundamental principles defended by the WEF. The basic principle it affirmed is that: 'Public education for everyone is an inalienable right guaranteed and paid for by the state. It must not be treated as a commodity. It must be radically democratic, egalitarian and fair'. This view of education goes against that imposed by some international organizations, which has ended up by driving a growing number of countries into a dilemma: should they choose to pay the external debt or give their citizens education?

Charlot identifies seven major consequences of this dilemma.

1 The neoliberal reduction of education to the status of a commodity threatens humankind in its universal condition, in its cultural diversity and in its construction as a subject of rights.

2 Education starts to be conceived by the state as a form of social assistance and ceases to be seen as a human right applicable to all and an essential component in effective citizenship.

3 The increase in private schooling and the market logic of putting public educational institutions into competition with one another, and, worse, companies getting into schools to sell or advertise their products and services.

4 Social inclusion is one of the roles of the public school, yet the

logic of neoliberalism prevents sufficient financial investment in education. The result is widespread illiteracy, school truancy, etc.

5   The most important victims of this situation are those in most need: poor people, immigrants, indigenous people, ethnic, religious and cultural minorities, as well as teachers themselves, because of bad working conditions and low morale.

6   Digital exclusion, where the new information and communication technologies are not accessible to everyone, and work according to the profit motive.

7   Values such as freedom, autonomy and decentralization have been appropriated by neoliberal thought. It is necessary to rescue and redefine those values, linking them to the project of the construction of a new world. Is this possible?

Two principles inform these reflections and goals. First – and this bears repeating – education is not a commodity. It is a universal right, linked to the human condition itself. Professor Charlot then demonstrated three fundamental educational processes: humanization, socialization and individualization (the latter meaning the universal right to be culturally different and original as a person). The integration of these processes is possible when education is linked to progressive movements campaigning for more solidarity, more equality and more justice. Secondly, education is an important instrument of struggle against all forms of violence, prejudice, exploitation, human degradation, and so in the building of another form of globalization.

The right to education is the right to the effective appropriation of all serious knowledge and not simply basic information given by some boss or by the internet. It is the right to intellectual activity, to express oneself, to imagination and to the arts, to the domain of one's body, and to understanding one's natural and social environment. It is the right to an understanding of one's relationship with the world, with others and with oneself. Such a kind of education requires transforming public schools and many of their practices. This transformation should occur alongside educating teachers about principles of democratic organization – democratic participation in setting the curriculum, in management (along with the participation of all groups in the school community); and interdisciplinary exchanges over teaching methods; and team work.

Charlot reaffirmed the importance of public policy relating to children's education; the necessity of public provision for special needs students; and the right to education of young people and adults who are socially excluded.

Action by Civil Society

The next presenter, Paul Bélanger, declared that there are two competing tendencies – the arbitrary process of economic globalization, and the growth of an intercontinental dialogue on rights among different people. Both demonstrate the urgency of every single man and woman exercising their right to learning, questioning and creating throughout their lives.

The threat of the imposition of a single social and economic model is very real. This worldwide tendency involves privatization in both health and education. There is also a danger of denying the world's children and adults access to formal education, or not letting them have it in their own culture. This retards their personal development and denies that intelligence and creativity constitute unique tools for sustainable development. Modern globalization can, as a result, have tragic consequences, including the possibility of a world where many people have their intelligence stunted. When it comes to new technologies, development nowadays tends to humour the dominant market forces. This can generate perverse asymmetries and monopolies of thought. On the other hand, the ease and speed of communication means these new technologies can also favour cultural pluralism, creativity and the development of decentralized, autonomous networks. This contains the seeds of an unimaginable democratic potential.

Bélanger argues that we are facing a moment both dangerous and promising. But evidence shows that governments and the private sector will not implement goals adopted by the UN unless there is autonomous supervision by non-governmental networks. It is also essential, if new challenges are to be taken up, that spaces are created in which alternatives and counter-projects can be tried out. Only if there is active community involvement and a continuous expansion of skills will the right to learn have a better prospect. Obviously, all this is not enough to reverse the direction of the dominant neoliberal system. A growing number of children are still being left unprepared to deal with economic changes or to cope with a complex urban environment. The irony is that only 4 per cent of the world's biggest 225 fortunes could guarantee a formal education for everyone.

Lifelong learning is an equally important goal since it has the potential to strengthen the individual's autonomy. The key element is the development of the capacity of adults to develop their potential and release hitherto undeveloped creative forces throughout an individual's lifetime. Developing the intelligence of a society as a whole is a universal source of richness and, more than ever, something to be universally encouraged.

Education as a Liberating Tool

Jocelyn Berthelot, a teacher and discussant, expressed her agreement with the ideas put forward by the presenters, underlining some specific points:

- The right to education cannot be detached from social rights.

- It is not possible to pursue a new world without liberating formal education from old models of upbringing.

- Education is not a commodity, and opposition to different forms of commercializing education must be a central part of a democratic educational project.

Over the years, despite countless agreements at the international level guaranteeing education for every citizen, governments have not committed themselves to it. These agreements could be used to show up the contradictions between what is really happening, and the promises made, in order to demand a real commitment from governments.

Berthelot identified other important themes:

- Inequality between women and men remains dramatic in many countries, and it is known that education can have positive consequences for women's lives, as well as for their families and society generally.

- Native peoples, especially in parts of Latin America, represent the biggest part of the population and their struggle should be supported by everyone, so that they can control their schools as a way of ensuring the respect due to their cultures, languages and ways of life.

- In many countries, the situation of professional teachers is humiliating and degrading. The struggles for union rights, proper salaries and professionalization are part of the fight for a democratic public education.

- Education is highly important to campaigns against AIDS, which is killing thousands of people every year, and damaging many countries' prospects for development.

There are many wider campaigns that educationists need to support, such as the ones against child labour, for a quality public education system for everyone, and the campaigns to exclude education from free trade agreements. In the same way, campaigns along the following lines, need to be developed in each country:

- Demand that 8 per cent of the gross domestic product of each country be used for public education.

- Pressure countries in the north to stick to their promise of using 0.7 per cent of their gross domestic product on helping poor countries' development.

- Support campaigns to strengthen teachers' unions, and increase cooperation among civil society organizations for education.

- Support mobilizations against the North American Free Trade Agreement, the World Trade Organization and the external debt.

- Campaign for democratic control of financial resources and for a reduction in military expenditure.

- Support initiatives that strengthen UN action on education, through UNESCO, and resist the roles of the IMF and World Bank.

In conclusion, Jocelyn Berthelot reminded us that public education is not a problem but the solution for development and an instrument for the freedom of citizens and people. Knowledge is a common human good and should be accessible to all and shared by all.

Outrage over Poverty

Marta Maffei, the second discussant, agreed with Charlot, underlining the right to culture and the need to take into account some additional aspects. The world is marked by poverty, and access to knowledge does not necessarily help to avoid it. This is the situation of many teachers, who have a formal education and are working, but most of whom are poor.

It is important to understand that when people live in poverty for years, they also develop a culture of poverty that has its own values, rules and strategies. This way, child labour, premature motherhood, diseases caused by malnutrition, alcoholism and AIDS are problems that affect mostly poor people. Poverty can also generate a subversive culture that modifies other cultures. And how do teachers face this reality? Should a culture of poverty be defended? Most teachers ignore this situation. They are not even prepared for it. Two common attitudes towards the poor can be identified, indifference and condescension, both of which increase exclusion.

In order to advance in a different direction, as the World Social Forum wants, Marta Mattei argued that public education should prioritize the poor, so that their needs are met, and their opportunities broadened. Universities and teacher education centres have not yet focused on that priority.

Referring to Bélanger's exposition, Marta Maffei pointed out that collective intelligence also requires adequate nutrition and the early introduction of children to a quality education. She agreed with the fact that capital can survive even where a society does not build up its collective intelligence, because it owns the key human, technological, financial, and communication resources. This is why international organizations, such as the UN, the ILO and others submit to the power of the dominant countries, which are not interested in building a collective intelligence. She concluded that we shouldn't naturalize poverty. However much we are surrounded by it, poverty is always an injustice and we need to recover our ability to be outraged. Only then will it be possible to make this other world we need so much.

Education and Emancipation

Paula Menezes, another discussant, highlighted the emancipatory role of education, drawing on experiences in Mozambique.

It is necessary to build a wider and more democratic notion of education that makes it possible for every member of a community (whether extended families, villages, religious associations, etc.) to feel like a citizen. Education is therefore an essential part of the construction of a new citizenship project. This project, founded upon social inclusion, can only be possible if based on a recognition of differences and diversity. In a country as diverse as Mozambique, which is a true cultural mosaic where so many languages are spoken, the question of a multicultural approach is particularly important. In this sense, it is necessary to pay attention to two principles that will ensure different forms of being and explaining the world: first, the right to be an equal even when difference leads to people being regarded as inferior; and, second, the right to be different when equality oppresses us by forcing everyone into the same mould.

Following this idea, it is important to recognize, as a central part of this new approach on education, the existence of several forms of knowledge. Scientific knowledge, which is the subject matter of formal teaching in general, is only a little part of this universe (in Mozambique, for instance, a significant part of the population uses traditional medicine). Yet this other knowledge is not recognized. It is also important to note that other systems of knowledge are not only distinct, but not really comprehended by modern Western knowledge, which is the one that is most used by public education. Different systems of knowledge also mean different forms of transmission like oral tradition, story telling, songs and theatre. These other forms should be respected and integrated into an educational system in which teaching is more democratic and emancipatory.

As people say in Mozambique, 'Every time one of our oldest people dies, another immense part of a library is lost'. And because libraries only preserve what is written, where is Africa, the continent of oral tradition? One of the most obvious but little noticed ways in which other knowledge systems are lost is the annihilation of local languages and cultures. In Mozambique, for example, discussions about national languages happen on two levels. On one level is the teaching of local languages to guarantee that the child will preserve the memory of their local culture. At the second level, the discussion is about which are languages and which are dialects.

The construction of a new world cannot limit itself to the academic world. Knowledge relevant to social action needs to be linked to politics and law. Samora Machel (the first president of Mozambique) declared that 'school should be the basis on which we all teach and learn'. Such an attitude is today, more than ever, essential, because recovering and preserving memory represents a form of struggle and emancipation against (neo)colonialism and neo-liberalism.

Essential Principles of this Fight

Translation allows one to operationalize differences. Horizontality recognizes that what is emancipation for some may not be such for others. Self-reflexivity is a way of combating authoritarianism and avoiding regulating all situations through a perspective produced only by a small part of society. Social justice is not possible without cognitive justice, without recognizing the presence of different forms of understanding, knowing and explaining the world. All forms of knowledge have to be present and valued in relation to one another. Faced with the endless map of knowledges, the conclusion is that it is impossible to have a single general theory about the meaning of education and knowledge. Education needs to be a central task of the political system, and political power should help, not only by funding it, but also by having as a priority the fight against the obscuring of non-Western knowledge and local forms of education.

CULTURE
Cultural Diversity, Cultural Production and Identity

FATMA ALLOO, LUIZA MONTEIRO,
AURELI ARGEMÍ, IMRUH BAKARI
and XAVI PEREZ

Introduction

The increasing demand by peoples and communities to have their cultural identity preserved comes in a world context we now call globalization, which many perceive as taking us towards a progressive homogenization at a global level. It is in this context that various networks request a discussion in the framework of the World Social Forum on the issue of cultural diversity and identity, in order to develop collective proposals that could facilitate a positive and just balance between the two phenomena.

Various persons representing networks and organizations have collaborated in order to produce the text and proposals here presented for discussion.

Context

The working group has agreed it should set out some fundamental facts for the guidance of this discussion. At the beginning of this new century:

- We are in a post–Cold War era in which one dominant hegemonic force exists – the US and the Western world generally;

- We have arrived at a political milestone whereby, after the world conference on racism in Durban 2001, there has been a grudging acceptance by the most powerful governments of the Western world that the enslavement of Africans which laid the foundation of the modern global economy was a crime against humanity;

- We now universally accept that the terrorist attack on the USA on 11 September 2001 was a monumental turning point in global relations.

Bearing these important factors in mind, it also seems worth pointing out that at this moment in human history we are not discussing colonialism or imperialism, nor are we discussing capitalism or socialism, though these may in some way inform the discussion. What is indisputable is that the world is characterized by economic imbalance, social inequality, an imbalance of political power, and a cultural hierarchy.

Also remember that, as we know, language as a cultural product is determined ideologically, hence the need for a cautious approach to defining an agenda that is truly consistent with the most authentic notion of diversity.

Globalization

As a historical process, globalization is as much a point of arrival as it is a point of departure.

The process of globalization manifests itself as a two-headed creature. One has an unprecedented capacity for communication and exchange on a global scale. In this sense, globalization favours multiple cultural permutations and the flourishing of new local cultures.

The other manifestation, in contrast, is the imposition of a Western socio-economic-cultural model throughout the world. By feeding our senses with particular images, rhythms, aesthetics, we are driven to the use of particular objects, clothes, machines, as well as being induced to have, for example, an accelerated perception of time, or to develop an indifference to violence. We tend to internalize a certain planetary imaginary imbued with a Western technology-focused face.

Culture

Culture remains a troublesome idea, and is one of those involving the greatest dispute.

It is therefore necessary to arrive at a definition which does full justice to all of human experience, since culture refers ultimately to a way of life. In particular, a definition of culture should explicitly include areas of human experience such as economics and politics, which form part of any cultural framework.

In this way we need to embrace three structural levels: values, institutions and practices. While institutions and practices are obvious, the idea of values is ambiguous to say the least. Put another way, one might ask, why values and not ideology? Is the issue of ideology not an important notion in understanding the socialization practices of societies? Or is ideology only a consideration when it is used to characterize a view opposed to the dominant Western idea?

We must abandon a notion of culture that is separate from politics, economics, education, religion, science and justice, or a definition that reduces the concept of culture to artistic and folklore statements or to the area of values and beliefs.

We can no longer talk of politics and culture, economics and culture, religion and culture, education and culture, etc., but of political culture, economic culture, educational culture, religious culture, social culture, artistic cultures, etc.

This inevitably involves speaking of cultural diversity as taking in each and every one of these basic activities of any human community, to the exclusion of none.

Culture is therefore conceived here as being the processes of human communication and interaction that should be capable of bringing the universal to the local context, and vice versa; as, ultimately, a method for action in the face of the destructive tendencies of globalization.

Cultural Diversity and Identity

It might be useful to consider that we all possess identities that at specific critical moments may be recognizable as *an* identity. Importantly, this identity may be determined by gender, ethnicity, nationality or politics, as well as the socializing (cultural) practices of a specific social location.

Cultural identities, despite the fact that each person articulates them in a particular manner, are not strictly individual, but also collective.

The construction of identity occurs within a social dynamic involving aspects of tradition, history and the present experience. While this is recognized in phrases like the 'framework of contemporary Western culture', identities categorized as being outside of this framework are not afforded the same dynamic possibility.

Becoming aware of the omnipresence of culture and cultural identity is essential to understanding the behaviour of others, not from one's own cultural matrix but, insofar as this is possible, from that of others.

Cultural Production, Diversity and Identity

The development of an international commerce in cultural goods and services favours some countries and imposes a specific cultural model (the Western one) on others, prompting the loss of identity and the tendency toward worldwide homogenization.

Cultural products end up being considered as entertainment products, comparable, in commercial terms, to any other product, and therefore entirely subject to the rules of international trade.

Over the past few years, many countries have begun to express their concern regarding this risk of losing their identity. They consider cultural output not just as commercial products, but as precious assets that transmit values, ideas and meanings – in other words, as instruments of social communication that contribute to the modelling of the cultural identity of a specific community. And as such, it should be excluded from commercial trade agreements.

The French government, concerned about the growing American-ization of its society, was one of the first to introduce the notion of cultural exception in international relations (the WTO General Agreement on Trade and Services). The notion of cultural exception, however, has not resolved the problem, nor does it seem likely to do so in the future.

At a local level, though, the space for cultural and artistic produc-tion takes on great value in the construction of identity and cultural diversity. From this perspective, preserving local space for cultural and artistic production is essential to the promotion of diversity and the building of identity. Some international networks, following guidelines laid down by artists themselves, have established contacts across a great diversity of cultures around the world. In theory, this is a positive development, and it is probably necessary to develop it further, although for this to be possible, a symmetrical exchange fostering a genuine interculturality must be guaranteed, where different identities can relate on equal terms.

Conclusion

The issue of cultural diversity sits side by side in importance with issues of peace, security, disarmament, poverty, democracy and human rights. Cultural justice should be promoted as part of the efforts to achieve political, economic and social justice.

Proposals

- To promote the development of a common Culture of Peace taking into account: the different cultural conceptions and practices related to conflict and peace; the different experiences of specific groups (such as refugees, displaced people, women victims of violence, and many other groups); the different notions around human security, in accordance with different cultural perspectives; and the different traditions of peaceful resistance developed in different cultures around the world and throughout history. Also, to promote a Culture of Peace, it should be a priority to use the arguments and experiences of demilitarization. It should also be a priority to confront the relationship between male culture and violence.

- To adopt the UNESCO proposal for a World Alliance for Cultural Diversity, which reaffirms the will to promote and preserve cultural diversity and to develop cooperation between North and South and especially South and South, understanding that, to achieve this, governments must wish to formulate new public policies with regard to cultural questions.

- Western culture is the currency of these exchanges. This should be countered with the development of an extensive citizens' network around the world, accompanied by a recognized legal framework that legitimizes it as the promoter of greater social cohesion, collective identities, the integration of different sensibilities, the development of projects with a global community dimension, and the application of the principle of social subsidiarity.

- It would also be necessary to safeguard the linguistic patrimony of humanity, supporting mother tongue education, and the learning of other languages in school.

18 VIOLENCE

(i) *Violence Against Women: The 'Other World' Must Act*

WORLD MARCH OF WOMEN

Introduction

It was decided that for the second meeting of the World Social Forum in Porto Alegre there would be a forum for reflection and debate on alternatives to the 'culture of violence'. The World March of Women agreed to write the paper that would serve as the basis of discussion for this Forum. We have deliberately chosen to talk about violence against women in order to illustrate how central this form of violence is to the so-called 'culture of violence'. It could be said that this is the original form of violence, even the paradigm on which other forms of violence are modelled. We chose to talk about violence against women precisely because feminists have always been the ones to speak about this phenomenon. Apart from the contributions of feminists and the pressure we have brought to bear, the public discussion on this issue has been like violence against women itself: invisible.

It is somehow terrible to talk about a 'culture of violence'. It seems paradoxical casually to pair the words culture and violence, one with its positive connotations and the other with all its negative associations. The very use of the word culture suggests, to varying degrees, social endorsement, assent and transmission. This is exactly what happens with violence against women.

Without denying the importance of other forms of violence, we believe that if the causes and consequences of violence against women are thoroughly understood, the groundwork can be laid for alternatives to construct another world based on equality and respect of others.

The aim of this paper, then, is to demonstrate the universality of violence and its diverse forms and, especially, to pinpoint its causes in order to succeed in eradicating it. We denounce patriarchy — a system which, for thousands of years, has imposed inequality, exploitation, privilege, discrimination, values, standards and policies, based on the presumed natural inferiority of women as human beings and on a hierarchy of social roles assigned to women and men. It is this system that generates violence. We denounce neoliberal capitalist globalization that is supported by a sexual division of labour that creates additional inequality between men and women and, concomitantly, the potential for increased violence. Our goal is to put an end to violence against women and we will list elements that must be changed in order to do so. Naturally, this directly concerns all who are active in the struggle against neoliberal globalization.

We hope that everyone who reads this paper will contribute to it with his or her thinking and proposals so that we will arrive in Porto Alegre in 2002 with a powerful text that invites action. We welcome your comments.

At the dawn of the twenty-first century there is deeply-rooted tolerance and complicity with all forms of violence against women.

Violence against Women: A Transnational and Transcultural Reality

Violence against women takes different forms depending on the society or culture in question, but it is a social phenomenon that cuts across all social classes, cultures, religions and geopolitical situations. There are no exceptions, and the rule is unfortunately confirmed every day. Indeed, every minute women are abused, humiliated, assaulted, raped, beaten, exploited and killed, most often by men close to them — and this has been true for thousands of years.

Violence occurs most often in the private realm (feminists have amply shown that the 'the personal is political'): for example, within the family, in the form of incestuous rape, genital mutilation, infanticide, preference for sons, forced marriage, etc.; and within marriage or a sexual relationship, in the form of marital rape, physical assault, psychological control, pimping, 'honour' crimes, femicide, etc. The public arena also exhibits violence against women in the form of sexual and psychological harassment in the workplace, sexual assault including gang rape, sex trafficking and slavery, pornography, organized procurement rings, forced sterilization, etc. Violence against women is most often an expression of one man's domination, but it may also be practised in an organized manner by several men or even by a state (remember the systematic raping in Bosnia and Haiti). Too often it is tolerated, excused or encouraged by silence, discrimination, women's dependence on men, theoretical justifications and psychological approaches that support various stereotypes and myths – men allegedly unable to control themselves, especially their sexual impulses; rapists being mentally ill; women loving 'real' men, etc.

The Multiple Manifestations of Violence against Women

Here are some global statistics on violence against women (taken from *Sexism and Globalization*, World March of Women, 2000):

- Between 20 and 50 per cent of women are, to varying degrees, victims of assault by their spouses;

- An estimated 5,000 women and girls in the world are victims of 'honour' crimes every year;

- According to UNICEF, one in ten women is raped at least once in her lifetime;

- According to most published studies on the subject, women are most often raped by a man they know;

- There are an estimated 130 million women in the world who

have suffered genital excision; every year nearly two million more women are subjected to this custom, at a rate of roughly 6,000 per day, or five girls per minute;

• Estimates of the number of women in the sex industry range from a low of nine million to as high as 40 million women worldwide;

• It is estimated that the sex trade generates $52 billion every year for organized criminal networks;

• It is estimated that four million women and girls are bought and sold around the world every year, by future husbands, pimps or slave merchants;

• In the region of Southeast Asia alone, nearly 7 million women and children have been victims of sex trafficking over the last ten years;

• Over 100 million girls are missing around the world because of the preference for male children;

• In India, an average of five women are victims of dowry-related burnings every day, and many other cases are never reported;

• In 2000, a study conducted in the fifteen member states of the European Union revealed that 2 per cent of women workers (three million) have suffered sexual harassment at work and 9 per cent of women and men workers have experienced psychological harassment.

Fundamentalist Regimes: Extreme Examples of the Institutionalization of Violence against Women

Fundamentalist regimes like that of the Taliban in Afghanistan have institutionalized violence against women, conferring on all men the divine right to employ it at any time. Over the centuries, the absolute control of women and appropriation of women's bodies have manifested themselves in different ways, ranging from manipulation to acts of outright horror. The twentieth century saw progress in women's rights but no significant reduction in the violence of which women are the specific targets. We know about 'honour' crimes, dowry-related crimes against young women, and the levirate – all practices that give men in the family the power of life and death over women and girls. Furthermore, in the West, despite broad recognition of women's rights, violence and other forms of control persist – a woman is raped every six minutes in the United States; there is not yet a recognition of the fact of marital rape or the right to abortion in Switzerland; sex trafficking is expanding; there are occasional massacres of women like that in Montréal in 1989. No society is free of violence against women because there is no society where women and men are equal, even where formal equality of rights has been recognized.

On the international scene, the situation of Afghan women is probably the most striking example of the tolerance of the intolerable in societies claiming to respect fundamental human rights. Before September 11, few countries had actively called for an end to the Taliban's abuse of women that had gone on for years. Since the beginning of the war against Afghanistan, however, it has become popular in the West to justify the bombing by pointing to the lack of respect for women's fundamental rights. According to Amnesty International, the number of women victims of armed conflict has risen from 5 per cent of total casualties during the First World War, to 50 per cent during the Second World War, to almost 80 per cent during the 1990s. There is no reason why the present war should be any different. Women in Afghanistan, like the rest of the population, want the bombing to end and, with the departure of the Taliban, to see the institution of equal rights. Afghan women's groups also want to be actively involved in peace negotiations and in the restoration of democracy in their country.

Rape as a Weapon of War

Another manifestation of violence against women is the use of women's bodies as war booty or a weapon of war. In all armed conflict, from ancient times to the present, aggressors have used rape as a way of attacking their enemies. Rape camps were organized during the recent Balkan war, for example, as part of the ethnic cleansing campaign. It has now been revealed that during the Algerian war, French combatants committed rape on a massive scale. Between 1932 and the end of the Second World War, Japan set up camps so that its army could be 'serviced' by sex slaves. In these rape centres, termed Recreation Centres, 200,000 women were forced into sexual slavery. The slaves, known as comfort women, were kidnapped from neighbouring countries which were at war with Japan. To take another example, since the end of the war in Kosovo, women from Eastern Europe have been kidnapped, confined, terrorized and taken by organized crime networks into brothels in Pristina. Almost half of the men frequenting these brothels are international NGO workers and peacekeeping forces. The list goes on and on.

Women Fight Back and Organize

Despite the suffering they have endured, women everywhere fight back against violence every day. They organize with each other and protest to change laws, ensure their implementation, challenge the 'customs' for which women pay the price, and offer solidarity to women who are victims of violence. Every day, women who have been violently attacked find the courage to rise up in loud and determined protest. They are the principal fighters against this social scourge. Here are just a few examples – the Mauritian women who mobilized against wife assault and had a law passed in 1997; the plays created by Filipina women to educate people about sex trafficking; Women in Black in Serbia, who protested Milosevic's militarist and nationalistic policy and supported women refugees in Kosovo; and groups in Burkina Faso who work with adolescent girls to prevent genital mutilation and forced or early marriage.

The Causes of Violence against Women

Violence against women is rooted in the hatred of otherness and the belief that domination is a viable means of survival. Patriarchy instituted a system of masculine domination (social, economic and political) over women. Despite the progress of feminism in the last few years, men and boys in all societies and social classes still derive large benefits and concrete privileges from this system of domination – for example, domestic work and the raising of children are everywhere the almost exclusive domain of women and girls, who do it for free. Boys and men everywhere are accorded more value than women and girls. In order to impose and maintain what is the oldest and most persistent system of exploitation and oppression, violence, or the threat of violence, is used as a tool of control and punishment for disregarding patriarchy's established rules (hierarchy, submission, obedience, etc.). Our societies have developed (and continue to develop) from a foundation that espouses a hierarchy of individuals according to gender. In this context, otherness is seen and constructed as a threat rather than as an advantage. From this springs the need to dominate in order to survive that is the basis of patriarchy. The desire to preserve the privilege inherent in the status of the oppressor leads to the use of violence as an affirmation of masculinity and as a tool for maintaining dominance. A bond of solidarity is thus constructed among men to make sure this situation continues. As long as we refuse to challenge these realities, we will not succeed in eliminating violence against women.

Patriarchal domination generally models itself on the dominant economic system or existing mode of production. The mode of capitalist production therefore coexists with its forerunner, patriarchal domination, and uses it to great profit. Regimes that were supposedly socialist have also operated hand in glove with patriarchy and women's historical experience with these types of societies has convinced us that a progressive regime will not automatically guarantee women's equality and act to eradicate sexist violence. Women are obviously present in all social classes. It is women, however, who constitute the majority of workers in the informal economy, the free economic zones, and those without paid work in the South. In the North, women form the majority in the ranks of the unemployed and those with casual, flexible and part-time jobs. Women – in the South and the North – still perform virtually all domestic labour for free. These areas of heightened vulnerability may also present the risk of increased violence and make it harder for women to escape violence.

Women are further rendered vulnerable by racist discrimination. These different modes of oppression intersect, interpenetrate and mutually reinforce one another. Having a disability, being very young or very old, being lesbian or a prostitute, increases the likelihood for a woman of being targeted.

The Consequences of Violence against Women

The repercussions of sexist violence on the lives of women victims are never negligible. One's entire being is profoundly shaken, with every thing that was previously taken for granted now thrown into question. Paradoxically, whatever the circumstances or forms of violence we women have suffered, we feel ashamed and guilty. We feel shame for the invasion of our intimate selves, for being robbed of control and of our physical and psychological integrity. We feel guilty for our supposed failure to offer resistance (the reality is always more complex than it appears). This is true in every part of the world – South and North, East and West.

The repercussions of violence are most obvious in women's health – the physical consequences of genital mutilation, for example, such as repeated haemorrhages and even septicaemia; or multiple contusions, broken bones, etc. from repeated blows.

By definition, violence can also result in death – the murder of newborn girls in China, 'honour' crimes in Jordan and Morocco, the murder of women in Ciudad Juarez, Mexico. But death can also result from wife battery: a blow struck a little harder than usual by a husband, in a particularly vulnerable spot. Even the World Bank has to admit that violence against women, as much as cancer, is responsible for death and incapacity in women of reproductive age, and causes more health problems than road accidents and malaria combined.

The consequences are also psychological: loss of self-esteem, depression, suicidal feelings, nightmares, anxiety attacks, psychosis, fear of sexual relations, vulnerability to sexual exploitation (prostitution), etc.

Consequences are often also material in nature – forced relocation, job loss, termination of studies, etc. Relations with intimates may be disrupted: separation from one's spouse, distancing from erstwhile friends, etc. The primary consequence of violence against women, even the threat of violence, is that it maintains women in a state of constant fear and vulnerability, and restricts our movements (especially in the evening or at night), as well as our access to public spaces where we can feel safe, and limits our social participation and autonomy. Women are thereby denied access to full citizenship. Violence fulfils the role of social control of women – quite apart from economic costs.

Violence against Women and Liberal Globalization

One of the results of liberal globalization is the relocation of businesses from the North to the South in the quest for cheaper labour. The labour market is thereby opened up to women, but under the most severe conditions – pay that is not adequate to live on, intolerable working conditions presenting grave health risks, non-existent labour rights, and prohibition of unionization. The precariousness of their situation in the labour market renders these women extremely vulnerable. For example, during hiring interviews in the *maquiladoras* of Mexico, women workers must answer questions concerning their sexual practice, menstrual cycle and birth-control measures.

Companies also demand pregnancy tests. Because most of these women are single mothers or are the main source of income for their families, they submit to these humiliating controls over their bodies. In plants that have been relocated to Bangladesh, women workers have two big fears: fire and rape. In June 1996, 32 women were burned to death in Dhaka because the factory had no emergency exit or fire extinguishers. Women in this kind of factory routinely suffer sexual harassment and are threatened with dismissal if they do not submit to their male bosses. A veritable law of silence is forced upon them.

In the North, changes in work organization (increased duties, accelerated work pace, more pressure on employees, etc.) and the development of all kinds of temporary and atypical jobs have led to rising psychological harassment, with women being the principal victims because they form the majority of people in these jobs.

As capitalist globalization evolves, we see a growing feminization of migration, for the most part towards industrialized countries. These women are forced to emigrate because they can no longer support themselves at home and must help their families with regular ship-ments of money back home. Some countries, like the Philippines, even encourage this migration. Women are often employed as domestic servants in the home, where they may be forced to endure sexual harassment and rape by their employers in addition to being depen-dent because of their often undocumented status. This was the case of the Filipina Sarah Balabagan (fourteen years old) in Saudi Arabia, and Véronique Akobé from the Ivory Coast. Both were tried and sentenced for (attempted) murder of employers who had raped them.

The international financial institutions (IMF and World Bank) impose structural adjustment programmes on indebted countries in order to 'restore' their economies. These programmes demand the destruction of public services, a drastic reduction of the civil service, major increases in the prices of essential goods, etc. They force women into even more unpaid work to compensate for the now non-existent services. They also throw thousands of women and men into unemployment, and impoverish and starve entire populations. These pernicious policies destroy the social fabric, thereby setting the stage for the emergence of yet more violence against women, in particular within intimate relationships. They promote the commodification of women's and children's (mainly girls') bodies – the only thing they have left to sell – in prostitution, domestic slavery, trafficking in human organs, etc.

The Sex Trade: A Vastly Profitable Industry

Liberal globalization has bestowed a global dimension on the sex trade, which had already morphed from a neighbourhood phenomenon into an industry. Internationalization has generated a huge sex trade where women and children have become consumer items to meet male 'demand'. Prostitution has expanded considerably in the South during the past three decades, and in Eastern Europe since the fall of the Berlin Wall. It appears in different forms. There is rising prostitution within countries linked with the movement from the countryside to the cities. Women and children are prostituted in the 'red-light' districts of metropolises in their own countries, for example in Thailand, Philippines, Indonesia, India, etc. In addition, spurred on by the ease of transportation and communications, the attraction of the 'exotic', and the search for ever younger prostitutes who are supposedly not HIV-positive, sex tourism is steadily growing. Some countries even depend on the income from prostitution to assure their development. Sex tourism is not only a phenomenon of countries in the South. It is also practised in Europe: in Berlin, Hamburg and Amsterdam, which have become major destinations. These cities also happen to be in countries that have recognized prostitution as 'sex work'.

The international traffic in women and children has therefore exploded. In the cities of Japan, Western Europe and North America we now see hundreds of thousands of young women who have been displaced into prostitution. The largest contingent comes from countries in South and Southeast Asia – roughly 400,000 a year. Next is the former Soviet Union, followed by Latin America and the Caribbean. These women and children are sometimes kidnapped and sold from middleman to middleman until they reach their ultimate destination. Other women are forced, out of desperation, to leave their country, and subsequently fall prey to organized crime networks that arrange their passage across borders and promise well-paid work in a bar, or marriage with a man from the West. The construction of Fortress Europe, which drastically restricts the free immigration of persons, the vision of the West as some kind of El Dorado, and the desire to flee war are some of the reasons women resort to these strategies.

In the organized crime networks, women are conditioned into prostitution by the use of violence to force them into obedience and submission – blows, humiliation, repeated rapes, etc. These networks generate huge profits. Interpol has calculated that the income of a pimp living in Europe is roughly €108,000 a year. Trafficking women for the purposes of prostitution is now more profitable than drugs: drugs generate one-time profits, while a prostituted woman is a year-long source of income to the pimp.

Prostitution networks are supported by the huge and completely unchallenged growth of pornography – sex shops, pornographic web sites, videos, etc. These businesses transmit commercialized, degrading and violent images of women's bodies, most of the time with complete legal impunity. They do the same, this time illegally, with children. Women appearing in these films are often themselves the victims of rape, violence and even murder, as the demand for hardcore films and socalled reality shows skyrockets.

Alternatives, Perspectives and Directions to Take, Towards the Complete Elimination of All Forms of Violence against Women

How do we stop it? What needs to be done so that this age-old violence is eradicated? Discriminatory practices and sexual inequality are often, even today, entrenched and institutionalized in the laws of numerous countries. Throughout the twentieth century and right up to the present day, feminists have been struggling for recognition of our fundamental rights. We have demanded and lobbied to have our gains formally written into law. Recognition of our formal rights is indeed the first battle to be won, whether at national or international level. Our first demand, then, is that:

Violence against women be prohibited by law in every country

Also that the content of international and regional Conventions (where they exist) must be incorporated into domestic legislation (see demands of the World March of Women, at the end of this section).

Ensure that these laws prohibit all forms of violence

There are still some countries where marital rape is not a crime: for example, India, Malaysia, Papua New Guinea and Serbia. There are countries, like Haiti, where wife assault, both psychological and physical, is not recognized. There are still countries where the criminal code stipulates that if a rapist marries the woman he raped he will not be prosecuted, for example: Costa Rica, Ethiopia, Lebanon, Peru and Uruguay. There are still countries, France for example, where only a superior, not a colleague, can commit sexual harassment in the workplace.

We must continue to ensure that these laws are actually implemented

In almost all countries, laws prohibiting violence against women are poorly implemented due to the absence of a clear political will to ensure their enforcement. In practice, even in those countries where women have the possibility of doing so, very few report assaults out of fear of reprisals or simply out of fear of not being believed. The violence thus remains invisible. In all the countries of the world, it is feminists who have made it visible.

Some Western countries are old hands at double talk: shedding a few tears of compassion, they sincerely deplore violence against women; at the same time – in the name of freedom of expression – they allow the walls of their cities to be plastered with advertisements that degrade and debase the public image of women, and incite and give men permission to rape.

But laws do not solve everything

- It is the responsibility of the state in all countries of the world to create a climate where violence against women is unacceptable to all citizens.

- It is the responsibility of the state in all countries of the world to educate their population by every means possible towards this goal, starting with the youngest children.

- It is the responsibility of the state in all countries of the world to sensitize professionals who will have contact with victims (social services, health, education, law enforcement, and the justice system) to the reality of this particular form of violence.

- It is the responsibility of the state in all countries to recognize and promote sexual equality and women's fundamental rights.

- We have a long way to go, to be sure, when some states have even institutionalized violence against women. But we are here, after all, to press for utopia.

It is not only up to the states to assume responsibility

All social movements – organizations opposed to neoliberal globalization, trade unions and political organizations – must actively denounce violence against women. Unions, for example, must condemn sexual harassment at work and support any woman who has been the victim of wife assault and is facing the necessity of quitting her job because her spouse follows her to the workplace (this happens both in the North and South).

It is our individual and collective responsibility as women and men to speak out against violence wherever we see it, including within our own mixed activist organizations. We must work to prevent its occurrence. We must not repeat the behaviour of the people who, at six o'clock one evening in 1986, stood on a Paris métro platform and watched a young girl being raped and did not move to help her.

It is the responsibility of our male colleagues in social movements to show publicly their solidarity with feminists' struggle against violence against women, in the name of the very different kind of society we want to build together. How about a solemn declaration by social movements and the World March of Women in which we commit to a common struggle? Why not organize an international tribunal on violence against women for the third meeting of the World Social Forum?

Violence of all kinds deprives women of our autonomy and undermines our physical, psychological and intellectual integrity. It prevents us from working, from being politically active, from having fun – in short, from living. This must be heard and understood.

Violence against women is legitimized and generated by all forms of inequality, fanaticism, sexist discrimination, and the condition of inferiority and marginality in which society attempts to maintain us. Violence is the ultimate guarantee of women's oppression; at the same time, our unequal societies are the breeding-grounds of sexist violence. The struggle against inequality is also a struggle against the legitimization of violence.

Men will certainly lose a little privilege in the struggle against sexual inequality. But are we not gathering together to rid society of privilege, all privilege? Men, like women, stand to gain human relationships based on reciprocal trust and respect. They, like women, stand to gain as new individuals who have shed the garb of outdated tradition. Men, like women, will gain a society that is genuinely egalitarian, for which we are struggling in all other areas: racism, anti-colonialism, etc.

Many writers refer to the innate nature of violence, and its 'natural' aspect. Freud proposed the existence of a death wish. Some even believe there is a violence gene. None of this has been proven in our opinion. We argue instead that violence is a social construction. Free of all harmful influences, it is quite simple to educate a child to non-violence. Those arguing that violence is natural would seem to be looking for ideological justifications or a way to legitimize it.

What is clear, meanwhile, is that violence is used to dominate. One person cannot exert domination over another without violence. It need not always be explicit: ideology also serves to maintain the hierarchy of dominance.

One of the things that makes it possible to really live as a human being is the ability to relax in peace and not constantly be on one's guard. A permanent state of war is intolerable. But that presupposes a minimum of trust in the other – the basis of any normal human relationship. Some women do not even know what it is to trust in this way. For them, life consists of dealing with the unexpected: the violence of their partner or their superior at work. *Living* is virtually impossible. Their lives are reduced to mere survival and a slow psychological death.

When we will be able to stop it? It has been said: 'A people who oppresses another people is not a free people'. To paraphrase this: 'A person who oppresses another is not a free person'.

Our capacity to build another world is also dependent on this: social movements must commit to challenging the unequal relations between women and men; they must undertake to incorporate in their analysis the links between capitalism, sexism and racism; they must demand respect for women's rights and commit themselves to challenging the culture of violence in both individual and collective practice. It is only by so doing that we have a chance of shaking the foundations of patriarchy and liberal globalization.

Appendix: Demands of the World March of Women to Eliminate Violence against Women

1 That governments claiming to be defenders of human rights condemn any authority – political, religious, economic or cultural – that controls women and girls, and denounce any regime that violates their fundamental rights.

2 That states recognize, in their statutes and actions, that all forms of violence against women are violations of fundamental human rights and cannot be justified by any custom, religion, cultural practice or political power. Therefore, all states must recognize a woman's right to determine her own destiny, and to exercise control over her body and reproductive function. (Added in 2001: the right to abortion and contraception, freedom from forced sterilization, and the right to have children.)

3 That states implement action plans, effective policies and programmes equipped with adequate financial and other means to end all forms of violence against women. These action plans must include the following elements in particular: prevention, public education, legal action, 'treatment' of attackers, research and statistics on violence against women, assistance to and protection of victims, campaigns against pornography, procuring, and sexual assault including child rape, non-sexist education, easier access to the criminal justice system, training programmes for judges and police.

4 That the United Nations bring extraordinary pressure to bear on member states to ratify without reservation and implement the conventions and covenants relating to the rights of women and children, in particular, the International Covenant on Civil and Political Rights, the Convention on the Elimination of all Forms of Discrimination Against Women, the Convention on the Rights of the Child, the Convention on the Elimination of All Forms of Racial Discrimination and the International Convention on the Protection of the Rights of All Migrant Workers. That states harmonize their national laws with these different international instruments in addition to the Universal Declaration of Human Rights, the Declaration on the Elimination of Violence against Women, the Cairo and Vienna Declarations, and the Beijing Declaration and Platform for Action.

5 That, as soon as possible, protocols be adopted (and implementation mechanisms be established):
- to the Convention on the Elimination of all Forms of Discrimination Against Women;
- to the Convention on the Rights of the Child.

These protocols will permit individuals and groups to file complaints against a state. They constitute a means of exerting international pressure to force states to implement the rights mentioned in these pacts and conventions. Genuine sanctions against non-compliant states should be adopted.

6 That mechanisms be established to implement the 1949 Convention for the Suppression of the Traffic in Persons and of the Exploitation of the Prostitution of Others, taking into account recent relevant documents such as the two resolutions of the United Nations General Assembly (1996) concerning trafficking in women and girls and violence against migrant women. There will be an addition calling on states to ratify the Convention of December 2000 on transnational organized crime, in particular the two additional Protocols on the trafficking in persons.

7 That states recognize the jurisdiction of the International Criminal Court and conform in particular to its provisions, especially those that define rape and sexual abuse as war crimes and crimes against humanity.

8 That all states adopt and implement disarmament policies with respect to conventional, nuclear and biological weapons. That all countries ratify the Convention against Land Mines. That the United Nations end all forms of intervention, aggression and military occupation, assure the right of refugees to return to their homeland, and bring pressure to bear on governments to enforce the observance of human rights and to resolve conflicts.

9 That the right to asylum for women victims of sexist discrimination and persecution and sexual violence be adopted as soon as possible.

The next two demands did not receive the agreement of all the women present at the 1998 meeting where we adopted our world platform for actions in 2000. Certain national coordinating bodies did not defend them. They are, however, included in the world platform. At our October 2001 meeting, we decided to ask all national coordinating bodies to discuss their position on these demands during the next year.

10 That, based on the principle of equality of all persons, the United Nations and states of the international community recognize formally that a person's sexual orientation shall not bar them from the full exercise of the rights set out in the following international instruments: the Universal Declaration of Human Rights, the International Covenant on Civil and Political Rights, the International Covenant on Economic, Social and Cultural Rights and the Convention on the Elimination of All Forms of Discrimination against Women.

11 That the right to asylum for victims of discrimination and persecution based on sexual orientation be adopted as soon as possible.

18 (ii)
VIOLENCE
Conference Synthesis on the Culture of Violence and Domestic Violence

FÁTIMA MELLO

Facilitator
Fátima Mello ABONG, BRAZIL

Debate Leaders
World March of Women:
Diane Matte CANADA
Sashi Sail INDIA
Suzy Roitman FRANCE

Discussants
Jurandir Freire Costa UFRJ, BRAZIL

The panel members for the World March of Women opened the conference by presenting a wide-ranging diagnosis of violence against women, discussing its roots and its relation to neoliberal globalization and offering ideas towards building alternatives, to which participants reacted with comments and proposals.

Violence against women expresses a combination of two mutually reinforcing systems: patriarchy (based on the assertion that there is a natural inferiority in women and also a hierarchy of roles attributed to men and women), and neoliberal capitalist globalization (which relies on the sexual division of labour to create additional inequalities between men and women, thus creating an environment favourable to increasing violence). To keep this combination of systems in place, violence is used as a means of control. The so-called socialist regimes also coexisted with patriarchy, and women's past experience with this type of society has convinced them that a change to a 'progressive' regime does not automatically create equality and eradicate violence against them.

In this regard, Jurandir Freire Costa argued that violence against women reveals men's abuse of power and appropriation of the means of physical coercion of women. However, for this to become a culture of violence, there has to be much more than isolated or sporadic incidents. Costa distinguished between acts of violence committed consciously – and therefore recognized as unlawful – and those that are neither perceived nor recognized as such. The latter are much more difficult to fight, because men and women are internalizing behavioural standards and acquiescing in violence.

The panel members from the World March of Women emphasized that women are victims of violence in all social classes, cultures, religions and geopolitical situations, even if this violence takes different forms in different societies. It happens in both public and private spheres, and is often carried out both by individuals or in an organized fashion by groups of men and by states. In Afghanistan under the Taliban, violence against women was institutionalized and made a divine right granted to all men, but in Western countries, too, in many of which women's rights are recognized, diverse forms of violence and control persist, such as the growth in white slavery, non-recognition of marital rape and of the right to abortion. In the United States there is a rape every six minutes. In all wars, rape of women is used as a weapon against enemies.

Expanding capitalist globalization engenders violence against women in many ways. The relocation of businesses from North to South in search of cheap labour has resulted in large-scale absorption of female labour in dramatically substandard conditions, with frequent demands for pregnancy testing before hiring, sexual harassment, health hazards in the work environment, prohibition of unionization, and wages inadequate to live on. There is also a growing feminization of migration, mainly towards industrialized countries. Policies imposed by multilateral financial institutions tend to lead to a dissolution of public services, forcing women to do even more unpaid work to offset the lack of these services. By destroying the social fabric, these institutions contribute to creating favourable conditions for the emergence of additional violence against women, in particular within marital relationships, but also with an increase in domestic slavery and the sex trade. With neoliberal globalization, the latter has evolved from a craft occupation to a worldwide industry.

In this situation, what alternatives and perspectives would allow all forms of violence against women to be eliminated? One of the first dimensions to be addressed would be in the realm of legislation. Many countries still have laws that institutionalize discrimination against women and it is therefore essential to struggle for recognition of their formal rights. Furthermore, it is crucial to ensure that these laws repress all violence, and that they really are enforced.

However, laws by themselves are not enough. It is the responsibility of states to educate their populations by all means possible, from the first years of life, and to train civil servants to this reality.

States should not be the only ones to take responsibility for fighting violence. All social movements – groups fighting neoliberal globalization, trade unions and political organizations – should denounce violence against women, and commit themselves to integrating in their analyses the links between capitalism, sexism and racism, demand respect for women's rights and address the issue of the culture of violence. The panel members proposed that it should be men's and women's individual and collective responsibility to take a stand against violence, including inside our organizations. It is the responsibility of our male colleagues from social movements to act in solidarity with the feminists' fight against violence.

Jurandir Freire Costa proposed that the struggle against violence concentrate on two areas. First, we need to rethink the basis of education, where our individual and collective responsibility should be to fight sexist education and the idea that individuals are to be morally judged by reference to their gender. For this purpose he proposed to hold a seminar during the third annual gathering of the World Social Forum on the subject, 'What it costs to be a male chauvinist'. A second area of struggle would be advertising, where the culture of the woman's body and its commodification nurture the culture of violence – and here men have a crucial role to play.

The plenary participants' interventions raised innumerable issues that deserve to be dealt with in more detail in the future. Several contributions demonstrated that in war situations there is an increase in violence against women. In this connection several proposals were presented for declarations in solidarity with the women of Afghanistan and Palestine, as well as denouncing United States violence against women and peoples. Also pointed out was the medical profession's violence against women in the form of genetic manipulation, caesarean deliveries, sterilizations and the denial of abortion. Several interventions stressed the need to build a culture of peace, equality and women's emancipation.

Finally, the World March of Women proposed a declaration, jointly with the social movements, pledging to fight together against violence and to organize an international tribunal on violence against women for the third World Social Forum in 2003.

Translated by volunteer translator Helena El Masri, reviewed by Peter Lenny

19 DISCRIMINATION AND INTOLERANCE

(i) *Combating Discrimination and Intolerance*

NATIONAL CAMPAIGN ON DALIT HUMAN RIGHTS, INDIA

Over 200 million people in South Asia and others in certain parts of Africa are plagued by discrimination and intolerance based on caste (or descent-based discrimination), sanctioned by society and religion. Called 'hidden apartheid' it denies them human rights and severely curtails their right to development.

The World Social Forum is a crucial arena in which to raise the issue of discrimination against the Dalits and other descent-based communities in Asia and other parts of the world. It is essential that the Forum:

- Ensure the visibility of this grave discrimination which has been forced to remain invisible during all these past decades of UN interventions and mechanisms;

- Emphasize the need for international solidarity to combat this discrimination;

- Develop strategies and share them with the international network of activists and NGOs;

- Build and strengthen the solidarity links between similarly affected communities around the globe.

Background to the Situation of Dalits in India

Dalits, so-called 'untouchables' (in legal parlance 'Scheduled Castes'), are routinely discriminated against through the practice of untouchability. Dalits continue to live in segregated housing colonies outside the main villages. The caste system denies skills and resources to Dalits and the majority eke out a living as landless labourers (90 per cent) in agriculture and casual labourers in urban markets. Dalits work as forced and bonded labourers in many parts of the country. The caste system forces Dalits, and Dalits only, into such inhuman and degrading occupations as the manual clearing up of human excreta.

Continued Practice of Untouchability

Despite the fact that 'untouchability' was abolished under India's constitution in 1950, the imposition of social disabilities on persons by reason of birth remains very much part of the social system. 'Untouchables' may not use the same wells, visit the same temples, or drink from cups used by others in tea-stalls. Social interaction in terms of inter-caste marriage or even eating together is completely prohibited. Dalit children are frequently made to sit at the back of classrooms. Dalit women are frequent victims of sexual abuse.

The recent survey by SAKSHI-Human Rights Watch identified 46 different untouchability practices in 3,320 villages in the state of Andhra Pradesh in India: the system of untouchability prevails in all the villages in one form or other. These practices alienate the Dalits from sources of livelihood, land, employment and wages and education, and from the whole process of development.

Bias and lack of political will make Dalits the prime victims of police atrocities. Poor implementation of special provisions, non-implementation of development programmes and proactive laws, and diversion of funds earmarked for Dalit development, are additional evidence of the racist mindset in Indian society.

Extreme Poverty

Most Dalits continue to live in extreme poverty, without land or opportunities for better employment or education. With the exception of a minority who have benefited from India's policy of quotas in education and government jobs, Dalits are relegated to the most menial occupations as manual scavengers, removers of human excreta and dead animals, leather workers, street sweepers and cobblers. Dalit children make up the majority of those sold into bondage to pay off debts to upper-caste creditors.

Poverty Line: Dalits have been most vulnerable to the global economic forces unleashed by the New Economic Policy in 1991. From pre-NEP in 1987 to post-NEP in 1993, the percentage of Dalits living below the poverty line actually increased by 5 per cent, reversing a declining trend over the previous fifteen years. A full half of the population lived below the poverty line in 1993 compared to only a third of the general population, whose percentage below the poverty line has remained unchanged since 1987.

Access to Basic Amenities: The rapid progress India has made since 1991 in many areas such as technology, infrastructure, industrialization, science and space research has meant very little for the Dalits, most of whom are still without even such basic amenities as electricity, sanitation and safe drinking water. Just 31 per cent of Dalit households are equipped with electricity, as compared to 61 per cent of non-Dalit households. Only 10 per cent of their households have sanitation. In many villages, the government installs electricity, sanitation and safe drinking water in the upper-caste section, but neglects to do the same in the neighbouring Dalit colony.

Access to Primary Education: Enrolment among Dalit children in 1993 at primary level was an inexcusably low 16.2 per cent, while among the rest of the population it was 83.8 per cent. Ninety-nine per cent of Dalit children go to government schools that lack basic infrastructure, classrooms, teachers and teaching aids. The trend to privatization of education adds to the travails of Dalits in education.

Access to Land and Labour: 49 per cent of Dalits are agricultural labourers and only 25 per cent are cultivators. By contrast, in 1961, 38 per cent of Dalits were cultivators and only 34 per cent were agricultural labourers. In addition, Dalits are fast losing the little land they have access to, despite a host of land reforms. Today, over 86 per cent of their households are landless or near landless and 63 per cent are wage-labour households.

Dalit Women and Gender Equity: Whenever upper castes mete out violence upon Dalits, the women are often the ones who bear the brunt of their violence and brutality, including rape, mutilation, molestation and disrobing. An average of two Dalit women are raped each day. This number is only the tip of the iceberg as many cases of rape go unreported either due to fear, intimidation by the police, ignorance of legal procedure, or loss of faith in the law enforcement establishment. In addition, Dalit women have very low levels of literacy, are denied equal wages, and earn a pittance of Rs.15–20 (about half a dollar) a day. They are also victims of human rights violation through the *joginin* (temple prostitution) system.

Manual Scavenging: Today, even as we march into the twenty-first century as a nuclear power, and despite a law banning the practice, there are 400,000–800,000 Dalits manually carrying human excreta as part of the sanitation arrangements in various places, including our nation's capital. They earn a mere Rs. 50 to Rs. 300 a month, this being considered part-time work.

Atrocities – Caste (read 'Mob') Rule: In hundreds of districts and several states, Dalits live today in a constant state of alert and fear due to threats to their life and security from upper-caste militias, sometimes abetted or at least tacitly condoned by the police. Since it was founded in August 1994, the Ranavir Sena has perpetrated nineteen massacres killing 277 persons, almost all of them poor, landless Dalits. No important member of the Sena has yet been tried in court.

From 1995 to 1997, a total of 90,925 crimes against Dalits were registered by police, of which 1,617 were for murder, 12,591 for bodily injury, 2824 for rape, and 31,376 for offences listed under the Scheduled Castes (SC) and Scheduled Tribes (ST) Prevention of Atrocities Act, 1989. These numbers represent only registered crimes. Either due to intimidation, inaccessibility of police stations, or loss of faith in the law enforcement agencies, many cases go unreported.

Reservation and Employment: Reservation, instituted as a mechanism to provide minimum opportunities for communities that have been denied access to employment opportunities, has come under a lot of fire from dominant castes as 'anti-merit' and 'undemocratic'. Actual implementation falls far lower than what the dominant castes or government claim. The Brahmin community, which comprises 5 per cent of the population, occupies 70 per cent of all top ranking civil service and academic jobs. SC/ST representation is mainly in the lowest categories of employment in bureaucracy, while in the universities it is 1.2 per cent and 0.5 per cent for SCs and STs respectively. Of the total SC reservation quota in the central government, over 54 per cent remain unfilled. More than 88 per cent of jobs in the public sector and 45 per cent of posts in the banks remain unfilled while the list of educated and aspiring Dalits in the employment exchange registers of the state grows.

Recommended Strategies

1   Ensure that all necessary constitutional, legislative and administrative measures including appropriate forms of affirmative action are in place to prohibit and redress discrimination on the basis of occupation and descent related to caste, and that such measures are respected and implemented by state authorities at all levels;

2   Ensure that degrading practices such as manual scavenging are brought to an end and persons engaged in the same are

rehabilitated with adequate compensation and placed in occupations that can ensure human dignity;

3 Urge the international community to ensure that bilateral aid to such countries having discriminatory practices based on occupation and descent has built-in protective mechanisms so that the utilization of such aid ensures fulfillment of the rights of such people to benefit directly from such aid, in particular the women members of such communities;

4 Ensure that affirmative action with a view to bringing about equality and equal opportunity to all sections of society is strictly implemented without delay in all the sectors, including the private sector in this era of globalization;

5 Ensure that in all bilateral and international development cooperation with those countries that have the above-mentioned forms of discrimination, the issues are squarely addressed and tackled and a specific focus on the elimination and remediation of the discriminatory practices is ensured;

6 Ensure, following the Paris Principles of 1991, that all the national institutions for the protection of human rights, be it of women, children, minorities or any other category of peoples of the respective country, have representation from persons belonging to such groups as suffer discrimination on grounds of occupation or descent related to caste;

7 Ensure that all mechanisms for remediation, including the judiciary at all levels, have adequate representation from members of communities discriminated against on grounds of occupation and descent related to caste with a special focus on women.

19 DISCRIMINATION AND INTOLERANCE

(ii) *Conference Synthesis*

LILIAN CELIBERTI

Facilitator

Lilian Celiberti ARTICULACÍON FEMINISTA MARCOSUR, URUGUAY

Presentations

Ana Leah Saravia ILGA, PHILIPPINES

Suely Carneiro ALIANZA ESTRATÉGICA DE AFRODESCENDIENTES DE AMÉRICA LATINA Y EL CARIBE (STRATEGIC ALLIANCE FOR AFRICAN DESCENDANTS OF LATIN AMERICA AND THE CARIBBEAN), BRAZIL

Martin Macwan NATIONAL CAMPAIGN ON DALIT HUMAN RIGHTS, INDIA

Comments

Gioconda Belli WRITER, NICARAGUA

Phoebe Eng BREAKTHROUGH, USA

Questions

- What are we talking about when we refer to 'respecting differences'?

- Is the concept of diversity revolutionary, modern, democratic or, on the contrary, does it conceal a conservative strategy of accepting the plurality of differences with reference to an ideal norm? How is diversity represented from a conservative perspective?

- The intersection of the many forms of discrimination puts the human rights framework to the test. Does this framework serve all people of different ways of life and identities regardless of gender, sexual orientation, age, race, state of health, disability, etc.?

- If race, class, gender and sexual identity combine powerfully, what theoretical and political challenges are we faced with?

- How do we devise strategies for defending people's human rights from a perspective that may include all these different dimensions?

Social groups referred to:

- Untouchables: discrimination and violence against the Dalits, who are victims of the caste system (India);

- African descendants: racism in Latin America and the Caribbean;

- Women, lesbians, gays and other sexual minorities (Philippines);

- Civil populations under attack in military conflicts and undeclared wars (the 'war against terrorism').

Analysis

- Discrimination is based on the unequal distribution of resources and opportunities. When we say unequal distribution of resources we are talking about a social and economic order, and a responsible state, that instigates, tolerates, supports or leaves unpunished practices of discrimination, or that denies and suppresses discussion of the existence of this problem.

- Discrimination is based on a 'conspiracy of silence', which denies diversity, conceals practices of violence and discrimination, or minimizes them by engaging in a discourse of false equality and tolerance.

- The concept of diversity and the recognition of identities is a key aspect in understanding how discrimination functions. But it can also lead to an evening out of the different forms of discrimination, diminishing the magnitude that discrimination and social exclusion have for particular groups. The concept of diversity is used on many occasions to even out subjects, conditions, positions and social consequences. It is essential to recognize that there are fundamental determining factors in social contradictions; gender, race and ethnic group are variables that have an impact on the class and power structures of multiracial societies. Therefore it is essential to discuss the concept of diversity as a way of 'covering up' and evening out social contradictions.

- Women and men of different race, class, sexual orientation, ethnic and religious group, are classified according to the degree of inequality they suffer; this is the basis of discrimination.

- The notion of an assumed white, heterosexual, masculine and Western universality as a reference point for the 'others' – that is, everyone else who make up three-quarters of the world's population – is a way of diluting differences and evening out group needs and characteristics without recognizing their diversities.

- Discrimination is defined by power; the oppressor has the power to categorize, label, stereotype; condemnation and persecution are justified on that basis.

- Discrimination adopts many different forms, some more visible than others, but the main point is that they create a second-class citizenry. Violence against sexual minorities falls outside the protection of human rights because these minorities are classified as being not normal. If discrimination is not seen or cannot be described, it 'disappears' and cannot be subject to criminal penalties.

- Patriarchy as a system of domination defines difference as a threat, a transgression of its stereotyped definitions of normality. It places people and groups in a subordinate hierarchy, it labels people, and on this basis condemnation and persecution are justified. Violence against women and sexual minorities is the most obvious face of this ideological system.

- Violence and discrimination are the same thing, only with different degrees of intensity. If they do not like you, they make you disappear as a human being.

- Historical decisions and economic models turned African and African-descendant populations into excluded, subordinate and dispossessed populations.

- There exists in our societies a common lack of political will to confront social exclusion based on racism and discrimination.

Proposals That Have Been Identified

The following preventive actions limiting the process of exclusion and encouraging the process of inclusion were identified.

Quotas and Affirmative Action Policies

- Affirmative-action policies that guarantee that members of disadvantaged segments of the population have full access to their human rights (civil, political, economic, social, and cultural);

- A policy of quotas for the black population changes the state's traditional historical position and implies the recognition of historical exclusion. This, in itself, constitutes a step forward, but a quota policy, divorced from wider policies directed at disadvantaged segments of the population, cannot possibly have an effective impact. A quota policy on its own can do little to advance the prospects of those sections of the population ready to enter the labour market. There must be wide-ranging policies that address the overall conditions of the excluded population.

Awareness, Education, Communication and the Production of Knowledge

- Work to overcome the denial, concealment, and underestimation of discriminatory practices;

- Community education to promote tolerance and discourage all forms of discrimination;

- Working with the media to change the public's attitudes and eliminate negative stereotypes;

- Direct education of the public in schools, churches, communities, etc., including the training of educators;

- Analysing the processes of exclusion and their link with the different forms of power, the construction of subjectivities, and identifying who has the power to divide, classify and assign rankings to particular groups;

- Dismantling the patriarchy of subjectivities and social practices, building a culture of tolerance;

- Carrying out case studies on discrimination to be shared with other groups.

Promoting of Legal Standards and the Recognition of Human Rights

- Legal reforms that oblige the state to recognize officially as citizens those segments of the population that have been victimized by discrimination;

- Implementation of existing rules and laws (equality of protection and access to the courts), e.g., the case of the Dalits, where laws are violated by the state itself;

- Freedom from discrimination based on sexual orientation should be explicitly included within the human rights framework;

- Recognition of the racial problem in Latin America and the Caribbean. This problem is concealed beneath the regional myth of racial democracy and prevents racial identity from taking shape politically;

- Making discrimination a criminal offence;

- Advancing the need for gender equity as a means of combating discrimination against women.

Links, Strategic Alliances and Mobilization

- Regional/international links, in principle between those who suffer from the same type of discrimination; these links will also connect different sectors;

- Exposing and denouncing governments and institutions that support and uphold situations in which discrimination exists (cf. the Dalits);

- The need for international cooperation to confront different types of discrimination, which cannot remain an isolated, 'untouchable' issue in the interior of the affected countries (viz. the Dalits);

- Standing united in the denunciation of all forms of discrimination and promoting sanctions against those countries that uphold the caste system;

- Strengthening the African, Latin American and Caribbean Alliance as a means of developing a regional perspective to combat discrimination;

- The anti–globalization movements must reject the centralization of power and formulate a new concept of power that includes diversity;

- Identifying what we can do to make a real impact in the fight against discrimination, basing our activity on human rights documents so that the more we use them the more effective they become;

- Using discrimination as a starting point of shared experience for establishing unconventional alliances;

- Supporting structures and agencies that promote equality and non-discrimination;

- Making our united case heard and promoting campaigns to end persecution and discrimination wherever they may exist;

- Every NGO to promote the formation of lesbian, gay, bisexual and transsexual (LGBT) groups or support these groups' local efforts; giving impetus to/collaborating on the organization of a Pride March in your city or town.

Strengthening of Democracy, Peace and Full Citizenship without Discrimination at All Levels

- Active commitment of peoples and NGOs to eliminate discriminatory practices in their own countries. Strengthening of participatory democracy in society and within the anti-globalization movement itself; rejecting the centralization of power and developing a new concept of power that allows greater flexibility and does not perpetuate the 'natural leadership' paradigms of the privileged segments of the population; trying to understand what it must be like to live under the same conditions as others;

- Reform of religious, judicial and other institutions that support discriminatory beliefs and practices;

- There are shared mechanisms of 'invisibilization' and exploitation of African descendants in the Latin American and Caribbean region. Racial problems derive from state actions since the denial of the existence of racism against African descendants strengthens inequalities. The social inferiority of black people has been essentialized, turning it into a kind of paradigm of social subordination;

- People's security and the fight against discrimination must be considered as prerequisites for achieving peace. Therefore, an anti-discrimination agenda is needed to confront the 'war against terrorism', which may encourage and legitimize practices that restrict the rights of those defined as the enemy;

- The debate must cover other forms of discrimination, such as the racial discrimination suffered by illegal workers in the USA and the situation of single mothers, amongst others.

Economic Measures

- Discrimination causes and is based on economic exclusion. Therefore, economic measures and concrete programmes, such as land reform, are needed; most violence is due to land issues in the case of the Dalits in India, for example;

- Financial reparations and cancellation of debts of African and African descendant peoples, acknowledging the bloodshed, genocide, centuries of slavery and exploitation they have endured in history;

- Acceptance that distribution of wealth, power and poverty is based on race, also influenced by gender, which, in the context of globalization, aggravates the process of the feminization of poverty.

Convergences and Differences: Points of Debate in Civil Society

- The struggle for an egalitarian globalization must break away from the logic of keeping dominated peoples in subordinate conditions by stereotyping their characteristics as quaint cultures and underestimating the extent of inequality.

- Discrimination and intolerance are institutional and represent the economic status quo. They are practised systematically both by individuals and institutions. It is an economic formula according to which the rich get richer and the poor get nothing.

- It is necessary to identify the different forms of discrimination and form alliances to fight them in an integrated way, without minimizing them, within social movements, because otherwise divisiveness and atomization occur.

- The issue of diversity has also led to a huge distortion within social movements, which are often unaware of the profound contradictions that come to the fore when they engage in mobilizing people in society. It is important to accept the contradictions and to learn how to negotiate them.

- There are other aspects of discrimination related to military conflicts. In this new millennium undeclared wars are being fought based on racism and intolerance. The wars we are witnessing are characterized by a depersonalization of the dead. The number of faceless deaths reported implies no emotion whatsoever as long as these people are the other, the enemy. This is a very dangerous ethic.

- Conventions such as the Geneva Convention on the treatment of prisoners of war, are not comprehensive enough and need to be redefined on the basis of a more appropriate ethics for the conduct of war.

Stakeholders

- **Social movements:** women's movement, LGBT, black and African-descendant movements, human rights movement.

Translated by volunteer translators Adam Henderson, Paula Zucherelli and Silas McCracken, reviewed by Adam Henderson

20 MIGRATION AND THE TRAFFIC IN PEOPLE

The Contradictions of Globalization

LORENZO PRENCIPE

'Today the World Is Global'

Since 1950, world production has increased fivefold and trade elevenfold. But who has profited from this growth? Of 6 billion human beings, 500 million live comfortably, while 5.5 billion are poor. In the 1960s and 1970s, there were 200 million persons among the world's poor – those who must survive on less than one dollar per day. By the beginning of the 1990s, the poor numbered 2 billion persons. Today worldwide there are 20 million refugees, 30 million 'displaced' persons, and 150 million 'economic' migrants (including 20 million in Europe and 50 million Africans). The African continent alone accounts for 5 million refugees and 20 million displaced persons.

Understanding Globalization

Globalization is the product of a confluence of three factors:

- Expansion of transaction space through the integration of new countries (new players);

- Globalization of large enterprises organizing their research, procurement, production, and sales activities on a global level (new games);

- Growth in trade as a result of liberalization and deregulation (new rules of the game).

One would have assumed that globalization would reduce the need to emigrate – but it is not a matter of the globalization of wealth. For, despite the significant opening of markets internationally, developing countries are increasingly the recipients of foreign consumer goods rather than stable societies capable of retaining workers, who are otherwise prospective emigrants, within their own borders.

From another perspective, the logic of globalization would dictate the free circulation of persons as well as that of capital and commodities. But this means the free circulation of people, reduced to so much labour power, to mere commodities that, like any other, are subject to no other law than the laws of the market. The extension of the liberal version of globalization to labour as a commodity implies the dismantling of social security systems. For liberalism cannot allow the completely free circulation of workers to be compromised by protective state-enforced measures, such as the minimum wage, limits on the length of the working day, minimal standards of hygiene and safety, and the prohibition of child labour.

A certain globalization of wealth, from which the dominant social strata of poor countries also benefit, corresponds with a globalization of poverty that afflicts vast segments of the populations of rich countries, most notably persons of foreign origin, particularly those who find themselves in violation of local immigration law. These victims of liberal globalization constitute a reservoir of cheap labour. Their situation is further aggravated by their dependence on organized criminal networks trafficking in human beings, without whose intervention it would be virtually impossible for these migrants to penetrate the borders of wealthy countries.

The current globalization context differs from that of 50 years ago (the industrial era): there is now a criminalization of clandestine migrants. The widespread closing of borders has transformed the nature of migration:

- from temporary to permanent;

- from individuals – mainly male – to whole families.

Western societies have been in deep crisis:

- unemployment has grown as a structural phenomenon;
- fear of the future has caused entire segments of these societies to become more closed vis-à-vis others;
- foreigners are widely seen as sources of insecurity and competitors on the labour market.

The Shifting Paradigm of Migration: from Industrialization to Globalization

We have moved:

- from industrial society to post-industrial society (globalization);
- from urbanization to relocation;
- from 'labouring classes' (with exceptions) to 'dangerous classes' (all);
- from inclusionary processes to exclusionary processes;
- from assimilating immigration to criminal immigration;
- from the welfare state to the penal state;
- from an 'open' world to a 'fortress' world.

Nearly everywhere, then, migration has become a crime in which both the source countries and the destination countries are complicit. This is the first factor in the criminalization of migration. It has brought along with it a transformation of European policies towards immigration into a kind of military-police fortification rather than an effort that promises a real possibility of integrating immigrants lawfully into the fabric of their host societies.

Characteristics of Current Migration Flows

Migrant Trafficking

No country is immune to illegal migration (consider, for example, the estimated eight million clandestine immigrants in the United States). It is a phenomenon that is inherent to all migratory flows, whether it takes the form of illegal entries, illegal overstays or illegal employment.

In Africa, given the increasingly reduced chance of reaching rich countries, the only alternative for migrants is to place themselves in the hands of traffickers who employ dangerous and illegal practices, including physical and sexual exploitation, confiscation of passports, forced prostitution and labour, and torture. Every year, one hears of hundreds of thousands of women and children in or of Africa being trafficked. Several African countries (Nigeria, Ghana, Ivory Coast, Senegal, Ethiopia, Kenya, Cameroon, Mali and Niger) are at once countries of origin, transit, and destination of migrant trafficking. Italy, Belgium, the Netherlands, the United States, the Middle East, and the Gulf states have become the destinations of choice for Africans who are the victims of migrant trafficking.

In East Asia, where the destination countries are not necessarily immediate neighbours of the countries of origin, illegal migration manifests itself in the form of persons who have overstayed their visas or who work illegally. In South and Southeast Asia, where the principal destination countries share borders with the countries of origin (Thailand and Burma or Malaysia and Indonesia), 250,000 illegal migrants in Japan, 220,000 in Korea, 600,000 to 1 million in Malaysia, 1 million in Thailand, and 1.9 million Filipinos reside abroad illegally.

Most countries have reinforced border controls, but the paltry success achieved in opposing illegal migration reveals that it is now a structural component of labour-force mobility. It has increased in numbers and in complexity as it has become intermeshed with trafficking in human beings. The latter is particularly flagrant in the case of children used for prostitution or for slave labour, or traded under the cover of adoption. Women are also victims of traffickers.

Recruited for legitimate jobs, they are subsequently forced to prostitute themselves, to marry against their will, or to labour in clandestine workshops. However, the trafficking that has increased most in recent years is that of Chinese migrants (50,000 each year, particularly from Fujian province) into North America and Europe.

In Europe, the phenomenon of clandestine immigration remains difficult to quantify and virtually insoluble. In the early 1990s, the number of illegal immigrants was estimated at 2.6 million persons. The immigration amnesties that have been granted in most European countries reveal that such migration flows are not temporary; nor are they a function of changes in the economic climate. Rather they are structural in character. Therefore, repressive policing measures will not suffice to control and manage them. Instead, the search for equality on a worldwide basis must be accompanied by policies encouraging integration of migrants within each country and by international agreements, cooperation, and development programmes externally.

One major appeal to clandestine immigrants lies in the informal economy, which is very much in evidence in Europe. The informal sector benefits significantly from the clandestine workforce, which is relatively more flexible and less costly.

The Transnational Character of Migrants

Current migration flows, deeply anchored in powerful social networks, are fluctuating in character, and maintain deep material and symbolic links between the countries of origin and the destination countries. These migration flows have developed cultural forms of their own. Thus new migrants exhibit a powerful resistance that hinders their integration into the host society.

The Feminization of Migration

One new feature of current migratory flows is their high feminine component, which has developed against the backdrop of the growing use of female labour, especially from the Third World. This labour-force has been absorbed into those parts of the manufacturing sector under stress (sweatshops, home employment) and low-cost urban services.

The Intensification of Social Exclusion

Migrants, like other vulnerable social groups, are victims of exclusion by the host society. Such exclusion may be active or passive. Mechanisms of passive exclusion are those that migrants share with other vulnerable groups by virtue of their social condition – a low standard of living, unemployment, or difficulties encountered in accessing the labour market.

Active exclusion is evidenced in the form of segregation or discrimination. Segregation forces the immigrant to isolate him- or herself in social, cultural and physical milieus removed from those occupied by the mainstream of the host society. Thus exclusion can be reflected in discriminatory practices such as the settling of the immigrant in marginal neighbourhoods, or through socio-cultural isolation. Discrimination is directly related to the unequal treatment that humiliates the immigrant in the many domains of social life in which he or she lives from day to day.

The European Case: Towards a 'Precarious Immigration'

The European Union bases free movement of persons within the Union on the strict control of external borders. It also envisages a selective openness intended only to satisfy the EU's economic needs. The manner in which work has become both more flexible and precarious in our societies is extended systematically to immigrants from poor countries who are permitted to come to work for a limited period of time in wealthy societies, only to be sent back home with the advent of economic crises. Of course, highly qualified workers will have the privilege of gaining permanent resident status or being naturalized rather quickly.

One also hears talk of immigration regulated through quotas, through the drawing of lots, or through contract assignments. In any event, states use a wide variety of mechanisms in order to maintain a certain relationship between legal and illegal immigrants. Among these mechanisms are periodic regularizations of the legal position of illegal migrant workers by means of amnesties, the occasional acceptance of large numbers of refugees, and selective humanitarian operations. All serve to fill temporary labour shortages in particular sectors.

Government officials in many countries argue that priority should be given to fighting the discrimination from which foreigners suffer rather than to action directed towards integrating immigrant workers into the host society. The struggle against discrimination is essential, but neglecting the integration component of immigration policy when talking of selectively opening borders implies that the new immigrants will not be allowed to stay for very long in the host society.

In reality, rather than fighting against so-called clandestine immigration – for if immigration is not prohibited it cannot be illegal – it would be better to make war on illegal employment and the undeclared employment of labour, whatever the nationality or status in the country of the persons involved.

Hitherto societies have been organized on the basis of a system that leads each person to accept the obligation to defend his or her own group in exchange for the protection that the group offers with respect to other groups. The member of the group is thus defined by opposition – not necessarily conflictual – to non-members of the same group. It is on the basis of this schema that the national is defined vis-à-vis the non-national, and the member of the community is defined by contrast to non-members of the community.

What Action is to be Taken vis-à-vis Globalization?

We must cease to be obsessed with the notion that 'everything is economic'. Globalization is also another way of seeing people and treating relations among peoples. Thus we must recast the balance between the global and the local.

21

THE GLOBAL CIVIL SOCIETY MOVEMENT

(i) *Discussion Document*

LATIN AMERICAN SOCIAL
OBSERVATORY (OSAL) and
LATIN AMERICAN SOCIAL
SCIENCE COUNCIL (CLACSO)

The Movement against Neoliberal Globalization

The rise of the movement against neoliberal globalization constitutes one of the most politically and socially important developments of the past decade. The formation and public appearance of this movement (one of its first manifestations was the Intercontinental Meeting for Humanity and against Neoliberalism in Chiapas, Mexico, 1996) must be understood in the context of a double crisis.

On the one hand, the emergence of this movement expresses the deep crisis of legitimacy of institutions and neoliberal policies across the globe. In this sense, the denunciation of, and the struggle against, the concentration of wealth created by the neoliberal order was closely linked to the struggle for a radical democratization of power on a global scale. A distinct feature of this movement was its great capacity to question, through its international campaigns, actions and debates, from Seattle to Genoa and Porto Alegre, the profoundly anti-democratic character of the institutions of global power, promoters of the free market ideology and world order.

But at the same time, the emergence and consolidation of the movement expressed the gradual exhaustion of the capitalist model – in its neoliberal version – in the 1990s. This final stage of the crisis manifested itself in successive financial shocks, which sped across the globe beginning in 1997 and which have reached the advanced capitalist countries at a time of growing economic recession, a recession increasingly taking on international dimensions. In this light, the critiques formulated against the financialization of capitalism and against rising foreign debt expressed the attempt to find a different solution to the crisis.

This double crisis – political and economic – created the breeding ground for the anti-globalization movement. Its vitality and power were manifest in the streets of Genoa in August 2001, where countless protests challenged the G8 summit.

Against the late twentieth century political-ideological backdrop and its dominant ideology, reflected in the apparent triumph of liberal ideologies announcing the end of history, the rise of the movement against neoliberal globalization allowed for an interrogation of the legitimacy of precisely these ideologies.

In a comparatively short time-span (during the second half of the 1990s), the anti-neoliberal movement was able to initiate a collective debate about the anti-democratic character of the neoliberal world order, and coordinate international protests (some of which were marked by radical militancy, like Seattle, Prague, Washington, Nice and Genoa) with great repercussions for the international public. These actions and meetings instigated by the movement (the World Social Forum 2001, among others) pointed to the degree of discontent generated by capitalism at the international level and demolished the illusions created by the simplistic idea of a harmonious progression towards a market society.

In the short time since its emergence, two points can be held up as preliminary triumphs of the movement. On the one hand, there is its ability to disrupt neoliberalism's cultural hegemony and the legitimacy of a world order that, supported by global liberalization of finance and trade, has produced over the past two decades a concentration of wealth on a global scale which has entrenched the divide between rich and poor countries, impoverished millions of workers, expanded armed conflicts and led to the indiscriminate expropriation of natural resources for the benefit of transnational capital. Its other triumph is its capacity to revive and resignify the importance of collective action and the internationalist tradition of the oppressed in the face of contemporary capitalism's profound transformations.

Heterogeneity and Diversity: A 'Movement of Movements'

Since its creation, and through numerous global protest actions, it has become evident that one of the salient features of the movement against neoliberal globalization is its heterogeneous constituency. This characteristic is intimately tied to the differential impact that the globalization of capital has had on economic decisions in different countries and regions, and on the essential diversity of human life. Neoliberalism, which constitutes a new strategy for capital to retain its capacity for accumulation, has been characterized by intensified subordination and exploitation of people around the world. The growing concentration of wealth and indiscriminate exploitation of natural resources – magnified in the past decades – are expressions of this phenomenon that has extended, deepened and diversified the groups, social classes and communities subject to oppression.

The surfacing and current dynamics of the movement against neoliberal globalization must be analysed in the context of a growing complexity and diversification of the responses to and struggles against the liberal economic order. It is imperative to escape from reductionist visions trying to downplay the wealth of experience of social movements and which seek to oppose 'old' and 'new' movements. One must remember that capital, as a product of social relations, expresses itself simultaneously in different forms. In the struggle against the effects of neoliberalism, the 'new' and the 'old' social movements are not mutually exclusive but reveal themselves to be complementary and supportive of collective action.

The movement against neoliberal globalization demonstrates in its makeup the complexity and diversity of contemporary social struggle. In this sense, it is a 'movement of movements' – an experience and confluence of articulations of resistance and social struggles, which, apart from their particular features of composition, reach, forms of protest and territorial claims, coincide in the fight against the devastating effects of capitalist globalization in its neoliberal phase.

The ability to construct in practice a single space of action that respects heterogeneity and does not suppress difference constitutes, in our understanding, one of the most novel aspects of this movement, compared to the historical experience of past decades. This characteristic diversity of the 'movement of movements' is, we think, one of the greatest assets and contributions of the recent experience of anti-globalization struggles.

The convergence of action, debate and programmatic agreement does not imply a weakening of each individual movement's particularities. On the contrary, and even though this might carry with it some friction and permanent tensions, the movement has developed a highly enriching ebb and flow between the perspectives of each constituent movement and social sector, and the greater framework.

The world which this international experience has built, and to which Porto Alegre was a response, has known how to turn its diversity, sparked by mutual learning and respect for difference, into a strength rather than a weakness. Moreover, these practices draw on a democratic and liberating spirit. It is not about ignoring debates and tensions existing within the movement, but rather affirming the strategic importance of establishing a common space beyond our differences. Respect for the movement's diversity needs to be the bedrock on which to build the process of convergence: of resistance, of struggles, and of radically democratic alternatives to the market order.

Porto Alegre: the Parliament of the People

In the recent (and not so recent) experience of the movement against neoliberal globalization, the first World Social Forum of Porto Alegre represents a point both of arrival and of departure. It is a point of arrival to the extent that the Forum was a moment of confluence and expression of multiple resistance processes that have developed since the second half of the 1990s. It was also a point of departure, because throughout 2002, the Forum served to launch these processes on the global level.

Two major themes dominated the debate: wealth and democracy (WSF, 2001). Surrounding these questions, intellectual activists and activist intellectuals exchanged visions of the need to preserve public access to humanity's common heritage, extracting it from the logic of the market; to build sustainable cities and habitats; and to redistribute wealth and the means to access it. They also discussed the nature of US political, economic and military hegemony and the architecture of world power; the usefulness of the notion of imperialism and the idea of socialism (debates which had been sidelined by the hegemony of liberal economic thought); gender equality; decentralization of power; guarantees of access to information and the democratization of communication media; and the need for regulating international capital flows, among other themes.

On the other hand, beyond the different points of view, sensibilities and strategies of each social movement, a focus on certain key questions has emerged that underlines the ultimate coherence of the movement and, to some degree, these were expressed in Porto Alegre. Perhaps one might group the concerns into five categories, which, though still relevant, have taken on a rather different complexion in the wake of September 11.

The first examines possible strategies to be developed in the face of the institutions of global power. An example would be the struggle to include social clauses in free trade agreements.

The second goes back to the relation between the social and the political, a question that raises the issue of how to define each of these concepts. From a 'fetishized' perspective, this relationship is usually presented as the tension between social movements on the one hand, and political parties and the state on the other.

The third refers to protest tactics. Opinions range from those defending the indispensability of direct, non-violent action to those advocating more traditional forms of mobilization.

The fourth relates to proposals to change the current concentration of wealth and power at the global level. This includes emphasizing the need for some form of regulation, especially in the finance sector.

The fifth is the ongoing debate surrounding the relationship between local experiences and national protests and the capacity for convergence of the two on an international level.

Porto Alegre introduced, at the beginning of the new millennium, a space for international encounter where social movements and anti-neoliberal politics convened to create the basis for a true parliament of the people. The process of international confluence has been strengthened in Porto Alegre through the declaration entitled *A Social Movements' Manifesto* [see Appendix to this book]. For the first time, a large number of organizations subscribed not only to a list of actions but also to a common set of programmatic goals ranging from the rejection of a sexist, exclusionary and patriarchal system to the demand for total cancellation of the debt; from the insistence on agrarian reform to a condemnation of all privatization; from the defence of workers' rights to the call for abolition of all genetically modified organisms and patents on living organisms. This represents a genuine international manifesto condemning neoliberal globalization.

From Porto Alegre to Genoa: International Convergence and the Vilification of the Movement

Porto Alegre demonstrated the will and ability of this global movement to debate and formulate democratic proposals aimed at building 'another possible world'. The World Social Forum (and the coming together of social movements for the actions of 2001) strengthened protests at the international level. A quick glance at the chronology of international activism between February and August 2001 makes clear the much publicized increase in coordinated action that took place in the spirit of Porto Alegre. Likewise, Latin America witnessed a rise in social conflict tied largely to the continuing devastating impact of neoliberal economic policy and structural adjustment in the region. In numerous cases, the protagonists of these conflicts were social movements that had participated in the Porto Alegre 'spring'.

The repression following the protests in Gothenburg (Sweden) and Barcelona (Catalonia, where the World Bank was forced to cancel its scheduled meeting), like the increase in local and national conflicts, highlighted the change in attitude of national governments and global organizations in response to the growing global discontent. The decision of the governments of the EU (taken immediately after the Gothenburg summit) to coordinate their repressive tactics against this kind of protest was a clear sign of what was to come at the Genoa demonstrations.

The increasing coordination of worldwide protests (itself an expression of an ongoing alternative globalization process) developed in a context marked by a general recession and the slowing of the US economy that had functioned as the engine of globalization over the past decades. This situation, added to the total indifference of international institutions to the demands of the movement, deepened the double crisis described at the beginning of this paper: the crisis of legitimacy of global institutions and the exhaustion of the neoliberal economic model's capacity to guarantee increasing profits for countries at the centre.

The many demonstrations and the Genoa Social Forum that took place during the meeting of the G8 in August 2001 were a new demonstration of the strength of the movement. The answer of those with power was decisive. Following a campaign of preliminary provocation by Silvio Berlusconi's right-wing government, the Italian police, with the complicity of the intelligence services of various European countries, engaged in a wave of repression which culminated in the death of a young man, Carlo Giuliani. The brutal repression in Genoa was a desperate attempt at criminalizing and delegitimating the protests of the democratic movement against neoliberalism. But it was abortive. The Genoa Social Forum found itself legitimated in Italy and elsewhere, and was able to dissociate itself from the violence committed by certain determined groups of protesters. 'If understanding the difficulties that the Genoa Social Forum had to confront seems useful, then understanding its unified functioning and integrative capacity is an example for the next mobilizations.'

Neo-Colonial War and New Challenges for the Movement

The criminal attacks of September 11 and the unilateral war against terrorism declared by the US and allied industrial powers now obscure the Battle of Genoa and its causes. Beyond the enormous challenges that the new situation poses for the movement, it is important to keep in sight the historical background to current events.

War against terrorism is part of a further expansion of the double crisis described above. Resorting to war can be conceived as an attempt at resolving the crisis. In historical terms, however, it constitutes a deepening of the cycle of neocolonial wars initiated by the US and allied Western countries following the fall of the communist regimes (the first Gulf War, the Balkans, Chechnya, conflicts in Africa, etc.).

On the economic level, similar to what occurred throughout most of the twentieth century, resorting to war could be an opportunity to try again a policy that favours deploying the military-industrial complex as a strategy for escaping the economic crisis. On the other hand, the neocolonial occupation of Afghanistan and other neighbouring areas creates a new possibility for controlling important energy sources for capitalist production (petroleum, gas, etc.), and for a chance for new financial investments. US military control of fossil fuels (and of the traffic in Afghan drugs, whose profits are recycled in the international financial system) is without doubt the principal reason for this 'civilizational crusade'. These diverse proceedings hope to find a way out of the economic crisis towards economic growth and further concentration of income and wealth, as the neoliberal model did in past decades. In this context, one must bear in mind the wave of lay-offs by numerous corporations, which has accelerated in both the industrialized countries and the capitalist periphery, and by means of which transnational corporations are attempting, at the cost of their employees, to recapture their competitiveness and regain part of the profits lost during the global crisis.

On the other hand, the absolute priority now being given to

'national security' is an attempt to reassure society through the adoption of increasingly authoritarian measures and restrictions of individual civil rights, in order to legitimate greater state control and the militarization of society.

On a geopolitical level, this post–September 11 situation is doing no more than deepen the tendencies, started in the 1990s, towards an ever-increasing militarization of international relationships that legitimates the neocolonial strength of the great powers, and most importantly, of the United States, and limits the already weakened role of the United Nations as the place to debate and take international decisions. The rapid succession of free market treaties signed in Latin America after the events of September 11, in the wake of the US Congress giving the president 'fast-track' negotiating powers, is a clear expression of the United States' attempt to benefit from the war context in order to consolidate its construction of the Free Trade Area of the Americas. This significantly increases US control of economic, political and military power in the Latin American continent.

The Western crusade against Islamic terrorism and the equation of Western civilizational values and capitalism are a further step towards criminalizing every protest or denunciation of neoliberal capitalism.

The challenges posed by the second World Social Forum in this context give new meaning to the debates and proposals that emerged from the first forum. We will try briefly to present some of these proposals:

1 Barbaric repression by armed police, evident in the recent demonstrations against military intervention in Afghanistan, poses the necessity of renewing international solidarity, rejecting war and affirming peace through a radical and effective democratization. The critical debate on colonial militarism demands finding the links between war and capitalism, whose emergence and development have been so intimately related to the production of wars.

2 On the other hand, the new international situation compels a redefinition of our criticism of international institutions in order to strengthen the World Social Forum as the soil of an alternative to globalization.

3 To strengthen debate and common action on a global scale we must elaborate an emancipatory vision which can transcend the barbarism of those who present the horrible facts as inevitable. We must put aside single national movements since these represent a regression in the growing internationalization of struggle, and instead renew debate on how to articulate the local, national and international arenas as essential perspectives for the movements.

4 Faced by the primacy of national security considerations and the consequent growing acceptance of authoritarian measures, we must debate how to defend public liberties and citizens' rights, which are essential to a radical democratization of social life and its link to the production and distribution of wealth.

5 It is equally necessary to deepen the debate on strategies for the social widening and geographical extension of the movement. Now more than ever, it is necessary to find ways to incorporate all organizations and groups that are not yet stably linked with the movement. This needs a model of how to articulate different organizations sharing a broad common objective that does not suppress differences, debates and disagreements.

6 The movement against neoliberal globalization is linked to the global protests at the meetings of the institutions of world power. The protests in Seattle, Prague, Nice and Genoa are a clear sign of this. The 'masters of the world' have understood this lesson and initiated a strategy of confining these meetings to geographical areas that are difficult for activists to access. Faced with this change in strategy, as evidenced at the most recent WTO meeting in Doha, and with the difficulty of keeping the whole movement visible, it is necessary to build a new agenda of global action for the movement that is not dependent on the schedules of the powerful. The Second World Social Forum is an occasion to deepen the convergence of the movements towards an agenda of renewed action. These are the reasons why we believe it is important to reflect critically on the modalities of action and public intervention in the new context.

Translated by Sonja Pieck

21

THE GLOBAL CIVIL SOCIETY MOVEMENT
(ii) *Conference Synthesis*

VITTORIO AGNOLETTO

Facilitator
Vittorio Agnoletto   GENOA SOCIAL FORUM, ITALY

Conference Leaders
Emilio Taddei   CLACSO, CONSEJO LATINOAMERICANO DE
CIENCIAS SOCIALES (LATIN AMERICAN COUNCIL OF SOCIAL
SCIENCES), ARGENTINA
Joseph Maria Antentas   MOVIMIENTO DE RESISTENCIA
GLOBAL (GLOBAL RESISTANCE MOVEMENT), SPAIN

Discussants
Eduardo Fernandes   COORDINADOR DE LAS CENTRALES
SINDICALES DEL CONO SUR (COORDINATOR OF THE TRADE
UNION HEADQUARTERS OF THE SOUTHERN CONE), URUGUAY
Naomi Klein   CANADA
Suwit Watnoo   FORUM OF THE POOR, THAILAND

Background to the Conference

In the last year the movement against globalization has grown. Spreading all over the world, this growth can be seen in the many regional social forums that took place recently – the Middle East Social Forum in Beirut, the African Social Forum in Bamako and the Pan-Amazonian Social Forum that was held in Belem. In many areas of the world, these movements have become the only real opposition to neoliberal globalization. After Genoa, it became clear that public acceptance of neoliberal policies is steadily declining and governments are more and more resorting to the use of force, repression and war. After September 11, the movement was accused in many countries of being a breeding-ground for terrorism and has been the target of strong repression, for example through new laws restricting civil liberties. Moreover, the war which is officially being waged against terrorism, is in actuality intended to establish US domination around the world in order to control the main energy resources.

The heterogeneity of the movement of the movements, its pluralism, its diverse social composition, alliances and ways of protesting constitute its richness; its convergence around broad programmatic agreements and the implementation of concrete actions does not cancel out these characteristics.

Key Questions

During the seminar, debate centred mainly on the following questions:

- Is it right to compare this 'new' movement to the 'old' movements that characterized past decades?

- What is/should be the relationship between this movement and politics and political parties?

- What are the priorities when choosing concrete methods of carrying out protests?

- What is the relationship between the movement against globalization and workers' organizations and trade unions?

- Is it correct to use the terms 'social movement' and 'civil society' interchangeably? What relationships should the movement have with neoliberal financial institutions (the World Bank, IMF, etc.)?

Leading Actors

Principal social groups that were referred to during the debate were:

- **Young people:** The presence of young people in the movement is important. In some European countries, this represents a reversal of the previous decade when young people, in the name of modernization, were mainly right-wing.

- **Women:** Their presence in the movement has also grown considerably in various geographical areas. Women are often the ones who suffer most from the effects of neoliberal globalization, for example, from the consequences of the privatization of social services and of course, from the effects of war.

- **Workers:** The importance of the full involvement of trade unions in the movement has been stressed, as has the recurring difficulty of involving younger workers, who differ from students.

Relevant Analyses

This movement is not against globalization in the abstract, but rather against a strictly neoliberal-based model of globalization. It must therefore emphasize strongly the concrete nature of its proposals.

The determination to be against war and against terrorism is a fundamental part of this movement.

It is essential to connect local struggles with global aims and perspectives, showing on every occasion the global interdependence of our economies and decisions affecting the environment, etc.

The Argentine situation is the most obvious result of the implementation of neoliberal World Bank and IMF policies and of widespread corruption in the political and business classes. Though this is a consequence of the dictatorship era as well, it stems also from the corruption fuelled by the infiltration of transnational companies, the selling off of public property, and by privatization.

There is no contradiction between the new and the old movement.

In fact, the present movement is a result of what was built in past decades by democratic and workers' movements, in daily life as well as on a cultural level.

Points of Agreement and Disagreement

Consensus

The term 'civil society' appears to be very inadequate and ambiguous. It can even serve as a way to limit the radical nature and the social reach of the movements.

It was noted that the attitude of trade unions towards the movement is very varied, not only in different parts of the world, but also among the various organizations that are present in only one place. A major criticism was made of those trade unions that keep their distance from the movement, as in several European countries and as happened in Genoa. The creation of a strong unified movement of workers against globalization is a fundamental goal.

Nearly Unanimous Consensus

A majority of those present agreed that the movement should be peaceable and non-violent and should practise civil disobedience. However, they reaffirmed that it is the international financial institutions and the most powerful states that carry out far greater violence than any riot could. A system that condemns billions to live in poverty and hundreds of millions of people to die of hunger or preventable illnesses is a structurally violent system.

Divergence

It has been stressed that this is a social movement, but with a strong political character. The relationship with the political powers that be is complex and locally differentiated. In some countries, there is no political party that could be a strong partner, and the movement is the only opposition; in other countries, there are organized political forces that are sympathetic to the movement, but they are small and such parties may need to change their approach. In other regions, there is considerable integration between the movement and political forces. Given this variation, the discussion, rather than centring on the inadequacies of the existing political parties and the centrality of the role of the movement, resulted in some disagreement about the degree of autonomy that should be granted to the movement by political forces and the role of political parties.

There were also differing opinions about the possibility of starting direct negotiations with neoliberal financial institutions such as the World Bank and IMF. Some participants believed that in doing this the movement would run the risk of being co-opted into the decision-making process and would lose its radical nature; others thought that, if concrete results are wanted, negotiations with such institutions cannot be avoided.

Translated by Nicoletta Zampriolio, revised by Frana J. Milan

PART
IV

POLITICAL POWER
& ETHICS
IN THE NEW SOCIETY

OVERVIEW

Key Questions, Critical Issues

WILLIAM F. FISHER AND THOMAS PONNIAH

Key Questions

The key questions in Part IV concern:

- International organizations and the architecture of world power;

- Globalization and militarism;

- The universal nature of human rights;

- Sovereignty, nation, empire;

- Participatory democracy; and

- Principles and values for a civilization of solidarity.

They centre on issues of global economics, human rights, international law and citizenship, the role of civil society and the difficulty of confronting views on neoliberal capitalism held with almost religious fervour. With respect to the global economy, these papers ask how the global economic architecture can be reorganized in light of the present hierarchical system of domination (Bello). Is the alternative a pluralist system of global governance, a World Parliament, global regional assemblies or an emphasis on the development of local institutions? How would a global Tobin Tax be implemented? Is the call by progressives for global governance simply the latest and most sophisticated form of extending Western leftist values? (International Organizations synthesis). The threat of cultural imperialism is matched by neoliberal capitalism's deployment of a 'neo-mercantilist' strategy to revive its economy and its control over key geopolitical regions. The Plan Colombia, the war in Afghanistan and the pursuit of the Free Trade Agreement of the Americas are cases in point and demonstrate that globalization is not just driven by corporations but is also enforced by the most powerful states in the world (Globalization and Militarism synthesis). What strategies must the movement for global justice and solidarity employ to counteract this new strategy? Should the movement shift from a focus on anti-globalization to anti-imperialism?

In terms of human rights, there is no legal infrastructure parallel to the legal infrastructure for economic globalization for the enforcement of the rights that are being violated by neoliberalism. There is a lack of awareness concerning economic, social and cultural rights. How can a permanent forum on these rights in relation to trade, finance and international justice be implemented as part of the United Nations structure? How can non-governmental organizations and social movements work together to establish such a forum? Would it simply set norms or request voluntary compliance? If the former, who will enforce its implementation? If the latter, how can its presence be more than symbolic? Could citizens use this forum to pressure their own states to abide by international commitments (Human Rights synthesis document)? How would such a forum respond to 'economic terrorism' or to the debt as an instrument of domination?

Corresponding to the lack of effective global rights machinery are the questions of how international law and citizenship should be articulated in light of the weakness of the current inter-state system, the rise of ethnic nationalism and the uneven emergence of a new global system. In a transitional era, international decisions are determined by the most powerful and not by a legal system. 'The right to interfere' becomes the law in reality. How do we conceptualize this transition? Is the solution a return to the ideals of national sovereignty? How should citizenship be framed in our age? Should it be nationally based, ethnically based or should we simply have global citizenship (Bensaid)?

How should civil society respond to the dilemmas of the reign of both the market and the state over society? The commodity as the essence of society satisfies neither human nor spiritual needs. Progress cannot be based on the social increase of consumption. The market cannot be the pole around which society revolves, yet neither can the state. The latter's inevitable bureaucratization has generated apathy and supplication to authority (Parameswaran). What procedures need to be established in order to overcome the limits of capitalism and statism? How can citizens move from being spectators who are dependent on elite-dominated institutions to becoming agents of change who construct their own institutions?

Last, in terms of principles and values, how do we confront a civilization that religiously believes in quantification, capital and the market? How do we confront a society that wants to transform the whole world into a commodity? How do we respond to a world whose dominant values are the dollar, the yen and the euro? What values are needed to build an alternative civilization of solidarity, that is, 'a world that can hold many worlds' (Löwy and Betto; Amorós)?

Critical Issues

The debates inherent in the papers of Part IV reflect some of the most critical divergences in the world movement: (1) the conflict between those who aspire to a reformed Bretton Woods system versus those who believe in a pluralist form of global governance; (2) civil society's relationship to the state and other institutions; and (3) the challenge of creating new values as counters to the neoliberal civilization.

Walden Bello forcefully argues that a pluralist system of global governance, a 'deglobalization', is preferable to the current hier-archical, monolithic structure of the International Monetary Fund, the World Bank and the World Trade Organization. Against the reformers' desire to salvage the potentially useful part of the inter-national financial institutions, Bello points out that the Global South experienced greater economic development between 1950 and 1970 than it did during the last 30 years under the expanded mandate of the Bretton Woods institutions. Therefore he argues for the strengthening of numerous other institutions in order to create a decentralized global order. Perhaps the solution to this contradiction between reformers and radicals is to continue to focus on delegitimating the current incarnation of the three global monoliths yet simultaneously strengthening other regional and international players such as the International Labour Organization (ILO) and the United Nations Conference on Trade and Development (UNCTAD), and creating new democratic institutions that can challenge entrenched power.

A second conflict, related to the one outlined above, has to do with civil society's relationship to the state, the inter-state system, international institutions and corporations. On the one hand, civil society is seen as a partner to these institutions, while on the other it is seen as the agent that should monitor the state to ensure that government enforces human rights behaviour on the part of other political-economic agents. Thus, on one side, it is wished that civil society is an equal partner at the negotiating table, whereas on the other side civil society is the prime player. The capacity to maintain this contradiction will allow human rights organizations to build a broad level of support for their discourse. Whether they will be successful in enforcing the actual implementation of human rights is less certain.

Civil society is perceived by many movements as separate from the state. In this view, civil society embodies participatory democracy against the 'supplicatory' democracy produced by both market and state ideologies (Parameswaran). It is the citizenry organizing itself locally, daily, and autonomously because the state is inherently oppressive. The documents do not explain how movements will convince the state or capital to allow for their autonomous development nor do they consider that the autonomy they are given is precisely to help them fill the gaps in service delivery that the state no longer aspires to fulfil. In addition, the conception of the state as an inefficient behemoth that serves the needs of the elite ignores the very concrete social benefits advanced by progressive states, like Kerala and the Scandinavian countries.

The third key conflict concerns alternative values countering the homogenization enacted by 'globo-colonization' (Löwy and Betto). In terms of an alternative ethics of development, these two authors propose an ethical system that brings together many of the themes in the other documents. Surprisingly, they call upon a Western and historically patriarchal scale of values ('liberty, equality, fraternity') to define the global movement, despite the fact that these values were devised precisely when the West began to colonize the rest of the world. In fact these values were often used to legitimate imperialism and sexism (Bhabha 1994: 66–85, Amorós). On the one hand, if 'liberty, equality, fraternity' are taken as the defining principles and values of a new civilization, then it is a project that is doomed to failure, precisely because of the resistance it will encounter from anti-imperialist radicals and many feminists who understand the importance of decolonizing the Northern and Southern imagination. On the other hand, if this document is taken as the first step towards opening a dialogue that will include movements and theorists, women and men, from all over the world in an effort to build universal values via a globally democratic process, then the appeal to past principles that have influenced all radicals over the past 200 years is an invaluable beginning towards the articulation of a new society. The ethical challenge of constructing universal values that simultaneously value difference constitutes the central dilemma in fashioning a new set of principles against those of our current civilization of numbers, money and the market.

These arguments for a pluralist governance against one overarching system, for a participatory democracy that grows out of civil society, and for a new civilization of solidarity that embraces diversity, imply an alternative form of development that encompasses an experimental conception of liberty. Freedom, in this definition, does not lie in certainty but rather in liberating ourselves from preconceived solutions. This attitude is a response to the fundamentalism of neo-liberalism and of the former Soviet Union. The notion that one size or strategy should fit all is rejected in this discussion and in most of the forum's conferences. That said, the implicit ethics of this set of documents do not collapse into relativism: the various members of the conferences and participants at the second World Social Forum do agree on the need for the universal application of human rights that can include the development of new planetary values. The key to the development of new values lies in the capacity to produce democratic processes and institutions that will allow for a genuinely international or global dialogue that will articulate a 'universalism of difference'.

22

THE INTERNATIONAL ARCHITECTURE OF POWER

(i) *International Organizations and the Architecture of World Power*

WALDEN BELLO
(FOCUS ON THE GLOBAL SOUTH)

Proposal for a Pluralistic System of Global Economic Governance

There is a crying need for an alternative system of global governance. We disagree with the view that thinking about an alternative system of global governance is a task that for the most part is still in a primitive state. In fact, we feel that many or most of the basic or broad principles for an alternative order are already with us, and it is really a question of applying these broad principles to concrete societies in ways that respect the diversity of societies.

Work on alternatives has been a collective past and present effort, one to which many, North and South, have contributed. Allow us to synthesize the key points of this collective effort under the rubric 'deglobalization'. While the following model addresses principally the situation of countries in the South, many points have relevance as well to societies and economies in the North.

What is Deglobalization?

We are not talking about withdrawing from the international economy. We are speaking about reorienting our economies away from the emphasis on production for export and towards production for the local market. This is all about:

- Drawing most of our financial resources for development from within rather than becoming dependent on foreign investment and foreign financial markets;

- Carrying out the long-postponed measures of income redistribution and land redistribution to create a vibrant internal market that would be the anchor of the economy;

- De-emphasizing growth and maximizing equity in order radically to reduce environmental disequilibrium;

- Not leaving strategic economic decisions to the market but making them subject to democratic choice;

- Subjecting the private sector and the state to constant monitoring by civil society;

- Creating a new production and exchange complex that includes community cooperatives, private enterprises, and state enterprises, and excludes TNCs;

- Enshrining the principle of subsidiarity in economic life by encouraging production of goods to take place at the community and national levels, if it can be done at reasonable cost in order to preserve community.

We are talking, moreover, about a strategy that consciously subordinates the logic of the market and the pursuit of cost efficiency to the values of security, equity and social solidarity. We are speaking, to use the language of the great social democratic scholar Karl Polanyi, about re-embedding the economy in society, rather than letting society be driven by the economy.

Pluralist Global Governance

Deglobalization, or the re-empowerment of the local and national, however, can only succeed if it takes place within an alternative system of global economic governance. What are the contours of such a world economic order? The answer to this is contained in our critique of the Bretton Woods-cum-WTO system as a monolithic system of universal rules imposed by highly centralized institutions to further the interests of corporations and, in particular, US corporations. To try to supplant this with another centralized global system of rules and institutions, even though these may be premised on different principles, is likely to reproduce the same Jurassic trap that ensnared organizations as different as IBM, the IMF and the Soviet state, and this is their inability to tolerate and profit from diversity. Incidentally, the idea that the need for one central set of global rules is unquestionable and that the challenge is to replace the neoliberal rules with social democratic ones is a remnant of a techno-optimist variant of Marxism that infused both the Social Democratic and Leninist visions of the world, producing what the Indian author Arundhati Roy calls the predilection for gigantism.

Today's need is not for another centralized global institution but the de-concentration and decentralization of institutional power and the creation of a pluralistic system of institutions and organizations interacting with one another, guided by broad and flexible agreements and understandings.

We are not talking about something completely new. For it was under such a more pluralistic system of global economic governance, where hegemonic power was still far from institutionalized in a set of all-encompassing and all-powerful multilateral organizations and institutions, that a number of Latin American and Asian countries were able to achieve a modicum of industrial development in the period from 1950 to 1970. It was under such a pluralistic system, under a General Agreement on Tariffs and Trade (GATT) that was limited in its power, flexible, and more sympathetic to the special status of developing countries, that the East and Southeast Asian countries were able to become newly industrializing countries through activist state trade and industrial policies that departed significantly from the free-market biases enshrined in the WTO.

Of course, economic relations among countries prior to the

attempt to institutionalize one global free market system beginning in the early 1980s were not ideal, nor were the Third World economies that resulted ideal. They failed to address a number of needs illuminated by recent advances in feminist, ecological, and post-post-development economics. All we wish to point out here is that the pre-1994 situation underlines the fact that the alternative to an economic Pax Romana built around the World Bank–IMF–WTO system is not a Hobbesian State of Nature. All we want to stress is that the reality of international relations in a world marked by a multiplicity of international and regional institutions that check one another is a far cry from the propaganda image of a 'nasty' and 'brutish' world. Of course, the threat of unilateral action by the powerful is ever present in such a system, but it is one that even the most powerful hesitated to take for fear of its consequences on their legitimacy as well as the reaction it would provoke in the form of opposing coalitions.

In other words, what developing countries and international civil society should aim at is not to reform the TNC-driven WTO and Bretton Woods institutions, but, through a combination of passive and active measures, to either (a) decommission them; (b) neutralize them (e.g., converting the IMF into a purely research institution monitoring exchange rates and global capital flows); or (c) radically reduce their powers and turn them into just another set of actors coexisting with and being checked by other international organizations, agreements, and regional groupings. This strategy would include strengthening such diverse actors and institutions as UNCTAD, multilateral environmental agreements, the ILO, and evolving economic blocs such as Mercosur in Latin America, SAARC in South Asia, SADCC in Southern Africa and a revitalized ASEAN in Southeast Asia.[1] A key aspect of 'strengthening', of course, is making sure these formations evolve in a people-oriented direction and cease to remain regional elite projects.

But above all, it would support the formation of new international and regional institutions that would be dedicated to creating and protecting the space for devolving the greater part of production, trade and economic decision-making to the national and local levels. The principal role of international organizations in a world where toleration of diversity is a central principle of economic organization would be, as the British philosopher John Gray puts it, 'to express and protect local and national cultures by embodying and sheltering their distinctive practices'.

More space, more flexibility, more compromise – these should be the goals of the Southern agenda and the international civil society effort to build a new system of global economic governance. It is in such a more fluid, less structured, more pluralistic world, with multiple checks and balances, that the nations and communities of the South – and the North – will be able to carve out the space they need to develop, based on their own values, their own rhythms and the strategies of their own choice.

Note

1   UNCTAD (United Nations' Conference on Trade and Development), SAARC (South Asian Association for Regional Cooperation), SADCC (Southern African Development Coordination Conference), and ASEAN (Association of Southeast Asian Nations).

22 THE INTERNATIONAL ARCHITECTURE OF POWER
(ii) *Conference Synthesis*

TEIVO TEIVAINEN

A background paper [see the previous paper in this volume] was prepared and presented by Walden Bello. The panel was also composed of Susan George, ATTAC, France; Peter Wahl, WEED; Aurelio Vianna, Rede Brasil sobre Instituições Financeiras Multilaterais; and Roberto Bissio, Social Watch. Maude Barlow, from the Council of Canadians, participated as a discussant. The Conference chair and facilitator was Teivo Teivainen, Network for Global Democratization.

Questions Prepared by the Facilitator

At the request of the World Social Forum Organizing Committee, the facilitator had prepared a page of questions which was distributed to the panellists before the conference and is reproduced here:

If we want to create a different world, we have to imagine and construct the institutional features of alternative futures. First, we need to ask to what extent existing institutions can be reformed. And to what extent we need to create new global or transnational institutions. What could they be like? How can they avoid what Walden Bello calls the Jurassic trap, the inability to tolerate and benefit from diversity?

Assuming that the institutions of the world we want to create should be as democratic as possible, the question of applying democratic principles in global and transnational contexts is one of the most important ones we face. What could democracy mean in global governance?

What are the limits of the 'one country, one vote' principle? What would applying 'one person, one vote' on a global level mean? Is, for example, the idea of a popularly controlled global parliament feasible? Is it desirable? If not, what is? Global civil society assemblies? Or should we rather aim at democratic regional institutions with no global structures?

One theme that many of the organizations gathered in Porto Alegre consider important is a tax on foreign currency trading, often called the Tobin Tax. It is, however, not sufficiently debated what kind of institution(s) should administer the tax. The IMF, as originally proposed by James Tobin? The UN? A new transnational institution – a currency transactions tax organization – with radically democratic decision-making principles?

These questions are also related to a basic question of political semantics. Is it analytically accurate and politically useful to define the organizations and movements gathered together in Porto Alegre as being against globalization, if the term is understood as the increasing transgression of nation-state borders on a worldwide level? Or is it rather that many of the organizations are looking for a *different* kind of globalization, perhaps formulated in the language of internationalism? Is deglobalization, as proposed by Walden Bello, an effective term to describe the aims of the movements?

It is frequently assumed in debates about globalization that being 'anti' globalization represents a more radical and revolutionary option, whereas those that aim at 'alternative' globalization are on the side of more superficial reforms. Is this assumption really helpful? Should we take into account that, while anti-globalization people can be pro-capitalist, pro-globalization people may be anti-capitalist?

While I am certainly in favour of aiming at radical transformations in the global space, the kind of cosmopolitanism of this attitude needs to be analysed also in cultural terms. To what extent are models of global democracy products of Western modernity, implying cultural imperialism or neocolonialism? Definitive answers are not easy to find, but it is time to start asking meaningful and concrete questions about what kinds of institutions we want to struggle for.

Proposals

This conference theme covered a huge terrain: the future of global governance. Correspondingly, the nature of the proposals was not as concrete and clearly defined as in many other WSF conferences dealing with more specific topics. Some key proposals were, however, presented. The dynamics of the debate allowed us to explore the different proposals critically and come to some provisional conclusions, though by no means a total consensus, on certain basic issues.

One of the main ideas of the conference and the way the debates were conducted was to emphasize differences and possible contradictions between different proposals. In the spirit of critical solidarity some lines of creative tension between the proposals were discussed. The idea was that people who share similar radically democratic aspirations should learn to debate openly and honestly.

For reasons of insufficient space these remarks cannot include all the lines of our rich debate. I shall focus first on two controversial proposals and then on more consensual themes. One of them was the main proposal of the background paper; the other emerged more from the audience and was extensively commented on by the panel.

Controversial Proposal 1: Deglobalization

Walden Bello's paper included a general proposal for a pluralistic system of global economic governance. The key term to describe his proposed strategy was deglobalization. This term created some controversy in the panel and also in the comments from the public. It was pointed out that it might be better to use less reactive terms. The political semantics around this term were recognized and commented on by various panellists.

While some disagreement on the usefulness of this term certainly remained, there was an understanding that those of us who use the terminology of anti-globlization or deglobalization can learn to work together with those who would prefer to use the language of alternative globalizations. Most also agreed that concepts are often specific to particular contexts and therefore it may not be wise to try to impose specific concepts to describe the overall aims of different movements. I felt that using terminology like 'globalization from below' got more expressions of support than using 'deglobalization', but there was no clear consensus on this issue. Most of the substantial points of Walden Bello's proposal, including decommissioning, neutralizing or radically reducing the powers of the Bretton Woods institutions, raised much less controversy than the terminological issue.

Controversial Proposal 2: World Parliament

The audience brought up various proposals. The one most often mentioned was the idea of a world parliament or some other democratically constituted global assembly. The idea was sometimes presented as part of a United Nations reform plan. These proposals did not receive overwhelming support either. Some of the panellists felt that because the objective conditions for establishing global democratic institutions do not yet exist, discussing issues like a world parliament was an unnecessary, even a harmful waste of time and energy for the movements. Panellists also raised some doubts as to the possibility of global democratic institutions on the grounds that democracy is only possible in relatively small communities.

The idea of a global parliamentary institution was more easily accepted as a long-term goal rather than a realistic plan for the movement's short-term concerns. However, Peter Wahl described it as a 'negative utopia', on the grounds that democracy on a worldwide scale is not possible and would only result in the creation of a global 'Leviathan'. Aurelio Vianna, along with most panellists, also pointed out that, even if one focuses on questions of global or transnational democracy, the role of the nation-state as an important space for democratic struggles should not be overlooked.

Points of Convergence

But some more consensual themes also emerged. Beyond the disagreements on the feasibility of global democratic institutions, organizing in the national context was still seen as important by most participants. Regional institutions could also play a role as an arena for democratic struggles, though it was pointed out that many of the existing structures of regional integration such as NAFTA are even more regressive than related global institutions.

The need for global rules was most clearly emphasized by Susan George, and even those who were sceptical of the vision of new centralized global institutions did not reject this need. Human rights, as emphasized by Roberto Bissio, was one area where nobody disagreed on the need for some global rules. Susan George also took up the need for global taxation. With rapidly declining official development aid and the increasing need for money for various, often global, purposes, developing global taxes was imperative. This point created no major controversies and seems to have been approved by the conference as a whole.

To sum up, there was some consensus that some global rules and corresponding institutions were needed in areas such as human rights and global taxation. This does not mean that we need a centralized world state. Quite the contrary: the principle of subsidiarity, according to which decision-making should be kept as close to the people as possible, was an essential point of convergence among the participants.

The exact nature and feasibility of global institutions is a theme that most panellists were unwilling to focus on in any specific detail. The debate was sometimes too premised on the idea that the only way to establish global democracy is through a simplistic idea of a world parliament. In my view, we clearly need more political imagination when we start talking about establishing some democratic rules for transnational and global issues. One of the challenges for future debates is to focus more on the concrete details of alternative possible institutional arrangements. If we want a radically democratized world to be possible, we also need to construct some democratic criteria on the basis of which different global governance proposals can be assessed.

Agents of Change

For a theme as overwhelming as the future of world power structures, the question of the agents of change is not easy. The role of the World Social Forum itself was pointed out as an important arena where different movements and other actors can create common strategies. It was also recognized that there is a need to get mass-based movements, including organized workers, to participate in the debates of the forum.

23 MILITARISM AND GLOBALIZATION
Conference Synthesis

MARCELA ESCRIBANO

Presenters
James Petras USA
Claude Serfati UNIVERSITY OF ST-QUENTIN-EN-YVELINES,
FRANCE

Moderator
Marcela Escribano ALTERNATIVES, CANADA

Discussants
Lily Traubman WOMEN IN BLACK, ISRAEL
Hector Mondragón ADVISOR TO THE NATIONAL RURAL
WORKERS COUNCIL (CONSEJO NACIONAL CAMPESINO),
COLOMBIA
Alfredo Wagner BRAZILIAN ANTHROPOLOGY ASSOCIATION
(ASSOCIAÇÃO BRASILEIRA DE ANTROPOLOGIA), BRAZIL
Dianne Luping LAW–SOCIETY, PALESTINE

The Central Question of the Conference

How and why do neoliberal globalization and domination by financial
capital cause increased insecurity and require an increase in militarism
to maintain their control?

James Petras

The decade of the 1990s marked the beginning of a plan to achieve US domination of the entire world, particularly in the Persian Gulf region.

The recent aggression in Afghanistan is part of a general offensive intended to impose unchallengeable US hegemony. It involves constructing an alliance with Europe by invoking as a pretext a global campaign against terrorism, a campaign that is in fact directed from within the United States, in response to its requirements of maintaining an internal political consensus. The US attack on Afghanistan represents an effort to reverse the trend of the relative decline of empire and to re-establish American dominion in a volatile area of the world. This is just one aspect of a broader offensive. The most obvious components of this general offensive are the following:

- Re-establishing the subordination of Europe to Washington.

- Reaffirming total US control in the Far East and the Persian Gulf region.

- Deepening and broadening US military intervention in Latin American and Asia.

- Intensifying the war in Colombia and extending US power to the rest of the continent.

- Reducing and repressing protest and opposition to the power of multinational corporations (MNCs) and the international financial institutions (IFIs), such as the World Bank, the International Monetary Fund, and the World Trade Organization, which are replacing democratic rights with dictatorial power.

- Putting state resources into the arms industry and subsidies to save multinational corporations (such as airlines, insurance companies and travel agencies, etc.) from virtual bankruptcy. The US has also implemented regressive taxation changes in order to limit a deep recession, which could undermine popular support for the project of the construction of empire.

The massive post-September 11 propaganda campaign magnified and distorted the nature of the attacks on the Twin Towers and the Pentagon, in an effort to create a global political consensus against 'terrorism' that would legitimate military action. The exhaustion of the model and a crisis of legitimacy are the true antecedents of the world crisis, for which September 11 serves merely as a point of reference.

From September 11 through the month of October 2001 the United States moved forward with preparing its forces for war and for the military offensive of its foreign policy. The paradox is that, despite its attacks, there has been no response of any kind on the part of the 'fanatical terrorists', including the presumed terrorists fleeing from Afghanistan itself. More importantly, the videos have shown only bin Laden's approval of the actions of September 11, but in no way do they demonstrate his participation or that of the al-Qaida network in those attacks. The group in question appears to be more an autonomous grouping. Nevertheless, without tangible proof, the US claimed to have valid cause for mounting an unlimited war of aggression. It can thus be deduced that the exhaustion of the model and a legitimization crisis are the true antecedents of the world crisis – for which September 11 simply serves as a reference point for precipitating the implementation of a plan that had already been designed prior to those events.

In the US, a political transition is occurring – from the liberal model to a neo-mercantilist model that is imperial in character, one which aspires to control completely the area of the world that provides it with the most profits and security, Latin America. The intervention in Colombia continues to deepen the imperial penetration of the continent in order to make this transition from a liberal to a mercantilist model by using the FTAA. The latter is a treaty that strengthens the US's hegemonic presence in Latin America, monopolizing all international trade in its own hands, excluding sectors of the exporting middle bourgeoisie. The latter is reserved the right to have export quotas, as in the case of Brazil. In practice, the

FTAA treaty is a return to the eighteenth century, with implementation of unilateral actions of all kinds, a total neo-mercantilism.

In reality we are facing a situation of permanent warfare, especially
in Latin America. This military definition of the current situation is
reflected in top-down decisions that are dividing the world in two:
those who are with us and those who are against us. On the basis of
this logic, the CIA (Central Intelligence Agency) can carry out
assassinations, contract bandits on its pay roll, provoke attacks such as
those that ensued in Brazil with the killing of the Workers' Party
mayors, and the boycott against Chavez in Venezuela in response to
his independence from the foreign policy of the United States. Even
though everyone knows that the government of Venezuela is
internally implementing a liberal model, it opposes Plan Colombia. It
is especially noteworthy that when Chavez affirmed after the events of
September 11 that 'one cannot respond to terrorism with terrorism', a
Washington official remarked, 'The Venezuelans will pay a very high
price for saying that'. The FARC (Revolutionary Armed Forces of
Colombia) are the most important military and political force in
South America opposing imperialism, and thus the US must attack in
Colombia. (It would seem that the organizers of the World Social
Forum have accepted the US version to the effect that the FARC are
terrorists and cannot be present at this event.)

To maintain the war in Colombia, it is imperative that an imperial
state be maintained; and in a context of profound economic crisis, we
can only count on the United States with Latin America to relieve this
crisis. Between $200 billion and $500 billion enter the US as a result
of money laundering, drug trafficking and capital flight with the
support of private banks based on ties with military and banking
circles in Latin American countries.

In any case, in Argentina, despite a search for political agreements,
it has been impossible to control the crisis. The crisis is also reflected in
other countries, where the mobilization of popular movements
enables us to predict volatile situations that will be difficult to defuse.
Because it has not suffered great setbacks in the last 25 years the left

can intervene in the current crisis produced by the exhaustion of the model. There is a potential for proposals arising from the left if it is capable of going beyond the struggle for reform. The progress in Argentina made by both the Socialist Workers' Party and other popular movements can serve as a stimulus, as models to be considered. We on the left have the capacity to intervene in the economic crisis if we make clear proposals.

Claude Serfati

The militarization of the international sphere is the product of the neoliberal model, a hopeless model that leaves in its wake only more death and devastation. Under these circumstances it is the United States that most benefits from the current crisis. More importantly, in the United States there is neither concern about nor interest in the consequences and negative repercussions of its foreign policy. It will be US and European experts reflecting vital US interests who will legitimate armed interventions in defence of globalization. Today we are all aware that petroleum will be decisive in this sense, but in strategic terms the defence of the market and of financial capital will be critical as well. The FTAA represents a violation of the people's human rights in Latin America, but the United States sees rejection of the FTAA as equivalent to opposition to globalization, and it is prepared to intervene directly, or through local forces of repression, in order to counter this opposition. The Argentine case could be one of the first instances of such interventions. It must be noted, finally, that the defence of globalization is the result of a meeting in Washington, from which Europe emerged as an auxiliary force subordinate to the US.

The NATO (North Atlantic Treaty Organization) coalition and the terrorist attacks of September 11, 2001 contributed to the accelerated militarization of the globe, as the US military budget is increased by another $40 billion. This increase in the budget, which had been rejected before September 11, found rapid approval following that date. The budget increases resources, including those to be used against Iraq, and expands military technology to defend the neoliberal economic model and private property. Ever since World War Two, the US defence budget has been increased with the consistent objective of defending imperial enterprise in the different phases of development.

The new objectives of American security policy support the manufacturing of weapons of mass destruction, with half the world's arms exports coming from the United States. The US is also prepared to use chemical and biological weapons against other nations, including such countries as Colombia and Ecuador. The international protocol on biological weapons is regarded as inapplicable to the armed forces of the United States, given its apocalyptic vision of the world, and US leaders are prepared to do whatever might be necessary to defend their dominance. They are also preparing themselves to repress those who protest in the streets. The US Air Force and Marines are preparing for the defence of financial capital worldwide.

The attacks of September 11 have resulted in legislation in Europe and North America in response to the 'terrorist attacks'. This has caused strong criticism because of the violation of civil liberties as a result. Neoliberal globalization creates chaos and poverty but defends the exploitation and peace of the market. It is precisely for this reason that it feels justified in making war both outside and within national borders.

We are experiencing a new militarization of the world, propelled by the US, which has converted itself into the world's new sole hegemonic power. But the liberty that the US is defending is its freedom to trade and to exploit natural resources. It is the principal beneficiary of globalization. Maintaining the stability of the global system of trade and financial networks enhances its need for national security. The FTAA and the WTO consider that a country's refusal to open up its borders to US products is a violation of the freedom of international trade and of the vital interests of the US. NATO is the guardian of this new world disorder and serves as a cover for North

American intervention. Peacekeeping! The international community is in fact imposing a new form of colonization on countries in difficulty!

The increase in the US defence budget will allow all the military plans for new weapons systems etc. that were once in question to proceed and a new military-industrial complex to develop in alliance with the financial system, the objective being to increase the profits of stockholders. The proliferation of weapons of mass destruction is the fruit not of globalization but of the powerful countries themselves. The US refuses to sign protocols providing for the destruction of chemical and bacteriological weapons. It is preparing to intervene, in the form of urban warfare, against anti-globalization groups. It will consider any act of urban violence to be terrorism along with the usual forms of struggle used by popular movements. Neoliberal organization is producing growing economic and social violence: if the prosperity of the dominant elite is to be assured, the ownership of capital must be maintained.

Lily Traubman

The violence in Israel has been structural since its birth: rooted in a nation-state, protected by an army based on Jewish national identity, and constructed to defend the State of Israel. The army is the people in uniform. The fact that there is no effective separation between civilian and military influences the entire society. Militarization expands militarism throughout society. Everyone participates in the army: three years for men, eighteen months for women. And for men, military service continues every year for one month until the age of 45. The army even has its own very popular radio station!

Security is a central aspect of daily life. Combatants occupy the top echelons of Israeli society. The army symbolizes all that is best in Israeli manhood. Continual conflict takes place under the shadow of the Holocaust: the belief that everyone is against us. Military spending is necessary, because war is always imminent. We are not responsible for this situation! It is the Palestinians who draw us into it. Militarism reinforces masculinity and violence against women, who are regarded as passive and in need of protection. Women are silenced and kept far away from sites of decision-making.

Women in Black and the Women's Coalition for Peace were the first to demonstrate in opposition to this militarism – 5,000 women ignored by the press. This reflects the degradation of humanistic values which are no longer considered legitimate, the disregarding of women, and the marginalization of non-violent action. Militarism is close to racism. The slaughter of 'others' is unimportant; there is always a justification for it.

The use of American-provided weaponry is very much in evidence. Israel receives $840 million in US military aid per year, a total of some $84 billion since 1949 (three-quarters of this for buying North American arms). Non-violent movements like Fathers Against Silence respond by advocating the demilitarization of society, and call on men and women not to go into the army. With demilitarization, the end of the occupation would finally be possible. But to date, negotiations between Israelis and Palestinians have been focused only on security and not on such equally essential issues as poverty, inequality, cooperation and the equitable distribution of resources.

Hector Mondragón

Why is there violence in Latin America? What US interests are being promoted by it? Why does the US want to extend its domination in Latin America? Drug trafficking and guerrilla warfare are consequences of the violence, rather than its causes. The violence itself dates back to the nineteenth century, to the expulsion and even extermination of thousands of peasants to make way for the rubber, petroleum, sugar, and cotton whose beneficiaries were the large landholders (a mere 6,000 persons, of whom 70 per cent were members of Congress, and who held almost half of the land in the country). Today many small farmers have no other alternative but to produce coca. Plan Colombia promotes the destruction of the forest, leaving the land in the hands of the big landowners. As the saying goes, 'Development is possible only with the expulsion of the peasants'.

In the year 2000, the United States approved $1.3 billion in additional aid to fund Plan Colombia. Some 83 per cent of these funds is dedicated to military purposes, primarily helicopters. But Plan Colombia has deeper purposes than selling helicopters: among them is petroleum.

As an oil-producing country, Ecuador is among those discussed in an article by US Senator Paul Coverdell (Republican). He argues that an organized and influential indigenous people's movement, in alliance with the unions and the Bolivian military, is seeking to govern the country, and that this is a threat to the multinationals and local Latin American *caciques*.

There is also the Andean Regional Initiative, for which another $700 million is being provided. The United States military base in Manta (Ecuador) and the bases in Dutch controlled Aruba and Curaçao are tools for preparing for war not only in Colombia, but also in Venezuela and Ecuador. And allegedly because of the need to replace the bases in Panama, Latin American countries are now required to accept 'visiting troops' from the United States, which they accept under the pretext that they will be helping to build highways and schools.

Deepening this militaristic drive, advisors to President Bush recommended to him last April (2001) to pursue the 1964 method [encouraging a military takeover] in Brazil, because he who controls Brazil controls South America. In Brazil, the Workers' Party (PT) had won the elections in the year 2000 with a one-third share of the vote in municipal elections, including the city of São Paulo, the largest in the country, while another opposition party, the Labour Party (victim of the 1964 coup) won the mayorship of Rio. It is clear that the PT could well win the next presidential elections while the Landless Workers peasant movement (MST) is more active and stronger with each election. Nor is Washington pleased that the current government of Brazil does not accept its proposal to advance the conclusion of the

Free Trade of the Americas Agreement (FTAA) from 2005 to 2003 and that Brazil insists – along with Venezuela – on strengthening Mercosur. The Pastrana government, on the other hand, has wanted the FTAA ever since the year 2000.

If neoliberalism arrived originally in Latin America in General Pinochet's boots, the proposed FTAA is seeking entry in the helicopters of Plan Colombia. In Paraguay there are already several dozen different military units from the United States supposedly on training and assistance missions. In reality, they aim to control not only the spirited Paraguayan peasant movement, but also Brazil, Argentina and the whole Mercosur region, in the heart of which they are stationed. The armies of Argentina, Paraguay, Uruguay and Chile are training in preparation for invading Colombia, while Argentina, amidst its own crisis, has accepted the installation of a US base for conducting 'nuclear research' in Tierra del Fuego.

Today, popular activism is increasing on the continent. The popular *argentinazo* rebellion signifies a forceful repudiation, by the masses, of the model imposed upon them in that country. In Bolivia, peasants paralysed urban centers with a large blockade that finally forced the Banzer government to backpedal on the privatization of water and negotiate about the eradication of the coca fields. Now they confront troops sent in by Quiroga. Earlier, miners armed with dynamite had occupied La Paz, and later other unions, supported by the middle classes, launched a general strike, which also obliged Banzer to negotiate. Also part of this scene of popular movements in Latin America is the indigenous people's uprising in Mexico.

The principal objective of Plan Colombia is allegedly the destruction of illegal coca fields by means of fumigation. In fact, fumigation, far from having eliminated all the illegal fields, resulted in an increase in the area sown with coca and poppies in 1999; although 16,000 hectares were destroyed, 38,000 new hectares were sown. The next year (2000), after another 30,000 hectares were destroyed, the fields increased yet again to some 60,000 hectares. We predict that illegal exports will continue to increase.

In reality, then, Plan Colombia has so exacerbated social conflict in the region that it threatens to engulf all South America in the conflict as a result of the US's irresponsible, militaristic adventure. Why does this Plan and its accompanying violence affect Colombia so much? The reason is that there exists in the country a regime that is stamping out social and political opposition. The regime is the product of a long history of violence that is closely correlated to the concentration of land ownership. The violence did not begin with the drug trafficking, but much earlier. Nor did it begin with the guerrilla movement, which was itself the product of violence on the part of the state: during the civil war (called *La Violencia*) from 1948 to 1958, two million peasants were displaced from their land, and 200,000 persons killed. At the same time, the sugar-cane plantations were extended in the department of the Valle del Cauca, the region which saw the largest numbers of peasants displaced (some 500,000) and in El Tolima, the department with the second largest number of displaced peasants, cotton production quintupled. This was truly a blood and fire model of 'development'. The regime that exists in Columbia today is based on a model of social and political genocide, a kind of 'genocidal democracy'.

Alfredo Wagner

Militarization of the Amazon region is being discussed as if it benefited the common good. It is necessary to carve out territory, to achieve domination redefining the concepts of national security and regional identities in the process. Only a new system of control can guarantee monopoly of the land, bioresources, minerals and water, and even outer space.

Satellite launches from an equatorial orbit reduce the fuel required by a third. A treaty with the US allows for entry into the country of containers that cannot be inspected and for rocket equipment under the sole supervision of American troops. It is not to be assumed that national sovereignty is in opposition to imperialism; in an empire sovereignties are transnational.

There are 20,000 persons living around the site of the Alcantara launch pad (six times the size of the Cuju base in Dutch Guyana); more than 300 families (black Quilombos) have already been expelled despite the fact that, under the terms of the constitution, their lands should be deeded to them forever since they have been free since 1778. The occupation of this land for the construction of the launch pad is an effort to destroy these peoples, as well as indigenous peoples.

Since 1990, the military's commercial ventures have expanded to include mining, genetic-resources and aerospace. While coercion on the part of the US is clearly evident, it is not only the Americans but Europeans as well who are engaged in this coercive activity. Let us work against such a global coalition of interests.

Dianne Luping

Democratic countries have recently enacted new laws that infringe civil rights. In Palestine, national security and the so-called war on terrorism are used to justify military occupation. In many other countries we are also witnessing a rise in violations of essential rights committed in the name of national security. The apartheid that the Palestinian people are experiencing is similar to that experienced in South Africa. It includes the expropriation of land and, in the end, denationalization. Palestinians living in the Occupied Territories are without basic citizenship rights – living in separate, isolated zones, ruled over by Israeli courts and curfews, and are the victims of propaganda intended to demonize the population.

Proposals

1 Campaign to end US military aid to Israel.

2 Campaign to support young people who refuse to go into the Israeli army (and go to prison as a result).

3 Support the call for international observers in Israel and Palestine.

4 Use the World Social Forum to prepare a plan to combat the US plans for strategic domination. Support popular struggles in Colombia, while trying to halt the genocidal democracy that exists there today.

5 The left has opportunities to act in the face of the US, which is not omnipotent. The crisis is structural, not merely the product of a temporary economic downturn. The possibilities for reform are very limited. Only on the basis of a transformation of the system can social welfare reforms be brought about. Mobilizations in one place can serve as models for other countries. The transformation required should be made on the basis of concrete actions, not just conferences.

6 Access to populations who are the victims of war must be attempted. If they are cut off from essential economic resources, another type of crime against humanity results.

7 Use national and international courts to investigate crimes against humanity and to end impunity for such crimes.

8 Organize contingents of peacekeepers that might provide protection in conflict zones or war-torn areas.

9 Civil society ought to campaign against the sale of arms to Israel.

10 Support Israelis who oppose intervention in the Occupied Territories.

11 There are no rights without legitimate force to defend them, and the use of force without justification is a crime.

12 Campaign against the embargo on Iraq (which is killing the same number of people every year as those who died on September 11 in New York).

Translated by volunteer translator Germaine A Hoston

24 HUMAN RIGHTS
*Conference Synthesis on
Economic, Social and Cultural Rights*

MARIA LUISA MENDONÇA

Facilitator
Maria Luisa Mendonça SOCIAL NETWORK FOR JUSTICE
AND HUMAN RIGHTS, BRAZIL

Discussants
Adolfo Perez Esquivel NOBEL PRIZE LAUREATE (1980),
ARGENTINA
Adalid Contreras Baspinero EXECUTIVE SECRETARY,
INTERAMERICAN PLATFORM OF THE HUMAN RIGHTS:
DEMOCRACY AND DEVELOPMENT, BOLIVIA
Koumba Touré INSTITUTE FOR POPULAR EDUCATION, MALI
Muchtar Pakpahan PRESIDENT, SYNDICAL FEDERATION SBSI,
INDONESIA
Miloon Kothari HABITAT INTERNATIONAL COALITION'S
HOUSING AND LAND RIGHTS COMMITTEE, INDIA
Izzat Abdul Hadi BISAN CENTRE RAMALLAH, PALESTINE
Sidiki Kaba PRESIDENT OF THE INTERNATIONAL FEDERATION
FOR HUMAN RIGHTS, SENEGAL

Endorsed by
Dignity and Human Rights Caucus (COMPOSED OF:
CEDAR INTERNATIONAL, FIDH INTERNATIONAL, INCHRITI
INTERNATIONAL, PIDHDD INTERAMERICAN, MNDH BRAZIL,
DHESC BRAZIL)

Since the first World Social Forum in 2001, the city of Porto Alegre has become a symbol of the creation of viable proposals and alternatives on an international scale. Indeed, in elaborating global alternatives, the World Social Forum explicitly focuses on the social domain, where the impacts of economic, political and cultural globalization are being identified and challenged by a diversity of actors working on gender, the environment, the debt crisis, human rights and other issues.

The Dignity and Human Rights Caucus (Consórcio Dignidade e Direitos Humanos) contributes actively to the creation of global alternatives. The Caucus emerged at the Dakar meeting of the International Council of the second World Social Forum in October 2001. The Caucus is an initiative of various international human rights networks. Its main purpose is to join forces and ensure that the area of human rights is dealt with coherently at the second World Social Forum in Porto Alegre. On this basis, the Caucus works for the creation of viable proposals and alternatives on an international scale.

Since the meeting in Dakar, the Caucus has brought together networks and organizations to collaborate actively in the preparation of the second World Social Forum. Several events are being endorsed: a fullscale Conference on Human Rights – in particular on economic, social and cultural rights; four different seminars; and a public testimony by Virginia Dandan, the chair of the conference. Meanwhile, the list of organizations and networks that have subscribed to the Caucus is beyond all expectations. And the Caucus remains open to any other organizations to join that are committed to the realization of human dignity and human rights.

The networks that compose the Caucus core group have reached a consensus on three main proposals that are explained in this preparatory document for the conference. The intention is to have these proposals publicly launched and debated during the fullscale conference on human rights, and gradually developed during the four seminars.

The three main proposals endorsed by the Dignity and Human Rights Caucus are:

1 The establishment of a permanent forum on economic, social and cultural rights, in the broad context of trade, financial and international justice;

2 The declaration of the primacy of human rights so as to overcome the unacceptable gap between economic globalization and human rights;

3 Generate broad support for the draft Optional Protocol to the International Covenant on Economic, Social and Cultural Rights.

Establishment of a Permanent Forum on Economic, Social and Cultural Rights

There may be broad consensus, at the level of shared values and principles, with the statement that everyone has a right to food, health, housing and education. It may also be evident that development projects which unjustifiably displace people are a violation of the right to housing. The question is: how to move from a more general belief in the principle of human rights to effective human rights practices and instruments for implementation at local, national and international level?

We have to create institutional protection mechanisms at the same time as the particular contents of economic, social and cultural rights are developed and interpreted. There is a persistent lack of clarity regarding the meaning and implications of these rights. Furthermore, economic, social and cultural rights are not only systematically threatened and violated, they are also largely unknown and ignored. The implementation of these rights has therefore to be seen as a long-term struggle to develop both their content and institutionally recognized protection mechanisms. The latter will have to arise alongside with – and not in advance of – a clear understanding of the content of the different economic, social and cultural rights. In this struggle, the people whose rights have been violated need to be recognized as the primary movers. As in the field of civil and political rights, the institutional framework and its legal and social protection mechanisms emerge out of the struggles for human rights by those affected.

The Dignity and Human Rights Caucus intends to contribute actively to the creation and enhancement of such instruments and mechanisms. The formal UN instruments for implementation that now exist are the so-called state compliance reports and the treaty bodies. An informal instrument with widespread impact is the civil society reports on state compliance with the International Covenant on Economic, Social and Cultural Rights. The Caucus now proposes to go one step further and to establish a Permanent Forum on Economic, Social and Cultural Rights. This proposal is a response to the non-implementation of these rights. This Forum is inspired by the recently established Permanent Forum on Indigenous Issues which, on 28 July 2000, the United Nations Economic and Social Council decided to establish as a subsidiary organ of the Council (ECOSOC Res. 2000/22). This Permanent Forum formally integrates indigenous peoples into the structure of the United Nations. This is the first time that representatives of states and non-state actors have been accorded parity in a permanent representative body within the United Nations.

The proposed Permanent Forum on Economic, Social and Cultural Rights is also inspired by the initiative of the UN Sub-Commission on the Promotion and Protection of Human Rights which wants to create a so-called Social Forum, intended to provide a new space for civil society within the UN human rights system. The forum would provide a space for exchanging views among a broad cross-section of actors (including the IMF, World Bank, WTO, trade unions, business representatives and social movements) on economic, social and cultural rights, especially in the context of globalization. The mandate of the proposed Permanent Forum might establish the truth concerning the most serious violations of economic, social and cultural rights and simultaneously create more effective conditions for people to get access to their rights.

Many questions need to be further explored and debated during the conference at the World Social Forum:

- Would such a Permanent Forum be realized on a national basis, or indeed, as suggested here, on an international scale, under the auspices of the United Nations?

- Who would be the members of such a Permanent Forum and who would define its overall composition?

- What would be its legal basis?

- How could one envisage the relation of this Permanent Forum to the UN Committee on Economic, Social and Cultural Rights?

The Primacy of Human Rights

The impact of trade liberalization on fundamental rights is very serious. Yet, the international legal regimes governing trade and human rights have been developed on parallel tracks, separately and sometimes inconsistently. Few states are ready to recognize this contradiction, or to remedy it. How can we assess the impact of international trade on human rights, whether it be the bilateral or multilateral trade agreements, or the activity of transnational corporations? How can we achieve and articulate the subordination of international trade law to international human rights law? Today, the WTO interprets the principles of international law very selectively. Under a pretext of wanting to depoliticize trade, the WTO tries to distance itself from obligations stemming from what ought to be the primacy of international human rights law over other international treaties. Moreover, the actual functioning of the WTO gives priority to the wealthiest countries to a disproportionate extent and this prevents entire regions from reaping the benefits of international trade. How can we return to just and equitable trade? Would the insertion of 'human rights' provisions into trade treaties be preferable to a simple social clause? Would the insertion of a social clause be consistent with the primacy and indivisibility of human rights? Would a social clause become just another form of conditionality? Is it indeed possible to find a remedy for the endangering of human rights resulting from the opening up of markets? What should the role of human rights NGOs be in this debate? Should the NGOs already engaged in this debate link up with forces taking a more overtly ideological position? Would that contradict the traditional apolitical stance of human rights NGOs?

Transnational corporations play a growing role on the global economic scene, and the impact of their activities on human rights is not only more and more important but, equally, more and more recognized. Transnational corporations are also making use of their almost total impunity with regard to the consequences of their investments and activities when it comes to human rights. Voluntary codes of conduct multiply. At the same time, there are diverse initiatives at the intergovernmental level to develop legal instruments in order to make corporations accountable at the international level. Examples include the Global Compact of the United Nations, the OECD Code of Conduct, the drafting of a Human Rights Code of Conduct for companies at the UN Sub-Commission on Human Rights, and a similar initiative in the European Parliament. Many questions arise. What should be the form of such an instrument? Ought it to be binding? Which international agency ought to negotiate it? Is there a contradiction between voluntary and legally binding approaches, and how might they coexist?

Human rights NGOs are also being solicited more and more by corporations to carry out human rights and social audits in order to evaluate corporate compliance with international human rights standards. These often take place where binding international rules are lacking. Should not priority be given to the development of such an approach to hold multinationals accountable?

The principle of international cooperation in international instruments also involves obligations that developing countries can utilize to ensure that no action is taken, and no global policies adopted, that could inhibit the ability of states to implement the commitments they have to their people stemming from international human rights instruments. Moreover, these states could use these obligations as the argument to counter the negative consequences of the iniquitous debt, of structural adjustment programmes, and of trade, investment and financial agreements.

The past few years have witnessed the emergence of proposals for new international procedures in this area. Some of these proposals have actually taken shape, following the example of the Optional Additional Protocol to the European Social Charter, which sets up such a system.

Support for the Draft Optional Protocol to the ICESCR

There have been long-standing efforts to establish an Optional Protocol to the International Covenant on Economic, Social and Cultural Rights (ICESCR), which would provide a right of direct access and complaint by individuals and groups to the UN Committee on Economic, Social and Cultural Rights. What progress has been made? How must economic, social and cultural rights be clarified so that they can be really enforceable? What practical responses can legal remedies really give when the implementation of economic and social rights has huge financial implications for states? Can we actually force states to take some kind of action in this respect?

The idea that states are legally responsible for the implementation and protection of economic, social and cultural rights is becoming more widespread. Every individual, and not just society as a whole, ought legitimately to be able to expect the state to work towards the full realization of these rights. This implies one should be able to lodge a complaint against a state, not only in national courts but also in international courts or commissions – for violation of the right to health, food or education, for example.

While globalization has helped new actors in economic and social fields (such as the international financial institutions, the WTO and transnational corporations) to become even more powerful, it has at the same time reduced the scope of action of states, on whom rests the legal obligation to promote and fulfil economic, social and cultural rights. Therefore the question of the accountability of these new actors has become vital. This question concerns primarily transnational corporations, which have been granted an unprecedented amount of power because of globalization, and which, in conjunction with international trade and financial institutions, currently act with virtual impunity.

The Dignity and Human Rights Caucus urges everyone to give high priority to the consideration of a draft Optional Protocol to the International Covenant on Economic, Social and Cultural Rights. To achieve this, the mobilization and engagement of civil society will be of critical importance. Extensive awareness-raising and public education must take place in order to give people and their representatives an understanding of the issues involved. The political will to realize these proposals can only be created by the broad mobilization of civil society. And civil society participation in the proposed Permanent Forum, the UN Committee on Economic, Social and Cultural Rights, and other mechanisms for the realization of economic, social and cultural rights, is essential if they are to be effective in holding actors in economic globalization (including transnational corporations) accountable.

25 SOVEREIGNTY, NATION, EMPIRE

DANIEL BENSAID

The comparatively recent spread of the nation-state as a form of political organization has accompanied the birth and triumph of capitalism on a worldwide scale. Its development has been determined by a dialectic between the unification of markets, the construction of state institutions, and the formation of nations, a dialectic that has varied of course according to the particular histories of individual countries. The nation does not suddenly appear, therefore, as an original construct created by the state. It has rather been the product of a process of territorial, administrative and often linguistic unification. Thus national consciousness provides the territorial state with a 'cultural substratum which ensures solidarity among its citizens' (Habermas). The converse of (and, at the same time, a condition for) the emergence of the nation-state system in Europe has been the process of worldwide colonization and imperial domination.

What we today call the Westphalian international order, which emerged in Europe in the mid-seventeenth century, is a partial and unequal order. Some states have remained multinational in character. Some, such as Germany, underwent a late and bureaucratically driven unification, with little initial popular legitimacy. By contrast, many African and Arab countries, born of colonial divisions, remain just fragile skeletons of the modern nation-state, crippled from the outset by their dependence as a result of the way in which they were integrated into the world market. They have had neither the time nor the means to achieve a socio-economic development that would allow them to consolidate effective public institutions and a vibrant civil society. Thus, in Balibar's view, the formation of nation-states has in fact failed in most of the world.

International law, beginning in the seventeenth century under Dutch intellectual inspiration, has basically remained an inter-state legal system, based on treaties. Despite the current process of globalization, this inter-state system remains the dominant international legal form. The UN is an assembly of nation-states, and its Security Council is a closed club for those powers that emerged victorious in the Second World War. Decisions made at summits such as those held in Kyoto on the environment and in Rome in order to create a permanent international criminal court must be referred to the member states for ratification. The European Union itself represents an institutional compromise between the weakened inter-state system and an emerging supra-national order. During this perilous transition, world leaders must steer a difficult course between the laws of the individual states and a supranational legal order that is still in its formative stage. In the absence of any international legislative authority, during this transition it is the law of the strongest that will prevail, imposed with the backing of the UN where possible, but without it if necessary (as former US Secretary of State Madeleine Albright declared during the war in the Balkans). The more international law is invoked, the more problematical and vague it appears to be.

Equivocations about the right of states to interfere in the efforts of other sovereign states illustrate this contradiction. Its advocates vacillate between the legal notion of right and the moral notion of duty. This new body of international law is supposed to supersede increasingly obsolescent national sovereignties, which are to give way to the increasingly accepted universality of human rights. In reality, the right to intervene comes down to the strong interfering in the affairs of the weak, without the slightest reciprocity. It thus becomes the ethical alibi for new acts of imperial domination.

Those who champion liberal globalization (notably in France) have coined the derogatory term *souverainisme* (or separatism) to condemn any resistance to market globalization and its social consequences. We would agree that inward-looking nationalism, jingoism and xenophobia are deluded and reactionary responses to the legitimate fears that arise in response to the unfettered forces of the liberal jungle. But it is not only nationalism as a conservative national ideology which is under threat here. It is also the other face of sovereignty, the popular and democratic legitimation of political power. The crisis of sovereignty in fact most affects states that have not successfully constituted themselves as sovereign nations, including those that have difficulty remaining so and those that want to change the global hierarchy of domination and dependence. The *souverainisme* of the strong is actually doing rather well: Europe is glorified as a new power in its own right, NATO mandates are being redefined, and there is unilateral military intervention in all directions, with no international legitimacy.

The building blocks of modern politics inherited from the Enlightenment – the idea of nations, peoples, territories, frontiers – have been eviscerated under the impact of capitalist globalization. This is what Habermas calls 'the progressive dissolution of organized modernity', in which, incidentally, there is no cause for rejoicing, for it calls into question the very continuation of democratic politics 'The basis of the sovereignty crisis is the disappearance of the people' and the dialectic between the power that brings political legitimacy into being and power as actually constituted (Balibar). The notion of the people has fulfilled a dual function as an imaginary community on the one hand and the collective subject of democratic representation on the other. This notion expressed the tension between an aspiration to democratic universality and the closed character of particularistic national affinities. With the dissolution of the people under the pressures of globalization, the symbolic structure that rendered the modern state a nation-state falls into crisis as well. Now increasingly void of both substance and significance as a result of privatization worldwide, the public sector becomes ephemeral. *Souverainisme* has tried to respond to this decline of public space and undermining of the common good by claiming that the general will can only be expressed at the national level. We thus find ourselves in an 'untenable betwixt and between', according to Balibar – traditional national sovereignty is in decline, but post-national sovereignties still remain to be defined.

Disturbing responses to the painful uncertainty of this 'no longer' but 'not yet' are everywhere in evidence. The decline of the political nation is giving way to the reassertion of the zoological (or ethnic) nation, democratic legitimation to genealogical legitimacy, and the political community to primitive group identities and rights resting on blood lineage. The ethnicization of politics and fantasies of ethnic cleansing are part of this regressive dynamic. In contrast, the search for new, wider geo-political spaces constitutes another possible attempted resolution of this tension. In some regions, as in the Arab world, the community of believers can seem to offer a plausible alternative to the collapse of nation states and the weakness of national-based populisms. This confessionalization of politics is not confined to Islamic fundamentalism. It is equally at work in the deadly dilemma faced by Israel, torn between maintaining itself as a Jewish state and the claim to be a truly democratic state in which the Jews would accept finding themselves possibly in the minority some day.

Defending the (civic and republican) political nation represents, for some, the only possible alternative to either a withdrawal into the ethnic nation or the dissolution of politics in the cosmopolitanism of the market, between warlike communitarianism and humanitarian cosmopolitanism. Any third way appears unlikely in the face of concrete issues like immigration, the rights of foreigners, and the relationship of citizenship to nationality. And Habermas's call for 'a multicultural citizenship' of 'cosmopolitan identities' and a 'constitutional patriotism' seems only to be a communication theorist's utopia, doomed to failure by the neoliberal pressures towards social disintegration and fragmentation of loyalties. The claim that a new form of cosmopolitan democracy will emerge through a purely deliberative process and that human rights will comprise its normative framework, seems, then, like a wild profession of faith in an abstract rationalism and universalism.

'It is from their political constitutions that peoples are born.' This statement by Habermas seems to neglect the historical dimension of the popular basis of legitimacy. It is hardly surprising he should consider the 'alleged right to self-determination' as an 'absurdity' which, according to him, has been reduced to ethnocentric reaction and the disintegration of social ties. Indeed, the contradiction between the exercise of legitimate rights of social groups to education, their language and control of their land, and the fractious disintegration that we see worldwide, is simply the converse of the universal spread of the market.

The world is seeing major new divisions. The constant shift in spheres of influence, territories, and borders can never be resolved amicably around the negotiating table. Modern war may in future rain down from the stars ('Star Wars'), but it never comes from nothing. Warfare is transforming itself, and in doing so taking on new characteristics. The American doctrine of asymmetric war with zero casualties for its own forces is based on its monopoly of high-tech terror, prefigured and symbolized fifty years ago by the Hiroshima bomb which eliminated the distinction between combatants and non-combatants. Wars between nations are being transformed into total civil war. Civilian victims become collateral damage. Ostensibly ethical wars, fought in the name of the universal good and all humanity, become secular crusades where the adversary is excluded from the species, reduced to a beast, fit only to be tracked down and exterminated. This is war without limits. It may still be the pursuit of politics by other means, but where proportionality between means and ends becomes totally devoid of meaning.

The new era of capitalist globalization and its new military character calls for new political forms. Never has the concentration of wealth, capital, knowledge and armed power been more marked. Imperialism has not disappeared: rather it has transformed itself under the impact of the expanded circulation of capital, commodities, information and violence. Meanwhile, the segmentation of the labour market, the fragmentation of territory and the law of uneven and combined development persist. The severance of nations from their territories demands the formation of new continental, regional and sub-regional (tribal-level) territories. Borders are shifting, shrinking inward from the edges to the centre (as the South penetrates increasingly into the North), but borders themselves do not disappear. New borders, like Europe's Schengen area, are dotted with detention centres for would-be immigrants. Whether we call it imperialism or empire, this remains a system of domination – economic, military, cultural and environmental – as public goods are increasingly privatized.

The change in scale resulting from globalization does not signify the growth in the size of nation states to continental dimensions. The economic, legal, military and ecological spheres are in disharmony. The result is not a homogeneous, neat, single global space in which different regions can rebuild themselves into equality with one another. Rather, inequalities persist, not only between the European Union and Mercosur for example, but also within each region. The construction of the European Community offers a good example of the contradictions which newly evolving sovereign, democratic entities face. Europe remains 'an unsolved political problem' (Balibar), which may lead to an uneasy solution in which a new 'fictitious ethnicity' or new type of people is invented. Habermas, opposing the twin utopias of regressive closure and progressive opening, supports a constituent power free from the presuppositions attached to the concept of a people, which in Europe's case would lead to some kind of progression towards a common European area. This kind of moderate federalism would, in his view, prefigure post-national democracy. In practice, however, this concept will fail, because the neoliberal economy's destruction of social solidarity causes people to panic about their identities and widens the gap between the euro-federalism of the elites and the euro-scepticism of the people.

One result of the crisis of national sovereignty experienced by many states is that the concepts of citizenship and nationality are increasingly dissociated from one another as the public sphere is increasingly privatized in multinational political entities. The big modern equation of nationality with citizenship is actually now beginning not to work. One desirable response to this step backward would be to define more radically the right to citizenship of the country on whose territory one was born by means of a 'citizenship of residence' where community citizenship would be more important than national citizenship. One would have to 'either completely dismantle the definition of a state as a community and "community citizenship", or detach the concept of citizenship from its definition as national citizenship', according to Balibar. This poses the problem of a secularized, worldly citizenship, a citizenship without 'community'. This kind of citizenship as an organized form of plural group membership might provide a solution to the choice between abstract universalism and vindictive communitarianism.

Last but not least, there remains another significant problem. What social force today is likely to lead such a social citizenship project towards the political universalization of the human species? This is the monumental question of the link between relationships of class and gender (both achieving potential universality), community affiliation, and political forms (when those are eventually found) of social emancipation.

Translated by volunteer translators Isabel Brenner, Kathryn Dykstra, Penny Oliver, Tracey Williams, reviewed by Germaine Hoston.

# DEMOCRACY
Participatory Democracy

M.P. PARAMESWARAN

Two Opposing Views on the Future of Humankind

One view holds that finally humanity has discovered, after a number of grave mistakes – the gravest of which was the attempt to build socialism during the twentieth century – the correct path for a bright future, the path of market-controlled society! No more experiments are to be conducted. They will not be tolerated!

The opposing point of view is that market-controlled democracy is anarchic and unjust, and leads to:

- Impoverishment of the many and enrichment of the few;

- Resource depletion, waste accretion and catastrophic environmental changes; and

- Increasing conflicts which may escalate into all-destructive global wars.

This view argues for some form of social control as opposed to the control of the market. A few people still advocate the dictatorship of the proletariat as the form of social control; others opt for participatory democracy.

More and more people across the world are embracing participatory democracy. A number of experiments in Kerala, in Cuba, in

Porto Alegre, etc., are being conducted to broaden and deepen the idea of participatory democracy. These should be studied, experiences exchanged, networks established, and a world movement for participatory democracy built.

Democracy, if it is really to mean government by the people, demands participation. This participation has to be creative. If not, it is only mass slavery, to put it in strong words, or mass involvement in the execution of projects conceived by a few, to put it mildly. Such non-creative participation will not be just, and unjust things are not sustainable.

Sustainability is a concept that has been introduced into the development debate only in recent years. It can mean simply a delay in the date of resource exhaustion or total prevention of the same. This gets automatically linked to the understanding of the concept of development. Participatory democracy ought to ensure just and sustainable development.

Participation, obviously, has to be universal and not limited to a few individuals. This suggests that both economic and political activities have to be on a small enough scale – on a human scale – so that citizens can participate meaningfully in them. This goes against the actual trend of development, which has seen an ever-increasing scale of economic operations and concentration of economic and political power in fewer and fewer hands.

Participation also demands the ability to participate, the necessary knowledge and skills, and the willingness to participate. The majority of people in any country are historically conditioned to supplicate and not to participate. This attitude stems, also, from a practical inability to participate. How can the billion-plus citizens of China or India participate effectively in taking decisions that affect them all? What can ordinary US citizens do today in a country ruled by billionaires and corporate giants?

Participation Demands Political Decentralization and Devolution of Powers, both Political and Economic

The question often asked is, how can small economic and political units cope with competition from the larger ones? Competition is a rule of the game. Societies make the rules. There has never been, and even now there is not, a single society which allows completely free competition. It is always tempered by the interests of the ruling class. However, even if the rules of the game were made more favourable to the people at large, participation and the need for sustainability still demand smallness of scale. Small is not only beautiful, it must also be powerful. Power therefore must be devolved from the top to the bottom, and on a permanent basis. Decentralized powers are to be won and kept.

Therefore, true participatory democracy demands revolutionary changes in the economics, ethics and the politics of a society. These revolutionary changes have to be brought about through processes which in themselves are consonant with the changes desired. One cannot bring about democracy through dictatorship, just as one cannot enhance ethics through corruption.

Economics

The motive for economic activity must become the social good in place of private profit. This means:

- **Regulation:** social controls which allow room for individual initiative in a socially tempered market.

- **Production:** for consumption rather than for exchange. No dictatorship of the commodity.

- **Small-scale dispersed production:** in order to be economically viable and environmentally safe.

- **Small has to become powerful.**

- **R&D:** geared consciously to make the small powerful and not to help the large-scale or enrich the already rich.

- **Primacy restored to the primary sector**.

- **Increasing local self-sufficiency** and reduced long distance transport of people and commodities.

- **Increasing reliance on solar energy** and recycling.

Ethics

- **Increasing wisdom to differentiate need from greed.**

- **Human progress to be understood in human terms** and not in terms of material consumption.

- **Understand the physical and spiritual aspects** of the quality of life.

- Recognition of the fact that **participation is not only an economic and political necessity,** but a spiritual necessity too.

- **Recognition of and respect for the rights of women, children and unprivileged.**

Politics

- Every able-bodied citizen should undertake some responsibility, small or large, in the day-to-day management of society.

- Each citizen to acquire knowledge and skills to take up such responsibilities.

- Elections are not to be taken as a once-every-five-year phenomenon providing leaders with an irrevocable power of attorney: the right of recall is essential.

- Right to information, a willingness to look into and ability to understand what one sees.

- Inversion of the power pyramid and conversion into cooperative concentric circles – with the local community at the centre and bigger formations as the outer rings. Ultimate sovereignty to vest in the local community. The powers of larger ones to be agreed upon at local level.

- Conscious programmes to educate and enable citizens to take up the responsibility of governing themselves.

These are some of the ideas that are being discussed in various circles. They have to be developed through practical experimentation on a sufficiently large scale and under diverse conditions.

Perhaps a whole new type of ideology may emerge from this praxis which will be:

- Different from the market ideology;

- Different from Marxist ideology as it was practised in the twentieth century;

- The product of a collective wisdom rooted in experience;

- Unlikely to offer the possibility of becoming a dogma;

- Enabling sustained and sustainable development of the human species;

- And leading to a world where wars become unnecessary.

These and many similar issues could be and should be discussed on international platforms.

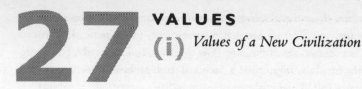

VALUES
(i) *Values of a New Civilization*

MICHAEL LÖWY and FREI BETTO

We propose here a few possible themes for debate on the question 'Principles and Values of a New Society'. These are not axioms, but working hypotheses and suggestions for reflection.

We of the World Social Forum believe in certain values, which guide and illuminate our project of social transformation and inspire our vision of a possible new world. The very different people gathered at Davos – bankers, corporate executives and heads of state, who direct neoliberal globalization (or globo-colonization) – also uphold values. We must not underestimate them, as they hold dear three great values and are willing to fight with any and all means to safeguard them – even by war, if need be. These three values of the Davos creed are at the heart of Western capitalist civilization in its current form. They are the dollar, the euro and the yen! Although they themselves come into contradiction, taken as a whole they constitute the globalized, neoliberal scale of values.

The main common characteristic of these values is their strictly quantitative nature: they know not good nor evil, fair nor unfair. They know only quantities, numbers, amounts: one, a hundred, a thousand, a million, a billion. Whoever has a billion – dollars, euros or yen – is worth more than someone who has only a million, and much more than those who have only a thousand. It goes without saying that whoever has nothing, or almost nothing, is worth nothing on the Davos scale of values. It is as if that person never existed. She or he is outside the market and, therefore, outside the civilized world.

Together, these three values constitute one of the divinities of liberal economic religion: its name is Currency or, in Aramaic, Mammon. The other two divinities are The Market and Capital. These are fetishes or idols, objects of a fanatical and exclusive, intolerant and dogmatic cult. This fetishism of commodities (according to Marx), or idolatry of the market (to use the expression of the liberation theologians Hugo Assmann and Franz Hinkelammert) and of money and capital, is a cult that has its churches (the stock markets), its Holy Offices (the IMF, the WTO, etc.), and that persecutes its heretics (who are all of us who believe in other values). These modern idols, just like the Canaanite gods Moloch and Baal, demand terrible human sacrifices: these are the victims of structural adjustment plans in the Third World, men, women and children sacrificed upon the altar of the World Market fetish and the Foreign Debt fetish.

An impressive body of canonical rules and orthodox principles serves to legitimize and sanctify these sacrificial rituals. A vast clergy of specialists and managers expounds the cult's dogmas to the heathen multitudes (keeping any heretical opinions they may have far away from the public sphere). The ethical rules of this religion were already established two centuries ago by the economic theologian, Saint Adam Smith, that each individual must pursue, in the most implacable manner possible, her or his selfish interest, in utter disregard of their fellow men and women, and the invisible hand of the Market-God will take care of the rest, bringing harmony and prosperity to the entire nation.

This civilization of money and capital transforms everything – land, water, air, life, feelings, convictions – into commodities, to be sold at the highest price. Even people become secondary in importance to merchandise. This civilization subverts the humanitarian conception of a person–commodity–person relationship. In this paradigm I put on a cotton shirt, which is a commodity, in order to humanize my social relations, as it would be strange indeed if I were to appear at work or a meeting of friends without a shirt. But now, the predominant relationship becomes commodity–person–commodity.

The brand of shirt I wear is what measures my human value. If I come to your house by bus or by bike, I have a value of Z. But if I arrive in a BMW, my value is A. I am the same person, yet the merchandise that I use is what assigns me more or less value. Hence I am reified.

As far back as the nineteenth century, a critic of liberal political economy had foreseen today's world with prophetic clarity:

> At last, the time has come in which all that human beings had considered as inalienable has become the object of exchange, of traffic, and may be alienated. It is a time when the very things which before were conveyed, but never bartered; given, but never sold; conquered, but never purchased – virtue, love, opinion, science, conscience etc. – when, in short, everything has finally become tradable. It is a time of generalized corruption, universal venality or, to speak in terms of political economy, the time when anything, moral or physical, once into a venal value, may be taken to market to be appraised for its appropriate value.[1]

Qualitative Values

Against the backdrop of this civilization of universal commodification, which drowns all human relations in the 'cold waters of selfish calculation',[2] the World Social Forum represents, first, a rejection: the world is not a commodity! Nature, life, the rights of people, freedom, love, culture are not merchandise. Secondly, the World Social Forum embodies the aspiration to another type of civilization, based on values that are neither money nor capital. These two civilizational projects and two scales of values confront each other, as completely irreconcilable antagonists, at the beginning of the twenty-first century.

What values inspire this alternative project of ours? Our values are qualitative. Our ethical, political, social and cultural values are not reducible to quantification in monetary terms. They are shared by the greater part of the groups and networks that constitute the huge world movement against neoliberal globalization.

Liberty

Our starting point in defining our values could be the three values that inspired the French Revolution of 1789 – Liberty, Equality and Fraternity. They have been present ever since in all the social emancipation movements of modern history. As Ernst Bloch points out in his book, *Natural Law and Human Dignity* (1961), these principles engraved so often by the ruling class on the fronts of public buildings in France may never have been fully realized. In practice, as Marx wrote, they were often replaced by Cavalry, Infantry and Artillery. But they are part of a great subversive tradition. They possess a concrete utopian force, that 'goes far beyond the bourgeois horizon', a force of human dignity that points to the future, to the 'march with heads held high' of humanity towards socialism.[3] If we examine these values more closely, from the standpoint of the victims of the system, we discover their explosive potential and their pertinence to the current struggle against the commodification of the world.

What does liberty mean? First and foremost, freedom of expression, organization, thought, criticism, protest – hard won through centuries of struggles against absolutism, fascism and dictatorship. More importantly – and now more so than ever – it means freedom from another form of absolutism: the dictatorship of the financial markets and the elite bankers and multinational businessmen who impose their interests on the whole of humanity. This is an imperial dictatorship. Under the economic, political and military hegemony of the only remaining global superpower, the United States, it hides behind the anonymous, blind laws of the market. Its global power is far superior to that of the Roman Empire or the colonial empires of the past. This dictatorship is wielded by the logic of capital itself, and imposes itself with the aid of profoundly anti-democratic institutions, such as the IMF or WTO, and under threat of its armed wing (NATO). The concept of national liberation is insufficient to express the current meaning of freedom, which is, at one and the same time, local, national and worldwide, as the profoundly original and innovative Zapatista movement so well demonstrates.

One of the great limitations of the French Revolution of 1789 was that it excluded women from citizenship. The republican feminist Olympe de Gouges, who wrote the *Declaration of Women's and Female Citizens' Rights*, was guillotined in 1793. The modern concept of freedom cannot ignore gender oppression that afflicts half of humanity, and the prime importance of women's struggle for liberation. Particularly significant in this struggle are women's rights to control over their own bodies.

Equality and Fraternity

What does equality mean? The first revolutionary constitutions guaranteed equality before the law. This is absolutely necessary – and far from existing in the reality of the world today – but it is woefully insufficient. The deeper problem is the monstrous inequality between people in the North and South of our planet and, within each country, between the small elite that monopolizes economic power and the means of production, and the great majority of the population, living from the force of their own labour – when not unemployed, and excluded from social life. The statistics are well known: concentrated in the hands of four US citizens – Bill Gates, Paul Allen, Warren Buffett and Larry Ellyson – is a fortune equivalent to the gross domestic product of 42 poor countries with a population of 600 million inhabitants. The international debt system, the logic of the world market and the unlimited power of financial capital have led to an aggravation of this inequality, which has worsened significantly over the last 20 years. The demand for equality and social justice – two inseparable values – inspires the various alternative socio-economic projects that are becoming more common today. From a broader point of view, this also entails a new mode of production and distribution.

Economic inequality is not the only form of injustice in liberal capitalist society. There is the persecution of the illegal immigrants and others without documents in Europe; the exclusion of the descendants of black slaves and indigenous peoples in the Americas; the oppression of millions of individuals that belong to the 'untouchables' castes in India; and so many other forms of racism or discrimination due to colour, religion or language, which are omnipresent, North and South, on our planet. An egalitarian society means the radical stamping out of these discriminations. It further means a different relationship between men and women, breaking with the ancient system of inequality that has reigned throughout human history and which is responsible for violence against women, and their exclusion from the public sphere and from the workplace. We must always remember the absolute majority of poor and unemployed people in the world are women.

What, finally, does fraternity mean? It is the modern translation of the old Judaeo-Christian tradition: love one's neighbour. It means replacing the relationship of competition, fierce dispute, war of all against all – which, in current society, makes the individual a *homo homini lupus* (a wolf to other human beings) – with a relationship of cooperation, sharing, mutual help, solidarity. This solidarity must include not only the brothers (*frater*, in Latin), but sisters too; it must extend beyond the limits of the family, clan, tribe, ethnic group, religious community or nation to become authentically universal, worldwide, international. In other words, this solidarity is internationalist, in the sense given by whole generations of militants in the socialist, workers' movement.

Neoliberal globalization produces tribal and ethnic conflicts, wars of ethnic cleansing, bellicose expansionism, intolerant religious conservatism and xenophobia. These types of panic, induced by the feeling of a loss of identity, are the reverse side of the same coin, the inevitable complement to imperial globalization. The civilization that we dream of will be a complete contrast – 'a world that can hold many worlds' (according to the beautiful formula of the Zapatistas), a worldwide civilization of solidarity and diversity. Faced with the economic and quantitative homogenization of the world and capitalism's false universalism, we must now, more than ever, reassert the wealth represented by cultural diversity, by the unique and irreplaceable contribution of each people, culture and individual.

Democracy as an Indispensable Value

Another value – democracy – has been inseparable from the other three ever since 1789. But democracy cannot be limited to the sense this political concept has in liberal democratic discourse: the free election of representatives every so many years, which, to be honest, has been deformed and distorted by the control that economic power exercises over the media. This representative democracy – which is also the fruit of many popular struggles, and which is still constantly threatened by the interests of the powerful, as demonstrated in the history of Latin America from 1964 to 1985 – is necessary, yet insufficient. What we need are superior, more participatory forms of democracy that allow the population to exercise directly their power to decide and to oversee – much in the way this happens in the participatory budgets of the city of Porto Alegre and the state of Rio Grande do Sul.

The greater challenge, from the point of view of a project for an alternative society, is to extend democracy to the economic and social spheres. Why should we allow an elite to wield exclusive power in these spheres if we reject it in the political arena? Social democracy means that the major socio-economic choices, investment priorities, and the fundamental orientation of production and distribution are democratically discussed and decided upon by the population itself, and not by a handful of exploiters or their supposed market laws or – in a variant that has proven bankrupt – by an all-powerful Politburo (the Soviet Union and its satellites).

The Environment

To these overarching values, one more must be added: respect for the environment. This product of modern revolutionary history is at the same time the oldest and the most recent. We see this value in the lifestyle of the indigenous tribes of the Americas and pre-capitalist rural communities of several continents, as well as at the heart of the modern ecological movement. Capitalist globalization – with its tendency to geometric growth – is responsible for the accelerated destruction and poisoning of the environment – pollution of the land, oceans, rivers and air; the greenhouse effect, with its catastrophic consequences; the threat of destruction of the ozone layer, which protects us from lethal ultraviolet rays; the devastation of forests and biodiversity. A civilization based on human solidarity cannot exist without also being a civilization in solidarity with nature, since the human species obviously cannot survive if the ecological balance of the planet is disrupted.

Socialism as an Alternative

The above list of values is by no means exhaustive. Each person may, based on her or his own experience and reflection, add more items. How, then, can we sum up in a single word the set of values present, in one form or another, in the movement against capitalist globalization, the street protests from Seattle to Genoa, and the debates of the World Social Forum? I believe that the expression 'a civilization of solidarity' is an appropriate synthesis of our alternative project. This phrase assumes not only a radically different economic and political structure, but first and foremost an alternative society that values the ideas of the common good, the public interest, universal rights, the non-profit motive.

We suggest that we define this society by the word socialism, which for almost two centuries has summarized humankind's aspirations for a new way of life, one with greater freedom, equality, democracy and solidarity. It is a term that – just like all the others (liberty, democracy, etc.) – has been manipulated by profoundly antigrassroots, authoritarian interests, but which nonetheless retains its original and authentic value.

In a recent opinion poll in Brazil, sponsored by the National Confederation of Industries (!), 55 per cent of respondents stated that Brazil needed a socialist revolution. When asked what they understood by socialism, they answered citing certain values: friendship, communion, sharing, respect, justice and solidarity. A civilization based on solidarity is a socialist civilization.

In conclusion, another world is possible, if based on other values, radically opposed to those that dominate the world today. We cannot forget, however, that the future begins now. These values are already prefigured in the initiatives that guide our movement today. They inspire the campaign against Third World debt and the resistance to new WTO agreements, the fight against GMOs and the proposals to tax financial speculation. They are present in social struggles, grassroots initiatives, experiences of solidarity, cooperation and participatory democracy – from the ecological struggle of peasants in India, to the participatory budget of Rio Grande do Sul; from the struggles for the right to form trade unions in South Korea, to the strikes in defence of public services in France; from the Zapatista villages of Chiapas, to the camps of the MST.

The future begins here and now, in these seeds of a new civilization which we are planting through our struggle, and with our efforts to build new men and women from the subjective and ethical values that we have embraced in our lives as militants.

Notes

1 Karl Marx, *Misère de la philosophie* (Paris Éditions Sociales, 1947), p. 33.
2 Marx's phrase in *The Communist Manifesto*.
3 Ernst Bloch, *Droit naturel et dignité humaine* (Paris, Payot, 1976), pp. 177–9.

Translated by volunteer translator Robert Finnegan with revisions by Thomas Ponniah

27 VALUES
(ii) *Feminism and the*
Three Enlightenment Ideals

CELIA AMORÓS

Relations between the feminist movement and what in a generic sense we shall call the left have been stormy, paradoxical and ambivalent. We can agree with Michael Löwy and Frei Betto (see the previous paper in this volume), that the reference point for the liberation movements of modern history has been provided by the three slogans of the French Revolution: liberty, fraternity and equality. There is no doubt that these three words sum up the fundamental values of the Enlightenment tradition. And, as could hardly be otherwise, feminism has drawn its nourishment from the Enlightenment ever since the beginning. We Spanish and Ibero-American researchers meeting in the Permanent Seminar on Feminism and the Enlightenment have made that clear.

In my book *Tiempo de feminismo: Sobre feminismo, proyecto ilustrado y post-modernidad* (The Feminist Era: On Feminism, the Enlightenment and Postmodernity), I have sought to recreate the genesis of European feminist thought by means of formulating 'claims', which is an emerging and typically Enlightenment procedure that can be contrasted with the lists of grievances, where, prior to the Enlightenment, women expressed their complaints at abuses by patriarchal power. John Stuart Mill had warned earlier that throughout history the oppressed have first of all denounced abuses by the powerful, only later calling into question the very basis of legitimacy of a given power. This warning in his *On the Subjection of Women* applies quite specifically to feminism. There is an abundant pre-Enlightenment literature, of which *The Book of the City of Ladies* is a good example. Written by Christine de Pisan in the fifteenth century, its author responds to the insults heaped on women as a whole by the Sorbonne professor Jean de Meun. Nevertheless, caught up in a logic according to which the Divinity wishes to be served in different ways by the different estates, Christine does not call for equal access for women to education or to jobs. Her work is a typical example of what we have called lists of grievances. Claims will be voiced only when a series of abstractions become available that, due to their universalizing potential, break down the estate structure of the Ancien Régime – which did not happen until Cartesianism and the Enlightenment. Abstractions such as subject, individual, citizen, and so on emerged in this way. These abstractions were formulated in universal terms, but nevertheless applied restrictively, and so important groups that did not fall within the ambit stated their dissatisfaction in terms of discrimination rather than of complaint. The author of *The Book of the City of Ladies* does not mention discrimination when referring to the manner in which Jean de Meun treats women collectively. And she fails to do so for the same reason that an outcast cannot feel discriminated against with regard to a Brahmin. The logic of the caste system, like the estates, is based on privileges of birth and not on universal rights. Only where a system of rights predominates are commensurable parameters established, on the basis of which one can speak of discrimination.

Nevertheless, we would be mistaken to think that feminism came into being merely by applying the principles of the Enlightenment to women, as if it were a fully armed Minerva sprouting from the head of Jupiter. On the contrary, feminism *avant la lettre* emerged from a laborious process of attributing meaning to the language of the Enlightenment and the Revolution. We can reconstruct this process, at least partly, by analysing the so-called *Cahiers des doléances*. These are documents written by the various estates – clergy, nobility, common folk or Third Estate – to voice their complaints and claims to the States General convened by Louis XVI. Women, too, wished to be heard and created their own literature. However, the writings that they entrusted to their representatives before the States General by and large got misplaced and ended up languishing in the writing desks of these illustrious delegates. Yet some have been recovered. The celebration of the bicentenary of the French Revolution provided an excellent opportunity to bring these writings to light, and they have been compiled in the Minutes of the Symposium on Women and the French Revolution held at the University of Toulouse le Mirail. In Spain, they were published by Alicia Puleo in an anthology of writings under the title *La Ilustración olvidada: La polémica de los sexos en el siglo XVIII* (The Forgotten Enlightenment: The Controversy of the Sexes in the Eighteenth Century). The degree of tension and conflict stirred up by this controversy can be seen by the fact that alongside the authentic writings there appeared texts considered apocryphal by critics. These apocrypha parodied the authentic writings, with the intention of casting derision on women's complaints and claims.

And so this valuable material offers us the chance tentatively to reconstruct the laborious process whereby women gave new meaning to the terms that the revolutionaries were using in confronting the *Ancien Régime*. Terms such as divine right, aristocrats, privileges and so forth became highly insulting during the revolutionary process. Women appropriated these terms in order to appeal to the revolutionaries themselves, as husbands, companions, and so on. By doing so, they were striving consciously or unconsciously to bring out the irrationality of the very basis of the patriarchal system: they labeled men who behave as the privileged sex 'the aristocrats of the home'. Thus they applied the insulting connotations of these terms to new referents. Just as the new revolutionary language was coined to strip the Ancien Régime of its legitimacy, so women's retooling of the significance of its terms came to represent a derationalizing of male domination.

By way of this shift in meaning, women were applying signs to themselves. You can appreciate what this implies if you realize that Simone de Beauvoir referred to 'the woman' as a hetero-designation: that is, as a product of men's discourse that set norms for women, determining what women are and what they should be. Accordingly, the author of one part of the *Cahiers des doléances*, with the pen name of Poor Javotte, refers to 'we women' – bringing out the new emerging awareness of women as a collectivity – as being the 'Third Estate within the Third Estate'. Here is a case pregnant with the power of the shift from the anti-estate logic towards an anti-patriarchal logic. The Third Estate does not set itself up as an estate, but instead represents the breakdown of the very logic that existed in the aristocratic system of estates. Because women's exclusion from the emerging citizenry was perceived, at least by some of them, as paradoxical to the nth degree, these women are saying that, by isolating us from the emerging public realm, you revolutionary men are restoring the (so often insulted!) estate-based logic of privileges by creating a hierarchy between 'two third estates' – the one you represent and the one you have awarded us. (Perhaps now is the time to recall that the Spanish philosopher Cristina Molina defines patriarchy as the power to award domains. It also comes to mind that Elizabeth Cady Stanton, one of the most important leaders of the North American suffragist movement, harangued those who denied women the right to vote: 'You, liberal men, treat your women as if you were feudal barons.')

So women were hetero-designated as 'the beautiful sex', i.e. under an aesthetic-sexual code. As Simone de Beauvoir puts it, the woman represents sex for a man, thus, to the extent that he alone assumes the position of subject, she is sex itself. The effect of this resignification of revolutionary language – 'we are the Third Estate within the Third Estate' – is to progress from hetero-designation to self-designation in the very same movement as from the aesthetic-sexual code to political language. By this linguistic manoeuvre, women set themselves up as a politicized collectivity, and are enabled to think of themselves as such. The transition from hetero-designation to self-designation can be made only by taking a self-reference that hitherto had mimicked hetero-designation and transposing it into the political register; for example, another writing of the time begins: 'To my sex. And we women are citizens too…'.

The controversy over citizenship for women during the French Revolution makes it clear that the relation between feminism and the left has never been one of pre-ordained harmony. (The relation with the right, naturally, has been and always will be one of irreducible conflict.) The idea of citizenship appears as a controversial abstraction with regard to the estate-based society. It means considering the fact of oneself belonging to a specific estate of society – that same estate-based society that one seeks to strip of its legitimacy – as irrelevant for the purpose of being considered a holder of rights. So women and their defenders (e.g. Condorcet) reasoned in a way we could reconstruct as follows. If being a noble or plebeian is a characteristic attributed on the basis of birth, which therefore should not be taken into account in attributing citizenship, then being a man or woman – also a characteristic attributed on the basis of birth and not merit – should be considered as making no difference in attaining that coveted citizenship. As heirs to the misogyny of Rousseau, the author of *The Education of Sophie*, the Jacobins rejected outright the analogy that female and male feminists drew between the distinction between the nobility and the peasantry and the difference between men and women. In the first instance, we find ourselves faced with an 'artificial' distinction – an insulting word for the enlightened – while in the second it is a question of a 'natural' difference. For the enlightened, the appeal to nature as a proper and desirable order of things has a normative sense, in that the term functions as a paradigm for legitimizing anything one wished to endorse. Thus to conceptualize the difference between sexes as 'natural' implies awarding women the private realm, which is theirs 'by nature'. In England, Mary Wollstonecraft, the author of *A Vindication of the Rights of Women*, represents the acceptance of the French Revolution by the group of radicals – Godwin, her husband and the father of philosophical anarchism; Thomas Paine, the father of the American Revolution; the poet Shelley, who would become her son-in-law, and others. She was to take issue with Rousseau, pointing out the incongruities between the democratic radicalism he espoused in *The Social Contract* and his oppressive proposals for women's education 'in accordance with nature' that can be read in *The Education of Sophie*, the fifth part of *Émile*. She made frequent use of resignified revolutionary language: 'It is to be hoped that the *divine right of husbands*, just like the divine right of kings, can be fought against without risk in this, the Age of Enlightenment'; 'men, proud of their power, should cease to use the same arguments as tyrannical kings'. It is difficult to express more fully than in these writings the extent to which the delegitimizing of the Ancien Régime brought with it a crisis of patriarchal legitimacy. Wollstonecraft was to make it clear that the woman educated in accordance with Rousseau's standards is nothing but a sham, the same sham that the author of *The Social Contract* denigrated in comparison to the 'natural' society. From a theoretical standpoint, I believe we can say that this entire controversy about the naturalness or artificiality of sex–gender *avant la lettre* was not brought to a conclusion until after the suffragist movement, when Simone de Beauvoir, in *The Second Sex*, proclaimed: 'Women aren't born, but made'.

In her 'Declaration of the Rights of Women and Women Citizens', Olympe de Gouges radicalizes the revolutionary idea of freedom of speech, extending it to the freedom of women to designate freely the father of their children. We will not go into the resignifications and re-elaborations that women have carried out on the idea of freedom. We refer to Carol Pateman, the Australian feminist political philosopher, who wrote *The Sexual Contract* in 1988. This work reviews the theories of social contract in order to answer the question: Why, if 'all of us' are born free and equal, do we always find women downtrodden? Pateman's answer is that we women are agreed on by men as a fundamental clause of the social contract. She explains that to think of women as free would involve imagining outside the scope of the contract because the logic of the social contract, as it took shape in bourgeois patriarchal society, also covers – paradoxically – the servitude contract.

While women have run up against such paradoxes as regards freedom, they have fared no better when it comes to equality. Sylvain

Maréchal, a member of the Baboeuf Club of Equals, drafted a law prohibiting women from learning to read (details of this inspired act in 1801 can be found in Geneviève Fraisse's book, *Muse of Reason*). There would be many advantages to it, not the least being the signing of a peace treaty between the sexes (women, of course, signing symbolically). So here we have the most radical Jacobin wing of the Revolution taking the most misogynist stance, as if men's mutual endorsement of one another was their yardstick for denigrating the status of women. It was the Jacobins too who ordered the closing of clubs for revolutionary women. The incipient democracy was shutting out women.

Feminist thought has particularly elaborated the idea of equality, perhaps because we women have suffered and continue to suffer from discrimination in various areas and at different levels. It has been broken down into synonyms and explanations, such as equipotency (Amelia Valcarcel), equiphony or equal access to public discourse (Isabel Santa Cruz), equivalence, and so on. On the whole, equality has been less fortunate than liberty in the way the great ideas of the French Revolution have panned out in practice, and it continues to be the test *sine qua non* by which the sensitivity and behaviour of the left are always compared. The feminization of poverty – 80 out of every 100 poor are women – should be a scandal for the left, at least of the same magnitude as the contrast between North and South (with which it does not overlap just like that), which very often blurs these horrendous figures. A phenomenon like this is no surprise if one bears in mind that throughout the world we women hold only 1 per cent of positions of responsibility. In this way, democracies will continue to suffer a legitimacy deficit as long as these imbalances are not corrected.

Lastly, there is fraternity. Right away there is a patriarchal bias as evidenced by the name itself, which refers to the status of brothers, not sisters. For that very reason it has a perverse effect by projecting this same bias on to liberty and equality, and because it appears to indicate that these noble ideas are applicable only to men. Indeed, within the imagination of the social contract we referred to, only men appear as its subjects. The painting by David, *Oath of the Horatii*, is emblematic of civic allegiance, with civic virtue and heroism represented by the male figures, who are sealing a pact under oath. Women, eternally under a different pact, are represented by a group in the background.

So it is not to be wondered at that we feminists have taken it on ourselves to elaborate the idea and practices of sorority, beginning by coining the name. For considering that we women have been, and to some extent continue to be, the transactional object of pacts among men, the practice of weaving networks and pacts among women will by necessity appear to be revolutionary.

Therefore the relationship of feminism with the three ideals of the French Revolution is complicated and paradoxical. On the one hand, this movement draws nourishment from its enlightened and revolutionary force; on the other, the patriarchal coinage of these ideals forms the basis for ongoing tension and permanent redefinition of these ideals in terms of feminist aspirations.

I do not know if this presentation may seem as if I wanted to deflate the balloon of pre-established harmony between the convictions and objectives of the left, and those of feminism. But the left has also had some harsh experiences of having its balloons deflated – all the more reason to think hard. I hope that these comments provide some food for thought in our debates.

Translated by volunteer translator Charles Johnson, reviewed by Peter Lenny

EPILOGUE

RESISTANCE TO NEOLIBERALISM, WAR AND MILITARISM; FOR PEACE AND SOCIAL JUSTICE

1 In the face of continuing deterioration in people's living conditions, we, social movements from all around the world, have come together in the tens of thousands at the second World Social Forum in Porto Alegre. We are here in spite of the attempts to break our solidarity. We come together again to continue our struggles against neoliberalism and war, to confirm the agreements of the last Forum and to reaffirm that another world is possible.

2 We are diverse – women and men, adults and youth, indigenous peoples, rural and urban, workers and unemployed, homeless, the elderly, students, migrants, professionals, peoples of every creed, colour and sexual orientation. The expression of this diversity is our strength and the basis of our unity. We are a global solidarity movement, united in our determination to fight against the concentration of wealth, the proliferation of poverty and inequalities, and the destruction of our earth. We are living and constructing alternative systems, and using creative ways to promote them. We are building a large alliance from our struggles and resistance against a system based on sexism, racism and violence, which privileges the interests of capital and patriarchy over the needs and aspirations of people.

3 This system produces a daily drama of women, children, and the elderly dying from hunger, lack of health care and preventable diseases. Families are forced to leave their homes because of wars,

the impact of 'big development', landlessness and environmental disasters, unemployment, attacks on public services and the destruction of social solidarity. Both in the South and in the North, vibrant struggles and resistance to uphold the dignity of life are flourishing.

4 September 11 marked a dramatic change. After the terrorist attacks, which we absolutely condemn, as we condemn all other attacks on civilians in other parts of the world, the governments of the United States and its allies have launched a massive military operation. In the name of the war on terrorism, civil and political rights are being attacked all over the world. The war against Afghanistan, in which terrorist methods are being used, is now being extended to other fronts. Thus there is the beginning of a permanent global war to cement the domination of the US government and its allies. This war reveals another face of neoliberalism, a face which is brutal and unacceptable. Islam is being demonized, while racism and xenophobia are deliberately propagated. The mass media are actively taking part in this belligerent campaign which divides the world into good and evil. Opposition to the war is at the heart of our movement.

5 The situation of war has further destabilized the Middle East, providing a pretext for further repression of the Palestinian people. An urgent task of our movement is to mobilize solidarity for the Palestinian people and their struggle for self-determination as they face brutal occupation by the Israeli state. This is vital to the collective security of all peoples in the region.

6 Further events also confirm the urgency of our struggles. In Argentina the financial crisis caused by the failure of IMF structural adjustment and mounting debt precipitated a social and political crisis. This crisis generated spontaneous protests of the middle and working classes, repression which caused deaths, failure of governments, and new alliances between different social

groups. With the backing of *cacerolazos* and *piquetes*, popular mobilizations have demanded their basic rights to food, jobs and housing. We reject the vilification of social movements in Argentina and the attacks on democratic rights and freedom. We also condemn the greed and blackmail of the multinational corporations supported by the governments of the rich countries.

7 The collapse of the multinational Enron exemplifies the bankruptcy of the casino economy and the corruption of businessmen and politicians, leaving workers without jobs and pensions. In developing countries this multinational engaged in fraudulent activities and its projects pushed people off their land and led to sharp increases in the price of water and electricity.

8 The United States government, in its efforts to protect the interests of big corporations, arrogantly walked away from negotiations on global warming, the anti-ballistic missile treaty, the Convention on Biodiversity, the UN conference on racism and intolerance, and the talks to reduce the supply of small arms, proving once again that US unilateralism undermines attempts to find multilateral solutions to global problems.

9 In Genoa the G8 failed completely in its self-assumed task of global government. In the face of massive mobilization and resistance, they responded with violence and repression, denouncing as criminals those who dared to protest. But they failed to intimidate our movement.

10 All this is happening in the context of a global recession. The neoliberal economic model is destroying the rights, living conditions and livelihoods of people. Using every means to protect the value of their shares, multinational companies lay off workers, slash wages and close factories, squeezing the last dollar from the workers. Governments faced with this economic crisis respond by privatizing, cutting social sector expenditures and permanently reducing workers' rights. This recession exposes the

fact that the neoliberal promise of growth and prosperity is a lie.

11 The global movement for social justice and solidarity faces enormous challenges: its fight for peace and collective security implies confronting poverty, discrimination and domination and working for the creation of an alternative sustainable society.

12 Social movements energetically condemn violence and militarism as a means of conflict resolution; the promotion of low-intensity conflicts and military operations in the Plan Colombia as part of the Andes regional initiative; the Puebla Panama Plan; the arms trade and increased military budgets; economic blockades against people and nations, especially against Cuba and Iraq; and the growing repression of trade unions, social movements and activists.

13 We support the trade unions and informal sector worker struggles as essential to maintain working and living conditions and to protect the genuine right to organize, to go on strike, to negotiate collective agreements, and to achieve equality in wages and working conditions between women and men. We reject slavery and the exploitation of children. We support workers' struggles and trade union fights against casualization, subcontracting of labour and lay-offs, and we demand new international rights for the employees of multinational companies and their affiliates, in particular the right to unionize, and space for collective bargaining. Equally we support the struggles of farmers and peoples' organizations for their rights to a livelihood, and to land, forests and water.

14 Neoliberal policies create tremendous misery and insecurity. They have dramatically increased the trafficking and sexual exploitation of women and children. Poverty and insecurity create millions of migrants who are denied their dignity, freedom and rights. We therefore demand the right of free movement; the right to physical integrity and legal status for all migrants. We support the

rights of indigenous peoples and the fulfilment of ILO article 169 in domestic legislation.

15 The external debt of the countries of the South has been repaid several times over. Illegitimate, unjust and fraudulent, debt functions as an instrument of domination, depriving people of their fundamental human rights with the sole aim of increasing international usury. We demand unconditional cancellation of the debt and reparation payments for historical, social and ecological debts. The countries demanding repayment of debt have engaged in exploitation of the natural resources and the traditional knowledge of the South.

16 Water, land, food, forests, seeds, culture and people's identities are common assets of humanity for present and future generations. It is essential to preserve biodiversity. People have the right to safe and permanent food free of genetically modified organisms. Food sovereignty at the local, national and regional level is a basic human right; in this regard, democratic land reforms and peasants' access to land are fundamental requirements.

17 The meeting in Doha confirmed the illegitimacy of the WTO. The adoption of a 'development agenda' only defends corporate interests. By launching a new round, the WTO is moving closer to its goal of converting everything into a commodity. For us, food, public services, agriculture, health and education are not for sale. Patenting must not to be used as a weapon against the poor countries and peoples. We reject the patenting and trading of life forms. The WTO agenda is perpetuated at the continental level by regional free trade and investment agreements. By organizing protests such as the huge demonstrations and plebiscites against the FTAA, people in Latin America have rejected these agreements as representing recolonization, and the destruction of fundamental social, economical, cultural and environmental rights and values.

18 We will strengthen our movement through common actions and
mobilizations for social justice, for the respect of rights and
liberties, for quality of life, equality, dignity and peace.

We are fighting for:

- Democracy: people have the right to know about and criticize the
decisions of their own governments, especially with respect to
dealings with international institutions. Governments are
ultimately accountable to their people. While we support the
establishment of electoral and participatory democracy across the
world, we emphasize the need for the democratization of states
and societies and for struggles against dictatorship.

- The abolition of external debt and the payment of reparations.

- Action against speculative activities. We demand the creation of
specific taxes such as the Tobin Tax, and the abolition of tax
havens.

- The right to information.

- Women's rights, freedom from violence, poverty and
exploitation.

- An end to war and militarism, foreign military bases and
interventions, and the systematic escalation of violence. We
choose to privilege negotiation and non-violent conflict
resolution. We affirm the right for all the people to ask for
international mediation, with the participation of independent
actors from civil society.

- The rights of youth, their access to free public education and
social autonomy, and the abolition of compulsory military service.

- The self-determination of all peoples, especially the rights of
indigenous peoples.

In the years to come, we will organize collective mobilizations including:

- 8 March: International Women's Day

- 17 April: International Day of Peasants' Struggle

- 1 May: Labour Day

- 7 October: World Day for the Homeless

- 12 October: Cry of the Excluded

- 16 October: World Food Day

Other global mobilizations will take place in 2002:

- 15–16 March: Barcelona (Spain), EU summit

- 18–22 March: Monterrey (Mexico), United Nations Conference on Financing for Development

- 17–18 May: Madrid (Spain), summit of Latin America, Caribbean and Europe

- May, Asia Development Bank Annual Meeting, Shanghai, China

- 1 May: International day of action against militarism and for peace

- End of May, fourth preparatory meeting for the World Summit on Sustainable Development, Indonesia

- June: Rome (Italy), World Food Summit

- 22–23 June: Seville (Spain), EU summit

- July: Toronto and Calgary (Canada), G8 summit

- 22 July: US campaign against Coca-Cola

- September: Johannesburg (South Africa), Rio+10

- September: Copenhagen (Denmark), Asia Europe Meeting (ASEM)

- October: Quito (Ecuador), World Social Forum, 'A New Integration is Possible'

- November: Cuba, second Hemispheric meeting against FTAA

- December: Copenhagen (Denmark), EU summit

In 2003:

- April: Buenos Aires (Argentina), FTAA summit

- June: Thessaloniki (Greece), EU Summit

- June: France, the G8

- WTO, IMF and the World Bank: they will meet somewhere, sometime. And we will be there!

APPENDIX 1

CHARTER OF PRINCIPLES

The committee of Brazilian organizations that conceived and organized the first World Social Forum, held in Porto Alegre, 25–30 January 2001, after evaluating the results of that Forum and the expectations it raised, consider it necessary and legitimate to draw up a Charter of Principles to guide the continued pursuit of that initiative. While the principles contained in this Charter – to be respected by all those who wish to take part in the process and to organize new meetings of the World Social Forum – are a consolidation of the decisions that informed the Porto Alegre Forum and ensured its success, they extend the scope of those decisions and define certain orientations that flow from their logic.

1 The World Social Forum is an open meeting place for reflective thinking, democratic debate of ideas, formulation of proposals, free exchange of experiences and linking up for effective action, by groups and movements of civil society that are opposed to neoliberalism and to domination of the world by capital and any form of imperialism, and are committed to building a global society of fruitful relationships among human beings and between humans and the Earth.

2 The World Social Forum at Porto Alegre was an event localized in time and place. From now on, in the certainty proclaimed at Porto Alegre that 'another world is possible', it becomes a permanent process of seeking and building alternatives, which

cannot be reduced to the events supporting it.

3 The World Social Forum is a global process. All the meetings that are held as part of this process have an international dimension.

4 The alternatives proposed at the World Social Forum stand in opposition to a process of globalization directed by the large multinational corporations and by the governments and international institutions at the service of those corporations' interests. They are designed to ensure that globalization in solidarity will prevail as a new stage in world history. This will respect universal human rights, and those of all citizens – men and women – of all nations, and the environment, and will rest on democratic international systems and institutions at the service of social justice, equality and the sovereignty of peoples.

5 The World Social Forum brings together and links organizations and movements of civil society from all the countries in the world, but does not intend to represent world civil society.

6 The meetings of the World Social Forum do not deliberate on behalf of the World Social Forum as a body. No one, therefore, will be authorized, on behalf of any of the meetings of the Forum, to express positions claiming to be those of all its participants. The participants in the Forum shall not be called on to make decisions as a body, whether by vote or acclamation, on declarations or proposals for action that would commit all, or the majority, of them, and that propose to be understood as establishing positions of the Forum as a body. It thus does not constitute a locus of power to be disputed by the participants in its meetings, nor does it intend to constitute the only option for interrelation and action by the organizations and movements that participate in it.

7 Nonetheless, organizations or groups of organizations that participate in the Forum's meetings must be assured the right, during such meetings, to deliberate on declarations or actions they may decide on, whether singly or in coordination with other participants. The World Social Forum undertakes to circulate such decisions widely by the means at its disposal, without directing, hierarchizing, censuring or restricting them, but as deliberations of the organizations or groups of organizations that made the decisions.

8 The World Social Forum is a plural, diversified, non-confessional, non-governmental and non-party context that, in a decentralized fashion, interrelates organizations and movements engaged in concrete action at levels from the local to the international in order to build another world.

9 The World Social Forum will always be a forum open to pluralism and to the diversity of activities and ways of engaging of the organizations and movements that decide to participate in it, as well as the diversity of genders, ethnicities, cultures, generations and physical capacities, providing they abide by this Charter of Principles. Neither party representatives nor military organizations shall participate in the Forum. Government leaders and members of legislatures who accept the commitments of this Charter may be invited to participate in a personal capacity.

10 The World Social Forum is opposed to all totalitarian and reductionist views of economy, development and history and to the use of violence as a means of social control by the state. It upholds respect for human rights, the practices of real democracy, participatory democracy, peaceful relations, in equality and solidarity, among people, ethnicities, genders and peoples, and condemns all forms of domination and all subjection of one person by another.

11 As a forum for debate, the World Social Forum is a movement of ideas that prompts reflection, and the transparent circulation of the results of that reflection, on the mechanisms and instruments of domination by capital, on the means and actions to resist and

overcome that domination, and on the alternatives proposed to solve the problems of exclusion and social inequality that the process of capitalist globalization with its racist, sexist and environmentally destructive dimensions is creating internationally and within countries.

12 As a framework for the exchange of experiences, the World Social Forum encourages understanding and mutual recognition among its participant organizations and movements, and places special value on the exchange among them, particularly on all that society is building to centre economic activity and political action on meeting the needs of people and respecting nature, in the present and for future generations.

13 As a context for interrelations, the World Social Forum seeks to strengthen and create new national and international links among organizations and movements of society, that – in both public and private life – will increase the capacity for non-violent social resistance to the process of dehumanization that the world is undergoing and to the violence used by the state, and reinforce the humanizing measures being taken by the action of these movements and organizations.

14 The World Social Forum is a process that encourages its participant organizations and movements to situate their actions from the local level to the national level, and to seek active participation in international contexts, as issues of planetary citizenship, and to introduce into the global agenda the change-inducing practices that they are experimenting with in building a new world in solidarity.

Approved and adopted in São Paulo, on 9 April 2001, by the organizations that make up the World Social Forum Organizing Committee, approved with modifications by the World Social Forum International Council on 10 June 2001.

APPENDIX 2

CONTACTS

Telephone/fax:	(+55 11) 3258-8914
Address:	Rua General Jardim, 660, 8° andar, sala 81
	Cep 01223-010
	São Paulo- SP
	Brazil
Coordination:	Alessandra Ceregatti
General Questions (International):	fsm2003ci@uol.com.br
Contact:	Carolina Gil
Workshops/Seminars:	fsm2003oficinas@uol.com.br
Contact:	Adriana Guimarães
Brazilian Council:	fsm2003cb@uol.com.br
Contact:	Luana Vilutis
National Committee and Regional Forum:	fsm2003nacional@uol.com.br
Contact:	Luana Vilutis
Press Assistant:	fsm2003imprensa@uol.com.br
Contact:	Verena Glass
Web Site Coordination:	fsm2003site@uol.com.br
Contact:	Patrícia Giuffrida
Web Designer:	informart@informart.com.br
Contact:	Eduardo Urzúa
Volunteers and Translators:	fsm2003trad@uol.com.br
Contact:	Adriana Guimarães

INDEX